At the
Coalface

At the Coalface

The heartwarming true story of
a Yorkshire pit nurse

JOAN HART

WITH

VERONICA CLARK

HarperElement
An imprint of HarperCollins*Publishers*
1 London Bridge Street
London SE1 9GF

www.harpercollins.co.uk

First published by HarperElement 2015

1 3 5 7 9 10 8 6 4 2

A catalogue record of this book is
available from the British Library

ISBN 978-0-00-759616-4

Printed and bound in Great Britain by
Clays Ltd, St Ives plc

MIX
Paper from
responsible sources
FSC C007454

For my husband, Peter

Prologue

Dropping the telephone receiver back down into its cradle, I jumped to my feet and closed the door. My pale blue overall was still grubby with coal dust from my pit inspection the day before. I was a nurse on call, in charge of thousands of miners, and right now one of them needed me. I clamped the palm of my hand against my hard hat and ran along the pathway towards the lamp cabin. With my metal checks jangling inside my pocket, I grabbed my lamp, battery pack and self-rescuer canister, and clipped them onto the side of my belt. It was still early and grey clouds swirled overhead. The air was thick with industrial noise and the threat of immediate rain. My pit boots picked up pace as I dashed from the lamp cabin towards the shaft side where the doctor was already waiting. The noise from the winding house groaned and creaked as the giant drum turned and toiled inside. The fans spat out air thick with coal dust as an avalanche of noise hissed above our heads like a steam train.

'Hello, Sister,' Dr Macdonald called.

'Hello, Doctor. I've brought the amputation kit,' I shouted above the din as I held the bag aloft to show him.

'Good. Are you all right?'

I nodded, although my heart was pounding with fear and adrenalin. My fingers trembled and the palm of my right hand was sweating as I clutched the handle of the surgical kit. It contained artery forceps, a tourniquet, sterile saw and knives of varying lengths. The thought of it alone made me sick with nerves, and I prayed that we wouldn't have to use it.

We approached the banksman, who checked we were ready to go.

'No flammables? No battery-operated devices?' he asked as a matter of course.

Dr Macdonald and I shook our heads. We knew the safety drill. He opened up the cage and loaded us into it. We switched off our headlamps as he pulled down the chain-mail shutters, enveloping us in virtual darkness. I felt reassured by the blackness because I didn't want Dr Macdonald to see the fear in my eyes. The cage rattled into life as we began our descent, hundreds of feet to the pit bottom below. Clouds of white steam billowed up around the edges, making it feel like a journey into the depths of hell.

'What information do we have, Sister?' Dr Macdonald asked.

I tried to remember what I'd just been told.

'It's a man, in his early twenties. He'd been riding on the conveyor belt at the end of his shift, but he didn't manage to jump off in time. His leg got mangled in the machinery.'

'Oh,' replied Dr Macdonald, his voice cutting through the darkness.

'It's an amputation,' I continued, 'though I still don't know if it's partial or complete. The deputy and first aiders are with him now.'

Moments later, the cage shuddered and chains rattled as we came to a halt – we'd reached the pit bottom.

'Ready, Sister?' Dr Macdonald asked. He switched his headlamp back on and my face was illuminated in a circle of golden light.

I reached out a hand and switched on my lamp too. The white circle of light waltzed around on the pit wall opposite.

'Ready,' I replied as we stepped out of the cage.

Suddenly a face loomed into view. It was the onsetter.

'The paddy train is waiting to take you inbye to district.'

I took a deep breath and climbed on board. As the train trundled off into the darkness I wondered what would be waiting to greet us at our destination.

1

The Year of the Floods

The boat was unsteady as it floated along the street. Inside the house my mother was huffing and panting as her contractions quickened with every minute.

'Where's the bloody midwife?' she screamed – her cries so loud that the neighbours heard every word.

Moments later, a small rowing boat bobbed outside.

'Hang on, I'll fetch the ladder,' my father called down from a bedroom window at the top of the house.

The midwife clambered out of the boat and placed an uncertain foot onto the ladder. The rungs felt slippy and unsure beneath her feet as her eyes darted nervously to the filthy brown water swirling below.

'I'll grab your hand when you reach the top,' Dad promised. He didn't care what it took to get her in; he just wanted her to hurry up.

A large bag dangled precariously from her arm as she climbed upwards, one rung at a time. My father was waiting to greet her. With one arm around her shoulder and the other to steady her, he helped the midwife climb in through the open bedroom window.

'I'm so glad you're here,' he gasped, smoothing a hand through his hair. His face was fraught with worry as his eyes signalled over towards the bed where my mother lay.

'I think the baby's on its way.'

The midwife nodded dutifully, took off her overcoat and rolled up her sleeves. I'd caused them all quite a lot of fuss, apparently, but less than an hour later I emerged naked and blinking against the harsh light of the world.

'It's a girl!' the midwife announced, wrapping me in a clean sheet. 'Congratulations.'

My dad later told me how he'd sighed with relief while my auntie Lucy had cleaned up. Meanwhile, Mum had sobbed quietly in the bed, glad it was over. I'd entered the world on 18 May 1932 and, true to form, I'd done it in quite a style. I was born in Bentley, a little pit village situated on the outskirts of Doncaster, South Yorkshire. The village was also near the River Don, which had a habit of flooding every time we suffered a heavy bout of rain, and May 1932 had been no exception. Rain it did, until floodwater had engulfed the entire village, including the residents and their terraced houses. The flooding was so severe that a boat service had to be brought in to transport the good people of Bentley in and out of the village, including the poor midwife.

Dad had been travelling to his job at Bentley Colliery in the same boat, day in, day out, for over a week. My father was a miner, but as soon as he discovered Mum was pregnant with me he took his deputy papers so he could become an overman, to bring in a better wage. Soon he'd passed his exams and moved to Brodsworth pit, where he was in charge of over 1,000 miners working the afternoon shift. Back then, Brodsworth was the biggest pit in Doncaster, employing thousands of men.

Standing at 6 feet 2 inches tall, my father was a gentle giant, but his solid stature gave him an air of authority and the men knew better than to mess with him. He had thick mousy-brown hair and he was incredibly handsome. My mother, on the other hand, was small and attractive, with natural red hair, which I'd inherited. She also saw herself as quite the little lady. But with a fractious baby and a house that constantly flooded, Mum was at her wits' end and threatened to drown me in the River Don just to shut me up, so Dad found us another house in a village called Woodlands. With a father in a good job and a stay-at-home mum, in many ways my life was idyllic. I was followed by a brother, Tony, just seven years later. Tony was a real screamer. One day, Mum, who was frazzled through lack of sleep, accidentally dropped his baby bottle. Back then, bottles were banana shaped with big ugly rubber teats at each end. They were also made of glass, so Tony's bottle smashed to smithereens as soon as it hit the floor.

'No!' she cried as she looked at the scattered pieces of glass.

Exasperated, she opened up her purse, handed me some pennies and told me to go straight to the chemist to buy another so she could feed the baby. The only problem was that, although it was April, it was bitterly cold and it'd been snowing heavily all week. The 10-minute walk to the village shop took me almost half an hour as I battled knee-deep through the snow, both there and back. Tony was a typical boy, and as long as he got fed he was happy. Our sister Ann was born three years later, so, as the eldest, I constantly ran errands for Mum. Every couple of days I'd be given enough money to buy a block of fresh yeast from the local baker. I loved the smell of the bakery, but more than that, I loved the taste of fresh yeast. The yeast looked pretty unappetising in a grey square lump, but curiosity made me crumble the edge of a corner off it one day. As soon as I put it inside my mouth it started to foam and I was hooked.

'Mmmm, lovely,' I sighed, breaking off another piece and hoping my mother wouldn't notice.

All my friends preferred sweets but I loved to nibble yeast. After a while, though, the crumbled block raised suspicion. Mum twigged what I was doing and forbade me to eat it ever again.

'It'll upset your stomach!' she snapped, but I didn't care.

As we grew, Mother settled into her role as the lady of the house. Dad doted on her and bought her everything her heart desired, and back then it desired a washing machine. In fact, it was such a coveted piece of machinery that we were the first family in Woodlands to have one. It was pretty basic by today's standards – a metal tub with a lid and a handle on top, which you moved backwards and forwards to create the 'wash'. But in Woodlands it was the height of sophistication, so much so that all our neighbours and their children crowded round our kitchen just to see it in action. Mum duly obliged, blinding them all with the marvels of modern science.

'Oh, you're so lucky, Ellen; I wish my husband would buy me one of them,' a neighbour cooed.

As she twisted the washing-machine handle back and forth we heard a swishing sound from within the tub and my friends were mesmerised.

'Oooh, can you hear that?' one cried. 'It sounds just like the waves of the sea!'

Mum lifted her head regally and smiled. She knew women in the village envied her with her handsome husband, three children and a brand new washing machine. However, unbeknownst to us, she had a secret – a yearning to return to her old life. Before she'd met Dad she'd worked as a barmaid at a pub on Fleet Street, London. The bar was always a bustling hive of activity, with journalists all hungry for the next big scoop. Mum loved everything about it – the buzz, the excitement and the fast pace of life. So, when she found herself stuck with three kids in the outskirts of a town in South Yorkshire, she wondered what might have been if she'd not married a miner. My parents had met quite by chance. Originally from Stafford, Mum had been in Doncaster visiting her brother when she landed a temporary job as a cashier on the reception of the local swimming baths. My father, Harry Smith, soon caught her eye. A few dates were followed by an engagement and ultimately marriage, but Mum soon felt trapped. Shortly after Ann was born, a group of her friends travelled up to Yorkshire to visit. I remember watching her eyes mist over as they spoke of London and past acquaintances.

'You'll have to come back and visit, Ellen. Everyone misses you. They all ask after you.'

'Really?' Mum gasped, her eyes lighting up. Little did we know then that she was already in the tunnel clawing her way towards a new life – one without us.

Weeks later, I'd wandered downstairs in my nightgown. My eyes were still blurry from sleep but I'd heard a noise and I'd gone to investigate. As I padded barefoot down the stairs I could hardly believe the sight that greeted me. It was my father. He was bent over double, sat in a chair in the front room, sobbing his heart out. It was a shock because my father was a strong man and I'd never seen him cry before. I knew something dreadful had happened. I automatically ran over to him and wrapped my arms around his neck, but it was no good; there was nothing I could say or do to make it better.

'She's gone, Joan,' he blurted out in between deep sobs. I pulled away from him with a puzzled look on my face.

Who's gone? What on earth was he talking about?

'It's your mother. She's gone and left me. She's left us all. She's packed up her things and gone back to London.'

I shook my head in disbelief. *Surely he'd got it wrong? There had to be some kind of mistake. Mum wouldn't just pack a bag and leave*

*us behind without a word. Ann was still a baby and a mother wouldn't
leave her baby!*

'Maybe she'll come home?' I whispered hopefully.

Dad shook his head. 'No, it's over, Joan. She's gone and she's
never coming back.'

That night I blinked back the tears and wondered how Mum
could be so heartless to just abandon us. She hadn't even bothered to say goodbye. But I was the eldest and I knew I could help
my father out with the little ones, so that's what I decided I
would do. Dad needed me to be strong, so I would be. I'd take as
long as necessary off school so he could keep his job, go to work
and bring in a wage to feed and clothe us all. I was 13 years old,
going on 14. A few months earlier I'd joined the St John
Ambulance Brigade as a young cadet, so I knew a little bit about
first aid.

Besides, how hard could cooking actually be? I pondered.

But cooking was a lot harder than I thought and, after cremat-
ing several family meals, a kindly neighbour called Lizzie Adams
took me under her wing. By then, I'd decided I would take care
of everything. Just because our mother had failed us, it didn't
mean I would. Lizzie was a wily woman in her sixties, but to a girl
my age she seemed absolutely ancient. However, what she didn't
know about cooking wasn't worth knowing, and I became her
willing pupil. Cooking, cleaning and looking after four people
was no mean feat, and soon I'd missed days, weeks, even months,
of school. But I was smart, and I knew I'd just have to work twice
as hard to catch up. In the meantime, Lizzie and I spent hours in
the kitchen where she taught me how to bake bread and boil
vegetables so that they didn't disintegrate as soon as I drained
the pan. She also showed me how to cook a tasty roast all the
way through, checking the juices ran clear, so that I didn't poison
anyone. Of course, my father was delighted to come home to a

piping hot meal and three happy, clean children, but he also felt guilty because he hated the idea of me missing school.

'We can't carry on like this, Joan,' he said, placing his knife and fork down firmly on the table. 'You need to go back to school so you can learn and do well in life. You can't stay here looking after us all; I won't allow it. Not any more.'

Dad was right, of course, but the thing was, after a year of playing housemaid, I quite liked the idea of caring for others. I'd enjoyed making sure the little ones got to school on time with a bellyful of food and clean faces and hands. I'd hated the house-work, but the satisfaction I felt when everything was neat, proper and in its place made it all worthwhile. In short, I knew it was what I wanted to do with the rest of my life.

'I want to be a nurse,' I told the St John cadet leader, a lovely woman called Mrs Hargreaves, later that evening. 'How do I go about it?'

She explained that at 14 years old I was much too young to be anything other than a child but, when the time was right, she'd make enquiries on my behalf.

In the meantime I tried to be the best cadet I could, and thankfully I discovered I had a natural talent for first aid.

With me back at school, Dad employed a husband-and-wife team – Harry and Emily – as live-in housekeepers. But the house was already too small and cramped, so Dad and Tony were forced to share a room. We were told we should call them Auntie Emily and Uncle Harry, even though we weren't related. Harry was an invalid. He suffered from pneumoconiosis, a restrictive lung disease commonly seen in miners, so the prospect of a regular wage and a roof over their heads appealed to Emily, who made it clear from the beginning that she had 'designs' on my father. Our 'aunt and uncle' soon made themselves at home, to the point where, as children, we were barely allowed to sit down in case we made the place look untidy. In some ways it was nice to live in a spotlessly clean house and be back at school, but I hated being told off for putting my feet up on the sofa. Emily wasn't only house-proud, she could also be very cruel. One day, she was cross because I'd moved something and put it back in the wrong place. Dad was out at work so she knew she could speak her mind.

'Your mother's run off with another man. She didn't love you. That's why I'm here, because someone has to look after you!' Emily hissed spitefully as she narrowed her eyes.

From that moment on I resented Emily with her tidy ways and vicious tongue. But she wasn't the only one who said things about my mother – other people gossiped too. In fact, so many rumours circulated around the village that they soon took on a life of their own, until, just by word of mouth, fiction became fact even if there wasn't an ounce of truth in it. I hated the other children when they said horrible things about her. Despite my own disappointment, I'd always stuck up for Mum and defended her honour. However, Ann had been a baby when Mum had left so she never, ever forgave her.

Seeing an absent mother and with her eyes on my father, Emily decided to step into the role, and she did, with aplomb. Instead of Mum, it'd be Emily at our school plays, dolled up to the nines. Emily was so sweet on Dad that I was convinced she was just waiting in the wings, ready to pounce once her husband had passed away. It was a thoroughly depressing situation.

The house was cramped not only with two extra people, but also because Harry and Emily had brought along their own furniture, most of it so much nicer than ours. To free up some space, Dad had decided to cut down our old kitchen table and use it as a bench inside his greenhouse, which he'd filled with chrysanthemums and tomato plants. He was so green-fingered he could turn his hand to anything. There were two Anderson air-raid shelters in the back lane, behind the row of terraced houses, but no one used them because there was a much safer and deeper one in the village park. With no takers, Dad saw his chance and filled the shelters with beds of manure and grew crops of mushrooms inside them. Even if anyone had wanted to use the shelters, they wouldn't because the smell was so pungent that, on a hot day, it carried all the way down the street. Mind you, the shelters were so exposed that they were eventually bombed, so I reckon my father's mushrooms saved a few lives along the way.

One day, quite without warning, Emily and Harry decided to leave. I never found out why, but I think the fact that Dad never acted on or picked up on Emily's many romantic hints was probably the final straw. He was miffed because he knew he'd have to find another housekeeper, but secretly I was relieved that we would have the place back to ourselves again. By this time, I was 15 years old and adept at making a mean Sunday dinner. A few days after Emily had left, taking her last pieces of furniture with her, something struck me – we had no kitchen table. I wasn't quite sure what to do, but then I remembered the one in the greenhouse. I knew it was a big job, but with Dad due home within the hour and the meat almost cooked in the stove, I needed everything to be perfect. I wanted him to think I could cope. Opening up the greenhouse door, I scratched my head as I contemplated the task in hand. The table was wide and heavy, and I wondered how I'd manage to get it down the garden – never mind how I'd lift it into the kitchen.

Blimey, it's heavier than it looks, I cursed silently as I dragged it along. *If only Emily hadn't taken her posh furniture with her, then we wouldn't be in this position.*

It took a bit of brute force but somehow I managed to push the table inside the house. But then I was faced with another problem

– it had no legs because Dad had sawn them off to fit it inside the greenhouse! The smell of roast beef filled the kitchen, making my mouth water. I had to think of something – fast. I nipped out into the backyard to look for something suitable to prop it up with. I stumbled upon a load of old house bricks. I collected as many as I could carry, stacked them on top of one another, and lowered the table top down onto them. It was hardly up to Emily's high standards – I could just imagine her shaking her head in despair – but at least it was a table once more. Moments later I heard the back door slam. We always used the back door – the front was reserved for funerals and weddings only – so I knew it was Dad. His footsteps sounded heavy as he came inside.

'Wash your hands and sit down. I've cooked you a lovely dinner,' I said as I loaded up some meat and vegetables onto a plate.

'Lovely. I'm starving!' he said as he grinned and wandered over to wash his hands at the kitchen sink. As he turned his head, he did a double take.

'Is that our old kitchen table?' he asked, pointing at it.

'Yes, I've brought it back inside. Now Emily's gone, we need a table, so I dragged it in. Don't worry – I've given it a good wipe.'

But he wasn't listening. Instead, he was looking underneath to see how I'd managed to prop it up.

'I've used some house bricks from the backyard so be careful, and whatever you do, don't cross your legs!'

'Rightio,' Dad said, chuckling, as he tucked into his meal. 'Ooh, Joan, tha cooks a great joint – this is lovely.' He smiled, chewing happily on a piece of meat.

But my father was enjoying his food so much that he forgot my warning and crossed his legs.

CRASH!

Dad was a giant of a man, and within seconds one end of the table had tipped up in the air and come crashing down with an almighty clatter. I watched as his dinner seemed to slide and then tip over in slow motion, landing neatly upside down in the middle of his lap. He glanced down at it and then up at me. He must've registered the horror on my face because he immediately burst out laughing. But I was absolutely furious; the dinner had taken me hours to prepare.

'I told you not to cross your legs!' I screamed like a demented housewife. 'Now look what you've done! There's gravy everywhere. And look at your trousers – they're ruined!'

But my anger tickled him even more and soon he couldn't speak for laughing. With tears of mirth streaming down his face he helped me clear up the mess from the floor. I was still fuming, so Dad tried his best to win me back around.

'I'll go and buy us a new table. As for this,' he said, tapping the old wooden table top, 'I think I'll shove it back inside the greenhouse where it belongs.'

I watched as he sheepishly carried it out through the back door, my arms folded and my foot tapping in annoyance. Eventually I saw the joke, but deep down Dad knew that at 15 years old, and with Emily gone, I was too young to play mother and full-time housewife. I needed to be back at school, but in order to do that he had to employ another housekeeper. The word went out and soon another woman knocked on our door. Her name was Elsie and she had the filthiest hands I'd ever seen. To this day, I still don't know why he took her on; but he did. Dad was lonely, so within weeks they began a relationship and soon Elsie became the ruin of us all. Even though Dad had given her a generous allowance to buy food, Elsie bought everything on credit or 'tick', as we called it. The shopkeeper added our family name to a long list of people who also owed him money.

Instead of using Dad's housekeeping money, Elsie spent it on goodness knows what and landed us in debt, but her deceit didn't stop there. One day, my favourite brown tweed coat vanished from the house. I was distraught because I'd always looked after my things, but it was nowhere to be seen. I asked Elsie and she just shrugged.

'It'll be wherever you left it,' she snapped.

I hated her but Dad was desperate – he didn't want me to miss any more time off, nor did he want to lose his job at the pit – so Elsie was the compromise. I didn't want to rock the boat or make his life harder, so I kept my mouth shut but vowed to leave home as soon as I could. My chance came sooner than I'd anticipated. True to her word, Mrs Hargreaves from St John Ambulance had remembered my request to become a nurse and had already started to make enquiries on my behalf.

'There's a college in Huddersfield. I've put your name forward because they take nursing recruits from the age of 16.'

My face lit up. Mrs Hargreaves had watched me progress as a young cadet. I'd worked hard to get my certificates in first aid and I'd left school as head girl. She paid my fare and travelled with me, taking two buses and changing at Leeds, so I could attend my interview in Huddersfield. It was such a long journey that it took up half the day, but as soon as we arrived at nursing college I knew I'd done the right thing.

'Tell me, why do you want to be a nurse, Joan?' the matron asked. She was a shrewd woman in her early fifties, tall and thin – the type you could never hope to fool – and she frightened the life out of me. Her hair was covered in a stiffened white head-dress, which she'd wrapped around her head at sharp angles, making her look a bit like a nun.

I twisted my hands nervously in my lap because I was unsure what to say. I spoke straight from my heart. 'I want to look after people; it's what I've always wanted to do. I just want to make a difference.'

The matron nodded and glanced down at my application form in her hands. She tried to hide it but I noticed the small flicker of a smile play across her lips, and I knew I'd done well. A few weeks later, a letter confirmed it when I was offered a place on the year-long course. I was excited beyond words as I made plans to move to nursing college. Although I felt a pang of guilt at leaving Dad, Tony and Ann behind with the horrid Elsie, I knew I had to do it because nursing college would be my escape route to a better life, and I was determined to grab it with both hands.

2

Nurse in Training

The nurses' training college was situated inside a large Victorian house, set in its own grounds. It was a tall and imposing building, and was a good ten-minute walk from Huddersfield Royal Infirmary. All our nursing training was done inside the house, which had enough room to accommodate a dozen people, but we travelled to the hospital one afternoon a week so that we could gain real work experience. I was one of ten live-in nurses in training. We were all aged between 16 and 17 years old. It was a new course and it taught would-be nurses everything from scratch, from cooking what we called wholesome 'invalid food' to how to launder sheets and clean and correctly disinfect a room. The cookery courses were fun but the food wasn't as joyful or, indeed, very appetising. We were taught how to make everything from junket – a type of blancmange using sour cream – to beef broth, and tripe and onions. On one occasion I forgot to soak my cut of salt beef overnight. The following day I prepared and cooked my 'beef tea' – or broth – as I'd been told, seasoning it along the way. But when I went to take a sip I almost gagged, and then I began to splutter and choke. Within seconds I'd spat it out, my face a sickly shade of green.

'Whatever's the matter, Joan?' one of my fellow students asked as I dashed over to the sink to try to rinse away the awful taste.

'Eurgh, it tastes like seawater!' I gasped.

I couldn't work out where I'd gone wrong until the teacher came over and sampled some using a spoon. She took a sip, pulled a disgusted face and shook her head in dismay.

'You forgot to soak your cut; that's why it tastes like a bag of salt. You'd kill a patient if you served this,' she said, plopping the spoon back inside the bubbling pan.

I bowed my head. I felt such a fool because, as usual, I'd tried to run before I could walk. Of course, I failed that particular task, but afterwards I vowed to always taste the food as I went along. A few months later, when it came to my cookery exam, I decided to prepare the same beef broth followed by some junket. I took my time, sampling it until it tasted absolutely perfect before setting it out on a tray. But when I looked around at the other trays I realised something vital was missing – a vase of flowers. I had no money, so I decided to improvise. I nipped outside into the garden where I 'borrowed' a small handful of pretty pansies. Standing them up inside a clean fish-paste jar, I added a sprinkle of water and then I was done. It was hardly a bouquet, but it did the trick. In spite of my last-minute DIY floral arrangement, I passed with flying colours and was allowed to move to the next stage of the course – cleaning. I could hardly wait.

My youth and inexperience had left me feeling a little home-sick, so I travelled back to Doncaster to visit my family. Of course, Elsie the horrid housekeeper was there and she didn't seem too impressed when she spotted me coming through the door. When I saw the state of the place I realised why – it was filthy. If anything, Elsie's low standards had slipped even more, so that I barely recognised my own home. I rolled up my sleeves and got stuck in, cleaning what I could. Ann, Tony and Dad were delighted to see me, even if Elsie hadn't been. By the end of the weekend, she pulled me to one side to speak with me. We were alone in the kitchen when she grabbed me roughly by the arm.

'If you want to come home then you're gonna have to pay your way,' she hissed, spitting out the words in my face.

'What do you mean? This is my home.'

'Yes, but you're a working woman now. You're earning, so you need to contribute. It's only fair on your poor father.'

I shook my head in disbelief. *Surely Dad didn't want me to pay to come home at weekends*. But Elsie was adamant.

'If you want to come home then it'll cost you 2 pounds, 12 shillings and 6 pence,' she demanded, holding out her grubby little hand.

'But that's what I earn in a month!'

She shrugged her shoulders as though it wasn't her problem.

'It's not up to me,' she insisted. 'It's what your dad says I should charge you.'

I was flabbergasted because Dad had never asked me to pay before. I felt a knot of anxiety clench inside my stomach. *What if things were more desperate than I thought?*

'I can't afford it,' I argued.

Elsie ran a hand through her unruly, thick grey hair. She tucked a greasy strand behind her right ear and turned back towards the sink. 'If you can't afford to pay then you can't come home, it's as simple as that.'

My heart plummeted like a stone. I'd only just received my first proper wage but I paid what I owed and left, knowing I'd never be able to afford to return. I wanted to ask Dad why he needed to charge me but I thought better of it because I didn't want to embarrass him. I also worried that he'd take Elsie's side instead of mine. *That must be why the house was in such a state. Dad must be broke*, I reasoned on the bus journey back to

Huddersfield. The rain pattered softly against the glass of the window, mirroring how I felt inside – both tearful and miserable. I stared at my reflection, trying my best not to cry. The bus slowly wound its way out of Doncaster, leaving my home far behind, and I returned to college where I threw myself into my studies. If I couldn't afford to go home then I'd use my time wisely and try to become the best nurse I could. Thankfully, my housemates were a joy to live with, and slowly, as each month passed, we learned the basics of nursing. One day, we decided we needed to get fit so we got up extra early, donned our shorts and went for a brisk run around the park. Feeling totally invigorated, we decided to run another circuit, and then another, until we'd jogged around constantly for two hours. We returned to the house en masse, where we washed, ate breakfast and got ready for our day's lectures. But we were so shattered by the run that we promptly fell asleep in the first lecture. The teacher was puzzled and asked why her class were so sleepy.

'We were trying to get fit, Miss,' a voice called from the back of the room.

The teacher looked across a dozen sets of bleary eyes as we began to yawn in unison.

'Well, it didn't seem to work, girls, did it?'

The following morning, I ached so much that I thought I'd broken something. My legs were too stiff at the knee to bend. I spent the rest of the day walking around like the Tin Man from *The Wizard of Oz*. After that, I decided that if I wanted to get fit then I'd have to do it in moderation, not all at once.

Our year-long pre-nursing studies were essentially split into an introduction course and three blocks of learning: three months in the hospital kitchen learning how to cook and prepare 'invalid food'; three in the laundry, washing the dirty and blood-ied sheets; and the final three with Home Sister, learning how to thoroughly clean the house to her incredibly high standards. Looking back, it sounds extreme, but it served a purpose, because by the time we'd finished we all had the same impeccably high standards. But it wasn't all work – far from it. It was also lots of fun. One day, we were kicking our heels after lectures when I decided to play a practical joke on the Sister in charge who, despite the house being huge, slept in a bedroom on the ground floor next to the main entrance. This was to ensure her young trainee nurses didn't leave or return at 'inappropriate hours'. There was a medical skeleton in the classroom, so I removed the skull, looped a piece of string around a bolt fastened on the top, unravelled the string and dangled it out of my bedroom window, which was situated directly above Sister's. I carefully lowered the skull until it was in line with her window. My friends stifled a giggle as I began to swing it to and fro like a pendulum. When it had gained enough momentum I swung it forward so that it tapped lightly against her windowpane.

TAP. TAP. TAP.

By now my mates were killing themselves laughing, so much so that they had tears streaming down their faces. Moments later, the sash window scraped open as Sister popped her head out and came face to face with the dangling skull. But she didn't scream; instead she craned her neck upwards and caught me holding onto the other end of the string.

'Hello, Sister.' I smiled weakly before pulling the skull up as fast as I could.

Thankfully she had a great sense of humour.

'Nurse Smith, you will be the death of me, I swear!' she said, laughing, as she popped her head back inside and closed her bedroom window.

From then on I became known as the joker of the house.

A few days later, Sister stopped me on the stairs.

'Nurse Smith,' she called. I stopped dead in my tracks and turned to face her, wondering what on earth I'd done wrong.

'I always know when you're on cleaning duties,' she sighed, tapping her foot against the step.

My mind raced. *Maybe my idea of cleanliness wasn't up to her high standards?*

I cleared my throat and spoke. 'Why, Sister?'

'Because you always make a clatter, dropping the hand brush down the stairs whenever you do it!' A smirk spread across her face and I watched as she turned and continued down the stairs. I could still hear her giggling away to herself as she walked into her bedroom and closed the door. I laughed too because I knew it was true – I loved the idea of being a nurse but sometimes I tried so hard that it made me clumsy.

I didn't want to go home at weekends because I didn't want to see Elsie, and Dad didn't rent a telephone then so I couldn't even call him. Instead, I went back to friends' houses. My pal Glenys lived close to the moor near Castle Hill, just outside Huddersfield. Glenys's father was a slaughterhouse man so they were poor and working class, just like me. However, her father also had the broadest Yorkshire accent I'd ever heard in my life. By the end of the weekend, as I gathered my things to leave, he mumbled something I didn't understand.

'Aht bahn ame,' he said gruffly.

I shook my head. I didn't have a clue what he was saying, so I looked to Glenys for translation.

'He asked when you were going home,' she explained.

I looked at him and shook my head. 'Oh no, I can't afford it,' I replied.

Glenys's dad shook his head; now it was his turn to look confused.

Only one girl left the nursing college. She was a sweet enough lass, but she couldn't keep up. Nursing was such a hands-on job that you had to be physically up to it, as well as mentally. But it did have its perks, namely the respect you got from members of the general public. As a trainee nurse in Huddersfield, I never had to pay a single bus fare. Instead, I was allowed to travel free, and often others would step aside in the queue to let me on the bus first. I valued both my occupation and outdoor uniform – a blue Mackintosh, cornflower-blue dress and black shoes – which I wore with immense pride.

After a year in training, and with only half a day per week working in the hospital, it was time for us to be let loose on the wards. At first the building had felt massive, but in reality it was just a regular-size town hospital. One of the first wards I worked on was the Ear, Nose and Throat, where children would come in to have their tonsils removed. As soon as they arrived we'd ply them with ice cream because it not only helped ease their sore throats, it also numbed the area. It was a pretty routine op and afterwards the hospital porter would collect the young patient from theatre, carrying them over his shoulder in a fireman's lift to prevent them from choking on their own blood. The children would usually stay in overnight. It was my job to care for them because I worked the night shift. Many of them were still young, only seven or eight years old, and, in some cases, it'd be their first night away from home, so I tried my best to comfort them throughout the night.

A month or so later, I was transferred to the casualty department where, because of the proximity of the hospital to the Pennines and the harsh winters there, lots of youngsters suffering from chest infections were admitted. Back in those days, no one had central heating; besides, these were the toughened children of farmers and land workers, so more often than not they'd be admitted wearing a 'liberty bodice'. The bodices were made out of a thick cotton material with a fleece liner. They would be permanently stitched around the children's bodies to help them survive the bleak, long winter. Underneath, their skin would be smeared with goose fat to create a disgusting type of body insulation. Most of my time in casualty was spent cutting poorly children out of these liberty bodices so that we could treat them, but inevitably, when the wrappers came off, they stunk to high heaven.

'All right?' I asked one little boy as I sliced some sharpened scissors through his outer bodice.

He nodded, his big, wide eyes looking straight up at me. I thought I'd been well prepared, but as soon as I removed the cloth the smell was so bad that it caught at the back of my throat, choking me. I held my breath to stop myself being sick. Soap, it seemed, only reached so far and didn't cut through goose fat.

Now we were working on the wards, my fellow student nurses and I had transferred from the college house to the nurses' home, where we slept in between shifts. The nurses' home was situated inside the hospital grounds, a stone's throw from the police college. It was down the road and housed lots of nice trainee police officers. Our official curfew time was 10 p.m., but we often broke the rule, returning an hour or two later. To get around this, I made friends with nurses who had a bedroom on the ground floor. As a group, we'd plan whose turn it was to leave their window open so that we could sneak back in through it. However, on one occasion it was so dark outside that all the windows looked exactly the same. I climbed in and fell on a poor unsuspecting nurse slumbering soundly in her bed. She screamed so loud that she woke up the entire block. Thankfully I was lithe and fast on my feet, so I was able to run to my room before anyone realised I was the intruder.

The casualty department was where I first fell in love. Shy and inexperienced, I became smitten with a male nurse called Stanley. He was almost ten years older than me, in his late twenties, but to me, a girl of 17, he was the height of male sophistication. Tall and with smouldering film-star looks, Stanley was so kind to me, and when he bought me flowers one day I was so thrilled I thought I would burst with joy. Afterwards, every time I cut my finger or felt a fishbone stick slightly inside my throat, I ran straight to the casualty department to seek immediate medical attention from the lovely Stanley. There was only one fly in the ointment: Stanley was homosexual. But I was young and naïve, and I'd never heard of a man being homosexual, so I was totally stumped as to why he didn't consider me in the same way. It was down to the lovely Sister le Fleur to set me straight and let me down gently. She quietly informed me that, sadly, Stanley's intentions were entirely honourable, and I had mistaken his friendship for love.

'You're just not his type, Nurse Smith,' she sighed, patting me kindly on the shoulder.

'What do you mean?' I asked, hurt and a little confused.

'It's Stanley. He doesn't go for girls. He's homosexual, so I'm afraid you are wasting your time.'

The news hit me like a sharp slap across the face. I was heartbroken, but I realised that, even with all the will in the world, Stanley and I would never be more than just good friends.

Stanley and the other male nurses were very protective of us young female nurses. One evening, I'd worked a particularly long and gruelling night shift when I was overcome with exhaustion.

'Why don't you go and have a kip?' another nurse, called David, suggested.

'But where?' I sighed. I was terrified Matron would catch me sleeping on the job.

'There's a side room, just down the corridor,' he said, pointing over to it. 'There's a bed in it. Go on, I'll wake you up in an hour if we get busy.'

I was so tired from standing on my feet for hours on end that I did as he said. I shut the door behind me, pulled back the covers and climbed into bed, where I fell into a deep sleep. I'd only been snoozing for a matter of minutes when David came bursting back in through the door.

'Joan, Joan, wake up!' His voice sounded panicked and urgent.

Bleary eyed, I sat up and stretched my arms above my head.

'Has it been an hour already?' I yawned.

'No!' David gasped as he proceeded to unceremoniously drag me out of the room with my legs trailing along the floor behind me. I looked up at him because, for a split second, I thought he'd gone completely mad! I was about to protest when he plonked me down and ran back to close the door.

'David, what on earth's going on?'

'It's the room,' he explained, trying to catch his breath. 'It's being fumigated. I've only just found out. They're burning some cones in there, but you must've been so tired that you didn't notice. As soon as I heard, I ran in to get you. Sorry, Joan, I didn't know, otherwise I wouldn't have told you to go in there.'

It transpired that the fumes had been highly toxic, and if David hadn't come to rescue me when he did I would have died in that bed. The whole episode shook me, and it made me think about my life, my family and my mum. I wondered what she looked like after all these years. *Had she changed? Did she still have the same distinctive red hair? Would she even recognise me? Did she miss us or think of us as often as I thought of her?* All these questions and many more burned inside me. They'd always been there, waiting, but now I was older I felt more able and prepared to meet with her to try to understand why she'd left us behind. I desperately wanted to make contact, but I was worried about Dad. I knew it'd hurt him because he'd see it as a betrayal. But then I thought of Elsie ruling the roost. In many ways I'd already lost him because I was unable to go back home. I felt rootless – as though I had no home. I wanted, no, I *needed* to see Mum, to know that I was still loved. I was fast approaching 18 years of age, and it'd been five long years since I'd last seen her.

A week or so later, I picked up a pen and wrote directly to my Uncle Albert to ask if he had an address. He passed my letter on to a lady, who turned out to be Mum's boyfriend's mother. She in turn gave my note to Mum. Weeks passed, so I presumed my request had fallen on deaf ears. I felt quite emotional because I missed my family, but I couldn't afford to hand over a month's wages for a weekend visit and I hated Elsie with a passion, so I was beginning to feel pretty desperate. To my complete shock and surprise, Mum not only replied, she even invited me down to London. As I boarded the train I felt a little apprehensive, but also a little excited because I knew this journey would change my life. Although it'd been years, the time melted away as soon as I spotted her walking towards me through steam billowing from the train along the platform at King's Cross station. She was still as petite as I remembered, and her hair was auburn, just like mine. In fact, standing there on the crowded platform, we could've been sisters.

'Hello, Mum,' I said as I instinctively held my arms out to greet her.

'You're the last person I expected to forgive me,' she admitted, before falling into my arms. As soon as we embraced I knew that I'd done the right thing.

We travelled back to her flat in Shepherd's Bush, where I met her boyfriend, Bill, who was a London bus driver. I liked Bill immediately. He was a lovely bloke and totally the right man for my mother. Ironically, Mum worked at a hospital, but as a kitchen assistant, in Roehampton. She also cleaned houses for the ladies of society, and used her previous skills as a barmaid to help organise cocktail parties. Mum was beautiful, bubbly and popular with everyone. I stayed there for a week, and when she suggested that I move to London permanently, my mind was already made up. I wrote to the General Nursing Council and transferred from Huddersfield to Hammersmith Hospital in London. I was told I'd start at the beginning of the next training year, so I moved into the London nurses' accommodation on New Year's Eve, 1950. It was miserable spending New Year's Eve alone but the hospital required that I sleep in the nurses' quarters the night before my first shift. I didn't mind because I knew it would be the beginning of a whole new life.

My snap decision to move from one end of the country to the other had left my father devastated because he felt I'd chosen Mum over him, but it wasn't that at all. I knew it wouldn't be easy to explain, so I went to see him before I left Yorkshire to break the news to him face to face. I thought he might take it badly, but not as bad as he actually did.

'You'll never see Ann or Tony again,' he threatened. I realised he was angry and still hurting over Mum. 'After all she's done, after all I've done for you …' he said, his voice choking with emotion.

'What? So why are you charging me to come home for the weekend, then?' I argued.

Dad looked at me and reeled back in horror. 'What on earth are you talking about?'

'Elsie? A month's wage just to come home for the weekend? Well, I couldn't afford it. That's why I've not been back to see you, even though I've been really, really homesick,' I snapped, willing my tears to go away.

It was clear that he didn't have a clue what I was talking about, so I explained all about Elsie and the monthly wage I'd handed over on my first visit home.

Dad gasped in disbelief. 'What? And you really thought I'd charge my own daughter to come home for the weekend?'

'Well, that's what she told me, so I paid her in full – my first month's salary!'

I could see Dad was trying to process what I was saying, and then the penny dropped. Elsie had lied to me and kept the money for herself. Dad vowed to deal with her later but I could tell he was hurt and disappointed in me.

'I can't believe you thought I'd charge you,' he said, slumping down into a chair at the kitchen table as though the stuffing had been knocked clean from him.

'I didn't know what to believe. That's why I never came home – I couldn't afford it.'

He was still trying to digest the news but he gave me a hug and promised to sort something out. Although we'd talked it through, it took him a few months before he eventually calmed down. He wished me well and insisted I was welcome home any time. To make matters worse, before I left the house I saw my coat. It was on the back of Elsie's daughter, who I presumed had also been hoodwinked by her wicked mother. Although I'd wanted to rip it off her, I held my head high, left the house and never said another word. I realised Dad was stuck with Elsie, because he needed to work to feed Tony and Ann. Still, after our conversation he watched her like a hawk. He slowly built a case against her, which was strengthened when she later stole and sold his best suit and gold pocket watch.

'I threw her out,' he later explained. 'You were right; I think she'd been stealing from me for a long time.'

I felt for Dad, because he'd only taken her on so that he could work to keep a roof over our heads. Now he was back to square one again.

3

Mishaps on the Wards

I returned to London and began work at Hammersmith Hospital, which, unlike Huddersfield, was a post-graduate school. Everything about it seemed better – the building, the wards and my wages, which doubled from a paltry £2 a month to almost £4.

The hospital was also massive in comparison – three times the size of Huddersfield. Before, I'd been able to navigate the wards in less than half an hour, but Hammersmith was so big that it took me three hours just to walk around it all. The main entrance was incredibly grand and housed a small shop just inside the foyer. The corridors cut through the building like arteries, carrying doctors, nurses and patients, and in some places they seemed up to half a mile long. The hospital had specialised units and modern wards spread out over four blocks, and you had to cross a yard to access each one. There was maternity at one end and A&E at the other, mirroring both life and death.

Unlike my old hospital, the maternity ward housed a neonatal unit for premature babies. This was cutting-edge medicine at the time. At Huddersfield, all premature babies had to be rushed to Sheffield for specialised treatment, but in London it was all under one roof. There were also units for radiotherapy and diabetes patients. The place was swarming with post-graduate students, nurses and doctors. Before, there'd been just one matron in charge, but at Hammersmith there was a deputy and a stand-in matron too. It was similar with the sister tutor. At Huddersfield there had been just one, but in London there was one with three under-tutors to support her. I felt totally out of my depth.

As students, we were expected to do everything, usually the jobs that no one else wanted to do. I worked on the children's ward, where I had the unenviable task of delousing young patients. Initially, I felt totally frustrated because I was treated like a country bumpkin, but after three months working in the children's ward I transferred to the geriatric ward, where I made a real name for myself after mixing up all the patients' false teeth. I'd spent three hours cleaning them, and once I'd finished I was delighted. I popped them back inside the sterilised bowl and made my way back up to the ward. However, the smile was soon wiped off my face by Sister.

'Er, how do you know whose teeth are whose?' she said, pointing towards the bucket.

I looked at her and then down at the dozen sets of teeth, all spotlessly clean but now hopelessly jumbled up.

'Oh,' I replied as my heart sank to my knees.

I spent the rest of the afternoon trying to match the rightful owner to each set, but it was an impossible and thankless task. Some of the patients were elderly and suffered with dementia, so, upon seeing a better pair of dentures, they claimed them even if they didn't fit. At one point a fight almost broke out. In the end, it took me the best part of the day to try to fit each person to each set, but it taught me the importance of labelling.

Shamed by the teeth débâcle, I transferred from geriatrics to the medical ward, where I worked a series of night shifts. But it wasn't long before I made a name for myself again. One evening, I was asked to clean out the sluice. It was a horrible task, and as soon as I entered I recoiled at the stench of urine. It was so strong that it choked the back of my throat. I immediately spotted the culprits, a dozen half-full Winchester bottles of urine that had stunk the place out. Pinching the end of my nose and trying not to breathe in too deeply, I emptied each and every one of them, sterilised the bottles, lined them up on the side in a neat row and wiped down the surfaces. Exhausted but satisfied I'd done a thorough job, I returned to the ward, where the nurses on the day shift were just about to take over. Once I was off duty, I headed back to my room where I flopped straight into bed. I was so tired that I fell asleep as soon as my head hit the pillow, but moments later I was woken by the sound of someone banging furiously at my door.

'You need to come to the ward – Sister wants to see you,' a voice called from the corridor.

'But I've just finished my shift and I'm in bed!' I protested, pulling the blanket up over my head.

'I don't care. Get dressed and come to the ward immediately!'

I didn't know who the voice had belonged to, but as I heard their footsteps disappear off down the corridor I sat upright in bed. Even in my hazy slumber I knew it was an order rather than a request. I was thoroughly shattered but I dragged myself up, pulled on my uniform and headed back up to the medical ward. By the time I arrived Sister was waiting for me with both arms folded. She looked absolutely furious.

'Is this her?' a man's voice called from behind. I dipped to the side to try to see where the voice was coming from, and that's when I spotted them – the professor and a line of junior doctors. They were all staring at me.

'Yes, this is the one,' she snapped, her eyes not leaving me for a second. 'When I asked you to clean the sluice, did you, er, throw anything away?'

I remembered the dozen stinky bottles on the side.

'Just some bottles of urine,' I muttered.

'Well, yes. And those bottles just happened to be 24-hour specimen samples that the professor and his doctors were waiting for the results from.'

My mouth formed the letter O as I felt my heart plummet, because I'd done it again. Once more, my exploits had become legendary. My distinctive red hair had marked me out from the other nurses, but not in a good way. Everyone, it seemed, remembered the young redhead nurse who'd thrown away a dozen important samples. It was such a serious offence that I was called in front of Matron to explain myself. I felt my legs tremble as I stood before her.

'In future, please would you enquire what is asked of you rather than take it upon yourself to decide what needs to be done,' she said, scowling at me from her desk.

'Yes, Matron. Sorry, Matron,' I replied, almost curtseying my way out of the door. I was just relieved to have escaped an even worse punishment.

In total there were fourteen nurses who, like me, had transferred from other hospitals. The other nurses had trained from scratch at Hammersmith and, because we were taught separately to them, they thought they were a cut above. In turn, there was a kind of camaraderie between the transfer nurses, who looked out for one another. At that time, the nurses' accommodation was situated directly across the road from Wormwood Scrubs. We were told to keep our curtains shut to stop the prisoners peeping in at us, and the prison siren would often sound to alert us every time a prisoner had escaped.

One evening, it'd just started to get dark outside when I heard the siren wail. I immediately went through the protocol of locking the fire-escape door in a bid to protect my patients and stop a would-be escapee from seeking refuge inside the hospital. But the latch on the door was broken and it wouldn't lock. To make matters worse, my ward was on the ground floor and, with only my patients for company, I felt extremely alone and vulnerable. In a panic, I ran to the ward telephone to call a friend who I knew was working in the ward above.

'I can't lock the door, Joyce. The latch is broken!' I gasped. 'Can you come down here and try to help me secure it?'

Joyce had already secured her ward and had a junior nurse working alongside her so she popped downstairs to see what she could do.

'I can't lock it either!' she said in a fluster. 'What shall we do?'

By now we were both terrified that the ward would be invaded by a dangerous criminal. I looked around for a weapon to protect us with, and that's when I spotted it resting up against the wall in a corner of the room – a long, old-fashioned umbrella with a big, heavy wooden handle.

'This should do the trick,' I said, sizing it up in my hands and gripping it like a rounders bat.

We stood there, one of us on either side of the door, watching, waiting and listening out for the escaped convict. My heart thumped hard inside my chest as adrenalin coursed through my veins, and that's when it happened. We heard a slight noise, then urgent footsteps on the other side. I held the umbrella aloft, poised and about to strike, when the door suddenly creaked open and a strange man stepped through. Joyce gasped out loud, so I shut my eyes and brought the weapon down with all my might. The force of the blow was astonishing as I struck the man bluntly on the top of his head, causing the wooden handle to reverberate through my hands.

WHACK!

'OWWWW!' the intruder cried as he staggered inside. He tried to regain his balance and put out a hand to grab against something, and that's when I noticed his bowler hat. It'd been smashed by the brolly and was sitting on top of his head like a squashed flat cap!

'What on earth …' I gasped. I realised that it wasn't a convict at all, but a gentleman – and a well-to-do one at that.

'You almost killed me!' he wailed dramatically, still staggering. Joyce and I ran over and, grabbing him under each arm, sat him down in a chair.

But I was still a little cross. He was right, I could've have killed him, but it was his own stupid fault for sneaking in through the fire exit!

'You shouldn't have come in through there,' I said, gesturing towards the door. 'What on earth were you thinking?'

'There's a prisoner on the loose!' he gasped. 'I knew the door was broken so I thought I'd get inside fast.' He winced as his fingers bobbed gently across the top of his head feeling for blood. There was none.

'I know there's a prisoner on the loose! That's why I hit you – I thought you were him!' I huffed.

But the more I looked, the more I thought I recognised him. I'd definitely seen his face somewhere before.

'Anyway, who are you?' I asked as I surveyed the top of his head for damage. There was none, but his bowler hat was ruined.

'I'm the dean of the hospital,' he replied curtly, 'and now I've got an almighty headache, thanks to you and that thing.' He pointed at the umbrella in my hand. I propped the offending item back against the wall, and took a guilty step away from it.

The dean stood up and stomped out of the ward as my jaw hit the floor. I turned to Joyce, my face a picture of pure horror. In the background a patient coughed but, other than that, you could've heard a pin drop as we all watched him leave.

'Joan,' Joyce gasped, putting her hand against her mouth. 'You're going to be in so much trouble.'

Thankfully, the dean never told a soul about my vicious assault on him, and after that I tried to keep my head down. A few weeks later, I was still trying to keep a low profile, when I wandered through a ward. I noticed a friend of mine standing at the other end of it, weighing a skinny old man on a large set of scales. This particular nurse was a good laugh and well known for practical jokes, so I decided to get my own back. Tiptoeing quietly behind them, I edged my shoe along the back of the scales as they both stared at the dial, waiting for it to settle. I suppressed a giggle and silently pushed down my foot to try to get a reaction. With enough force I'd managed to add on another stone to the skinny fella. My colleague spotted me lurking behind the patient and grinned, so the man turned to face me. You can imagine my shock when I recognised him – it was the dean of the hospital, again! He was being weighed before a minor operation.

'You!' he said, pointing a bony finger at me. 'What is it about me that you can't leave alone?'

I shook my head, trying to think of an explanation. Then I noticed the faint flicker of a smile as he began to laugh. Lucky for me, the dean had a good sense of humour.

'Oops!' I smirked as I walked away.

My reputation as Calamity Jane went before me and soon I was transferred again, this time to the surgical ward. A young man, who was the same age as me, had been admitted for an emergency appendix operation. At that time, patients had to be shaved down below for such things and normally it was a job for the male porter. However, on that particular day he was off, so it was left to me. I grabbed what I needed, including a razor, shaving cream and a bowl of warm water, and pushed the trolley towards his bed. Some of the other male patients had already been shaved and so, when they heard the telltale squeak of the trolley, they knew what was coming. They were also total wind-up merchants, and as soon as I'd drawn the curtain around the poor boy's bed the banter started.

'Hey, this is her first time. Watch out! She might nick you!' one called.

I pulled the curtain aside slightly and gave him a stern look. It didn't work.

'She's new to this sort of thing,' warned another, 'but don't worry, son, if anything drops off and falls on the floor, we'll pick it up for you.'

With that, the whole ward dissolved into fits of laughter. More comments followed but I held my nerve and tried to get on with the job in hand, namely shaving the poor lad's private parts. I tried not to look at him as the razor shook in my trembling hand. He flushed bright red and pulled the pillow out from underneath his head and covered his face with it. I wasn't sure if it was through embarrassment or downright fear! It took a little longer than expected, but eventually he was as smooth as a newborn babe.

'Thanks, Nurse,' he offered, smiling weakly as I popped the razor back into the bowl and covered him up with the bed sheet.

'You're welcome,' I replied, blushing a little.

As I drew the curtain, the metal rings scraped against the metal pole, signalling that I'd finished. The rest of the ward looked up and it started all over again. I walked out to a series of catcalls and light teasing.

'Look, Arthur, she's blushing!'

'No, I'm not. Now go to sleep. You're supposed to be ill!' I laughed, pretending to scold them.

The young lad had his operation, and a week later he was ready to leave hospital. Before he did, he beckoned me over.

'I just wondered if you'd like to go out with me some time, on a date or something,' he asked nervously.

His question jolted me because I hadn't expected it. At first I wasn't sure what to do, but I told myself that he was no longer a patient so what harm could it do?

'Er, that's fine,' I agreed.

'Great. Here's my number, if you want to call me.'

I took his number but I never got to go on the date. I didn't even make the call because, just days later, his mother was on the phone to Sister calling me all the names under the sun.

'She's corrupted my boy! She's shaved him downstairs and now she wants to go on a date with him!'

I was duly summoned to Sister's office, where I was asked to explain myself. Thankfully, Sister was sympathetic and nodded throughout. She was a natural blonde so knew what it was like to be me.

'It's the hair,' she remarked. 'People remember you. His mother certainly did because she told me she didn't want "that red-haired bitch" going anywhere near her son!'

I clasped a horrified hand to my chest – I was absolutely mortified.

'But he asked me out, not the other way around,' I protested.

'I know, but I also think he became a little bit infatuated with you after you shaved him down below. So I think it's best all round if you decline his offer, don't you?'

'Yes, Sister.'

She was right about the hair; it was a total hindrance.

One day, I'd accompanied Matron and the consultant on his ward rounds. The doctor examined a man who'd been having trouble with his hearing, and, after a few moments, he turned to me.

'Nurse, I need an auroscope.'

I nodded and went towards the office at the back of the ward. I returned clutching the morning paper, but Matron and the doctor looked at me a little baffled.

'What's this?' the consultant asked as I handed over the newspaper.

'Today's horoscopes … in the paper?' I muttered, realising in a split second that I'd just dropped another clanger.

He tried his best not to laugh but I could see that he was having great difficulty. It was a good job he saw the funny side because Matron's face looked like thunder – she was absolutely furious with me for showing her up.

'I want to make him better, Nurse, not tell his future!' the doctor chuckled.

I felt myself blush as he walked away.

The night shifts were long and sometimes seemed never-ending. Often, a few of us would wander down to an open-air swimming pool in White City to get a bit of fresh air. One day, I was with two colleagues when a chap named Peter came over to talk to us. He was tallish, around 5 feet 10 inches, with jet-black hair slicked back. He also wore glasses, which I thought made him look terribly sophisticated. He told us he was there with a friend called Bob who had a good job working for an oil company in Kuwait. Peter seemed keen on my friend, a beautiful brunette called 'Jimmy' James. I never did find out her Christian name because she insisted that everyone call her 'Jimmy' for short. Meanwhile, Bob was sweet on Jo, a blonde, so I was the redheaded gooseberry in between the four lovebirds. One day,

Bob asked if we'd like to go to a lido in Ruislip. I wasn't keen because I knew I'd be the odd one out, but Jimmy and Jo were so excited that I agreed to tag along. However, I soon became bored so I decided to burn the hairs off the legs of the men with a cigarette just to get them to move.

'Ouch!' Peter said, patting the scorched skin of his leg. It made me smile.

I wasn't a total lost cause because I had a sweetheart of my own, an American Air Force photographer called Bill. Mum had a holiday home down on the coast in Hastings, and that's where I'd arrange to meet Bill. He'd bring me coffee and endless supplies of stockings, but in London I was all alone. The five of us went out a few times but eventually Jimmy dumped Peter for a Guards officer, so one day we found ourselves thrown together. I secretly liked Peter because he was different to everyone else. He was strong-willed and knew his own mind. He also refused to be swayed by others, and I admired that in a man. However, it also meant that we always ended up doing what he wanted to do.

'Let's go to the pub,' he suggested one afternoon as we strolled past one.

'No, I don't really drink,' I explained.

'Oh, that's a shame. You'd better wait outside for me, then,' he replied, before heading inside the door.

I was so headstrong and independent that I wasn't used to having a man tell me what to do, so his manner had shocked me. But I also quite liked the fact that he was authoritative and good-looking, so I let it go and followed him inside.

'Why do you wear glasses? Are you short-sighted?' I asked as we sat down at a table with our drinks.

Peter adjusted his glasses and began to explain.

'No, when I was a baby I had a problem with one of my eyes – it turned inwards. I had it corrected but it didn't work, so now

I only have limited vision in it. Although this one,' he said, pointing towards his left eye, 'is absolutely perfect!'

I loved Peter's honesty and found his uncomplicated view on life totally refreshing. But Mum wasn't as keen. They were both strong characters, with big personalities to match, so they constantly clashed.

'He's an arrogant bastard!' she muttered underneath her breath one evening – loud enough for me to hear.

At that time, Peter was a qualified plumber working for the council, but Mum had always wanted me to marry a doctor, so she thought he was beneath me. To make matters worse, Peter's mum didn't like me very much either, so we had a battle on our hands just to stay together as the mum-in-laws plotted and planned to split us up.

'I wish we could get away from here,' I sighed as we sat together in the pub.

I knew I wanted to spend the rest of my life with Peter, and he with me, too, but the constant nagging and interference from both sides had put a strain on our relationship. Instead, we tried to stay out as much as possible. We'd go to the pictures, for drinks, or we'd simply take our bikes and cycle alongside the River Thames. Peter was a football fanatic, a QPR supporter. He lived close to their ground so he'd go down there every Saturday. In the evening, we'd go out for dinner – usually a fish restaurant because it was his favourite. Sometimes we'd take a picnic and meet up with our friends Bert and Joan. The four of us would take a bus to Uxbridge, which had wide-open spaces where Peter and I were able to kick off our shoes, run barefoot through the grass and relax in the sunshine – anything to stay out of our mothers' ways.

As it got closer to my SRN (State Registered Nurse) exams, Peter tried to help me revise. He'd look through the textbook and fire questions at me. Over the months, he'd become so knowledgeable about all things medical that I'm certain he knew just as much as I did.

'You'd make as good a nurse as me!' I teased, throwing a cushion at him.

'Well, I've got the legs,' he laughed, flashing me an ankle.

As my twenty-first birthday drew close, Peter decided that I should start saving up.

'Just a few bits … for your bottom drawer,' he suggested.

'Was that a marriage proposal?' I gasped.

Peter arched one eyebrow. 'Well, maybe I should get you a ring first?'

I tried not to laugh. Instead, I wrapped my arms around his neck and gave him a kiss. Peter wasn't the type to go in for the full bended-knee marriage-proposal bit, so this was as good as it got.

'All right, I do!'

We visited an old-fashioned jeweller on Uxbridge Road, where Peter spent £8 – a fifth of his monthly wage – on a single solitaire diamond ring. We were officially engaged on 23 February 1953, but we didn't have a party because we couldn't afford one. When he finally slipped the ring on my wedding finger I was so happy, I thought I would burst. I passed my SRN in June 1953, and 18 months later I married my beloved Peter the week before Christmas, on 18 December 1954. We were wed at St Luke's church in Shepherd's Bush. I bought my wedding dress from Shepherd's Bush market for £5 and 5 shillings. The veil and headdress cost me a further £3, but I didn't care.

Throughout the year I'd saved up enough to line my bottom drawer with things for our new home, but none more prized than a beautiful crystal fruit-bowl set. It comprised one big bowl and six smaller ones, but it didn't stay that way for long. Every time

Peter and I had an argument, his mother insisted he claim back some of our 'bottom drawer' goods, just in case. But more importantly, she'd always tell him to take back the fruit-bowl set. That set of bowls travelled constantly between Peter's mother and me, so much so that, by the time we'd married, there was only one small bowl left because all the others had been smashed.

We lived in rooms above Mum's flat, which was a big mistake; they were cramped quarters and the walls were paper-thin, so she heard every word. She tried her best to split us up. She bickered and constantly had a go at Peter. She'd ask him to bring up coal from the yard below to light the fire. He hated being told what to do so he'd refuse and dig his heels in, which only served to infuriate her even more. In the end, I'd collect the coal for a quiet life.

'But it's a man's job. You shouldn't be doing that – he should!' Mum protested. I simply couldn't win.

Peter's mum was also meddling but in a much more subtle way. If she knew I was cooking his dinner she'd go out of her way to invite him over, cook a meal and turn on the TV to delay him further. We didn't own a TV so, inevitably, I'd be sitting at home for him in front of a stone-cold dinner for two. I'd simmer away with anger, waiting to explode. The outside influence took its toll and eventually I decided enough was enough. I was 22 years old but, in many ways, I felt as though my life was already over. I loved Peter with all my heart. He'd supported me during my nursing exams and had always been my rock and shoulder to cry on when I'd had a tough day at work, but his meddling mother had made our relationship impossible.

By this time, my father had started a relationship with a widow, an old family friend called Polly. She was a wonderful woman and she loved and cared for my siblings as though they were her own. But just as Dad had started to move on with his life, mine had stalled to a halt. Polly had three children: Val, who was the same age as me; Harry, her eldest who'd already left home; and her youngest child, Meryl, who was the same age as Tony. It meant there was no room for me, but I wrote to Dad and Polly to tell them how unhappy I was in London.

Maybe it's time to come back home, Dad wrote in reply.

It made perfect sense. I loved Peter but he constantly argued with Mum and she'd retaliate. Neither of them would back down and I'd had enough. I bought a train ticket and travelled back to Yorkshire to visit Dad and Polly.

'You've lived Peter's way of life so perhaps it's time he tried your way of life for a change,' my father suggested.

I nodded my head because it was true. I was utterly miserable living in rooms above Mum, with Peter's mother constantly sticking her nose into our business. Each week it seemed as though the gulf between us had grown wider. My father was right; paradoxically, the only way to save my marriage was to leave Peter and return to Yorkshire.

4

Going Home

I went to see my doctor, who told me in no uncertain terms that I was so stressed out that I was on the verge of a nervous breakdown. I felt it too. Mum was always arguing with Peter over nothing. He refused to kowtow to her, so we lived in a permanent stalemate with me caught in the middle. Secretly, I'd started applying for jobs in Doncaster to see what came up, although I never told a soul, apart from Dad and a staff nurse at work called Maggie.

'We'll miss you if you go, Joan,' she sighed.

'It's just that no one will listen to me, Maggie. I feel as though I'm banging my head against a brick wall. It's got so bad that I dread going home because Peter's so headstrong that he won't listen to me, not any more. He just seems intent on winning the argument with Mum, and she's impossible to live with. I can't win.'

Maggie looked at me. We were standing in the corridor at work with people flying past us but, thankfully, everyone was too busy to stop and eavesdrop on our conversation. Maggie thought for a moment and then spoke quietly.

'If it's that bad then I think your dad is right, Joan. I think you need to go home.'

I looked up at her.

'Do you really think so?'

She nodded. 'If it's going to make you happy, then yes, I do.'

I knew I'd miss Hammersmith and my colleagues, but I felt caught between a rock and a hard place and I needed to escape for my own sanity. Weeks later, I received a response from a nursing home in Doncaster. I told Peter I was going home for the weekend when I was actually going for a job interview. I got the job, returned to London and handed in a month's notice at work. Of course, people were shocked when I told them I was leaving.

'We're moving back to Yorkshire,' I explained, only there was no 'we' about it.

One night, when Peter was still at work, I came home from the hospital and packed my suitcase. I worried he'd find it and stop me, so I hid it under some stuff at the back of the wardrobe, knowing he'd never think to look there. The following day, after everyone had left for work, I sat down and wrote Peter a note.

Dear Peter, I've been to see the doctor who says I'm on the verge of a nervous breakdown, I began. I read and reread the sentence. It sounded a little melodramatic written on the page, but it was true. My hand shook slightly as I continued. *He says I need to get away so I've decided to go back to my dad's house. I'll be in touch later, lots of love, Joan x*

The note was short and sweet but it said all it needed to say. I found it difficult to write because I hated the thought of running out on anyone, yet that's exactly what I was doing. Unlike my mother, I didn't have children and I was leaving purely because of the constant interference from both sides. I was convinced if I did stay it would only be ten times worse. But I was at the end of my tether and couldn't see another way out. I had to leave London for my own sanity. I read the note again, folded the paper in half and ran my fingers along it to form a neat crease. I placed it inside a small white envelope, sealed it and propped it up against the teapot in the middle of the kitchen table. I glanced up at the clock on the wall; only a few more hours until my train left for Yorkshire. Deep down, I was terrified that Peter would finish work early and find me at home. Less than half an hour later, I closed the door on our rooms in Brackenbury Road, Shepherd's Bush, and on my married life. I took the tube and headed over to King's Cross station, fraught with anxiety.

What if Peter comes home and dashes over to look for me? How would I explain myself?

But I hadn't thought that far ahead. All I knew was that, right then, I needed to go home so desperately that the homesickness ached inside my bones. I hid away in a corner of the café at King's Cross station, watching the hand of the brown Bakelite clock slowly tick by.

Dad knew I was coming, so he'd prepared a bed for me. He picked me up from Doncaster station when I arrived, and I stayed the first night with him. The following morning, I travelled to the nursing home. I'd been told I'd be responsible for running the home along with two other trained staff. Unfortunately, one of those was a decrepit 80-year-old nun. The owner wasn't much help either; she was bedridden due to a heart complaint, and she barked orders at me from her single bed. In many ways I felt sorry for her, but I soon realised, sick or not, she still wasn't a very nice person.

'I'll need you to work 12-hour night shifts, five times a week,' she informed me. The horror must have shown on my face because she quickly added, 'But, of course, I'll pay you a little extra.'

However, that was where her generosity started and ended. I discovered to my dismay that she kept the fridge firmly locked with a padlock and chain to stop staff from helping themselves. Not that there was much time to eat. She'd leave me a few slices of bacon and a drop of milk for my supper, but as the live-in help I felt I couldn't complain. My bedroom was situated on the top floor. It was a small but clean room, and all I needed at that moment in time. The nursing home housed twenty-four patients: twelve were private patients with their own rooms on the first floor, while the other dozen NHS ones were mixed in together according to gender. I was assigned an auxiliary nurse to help me, which was a blessing, because I needed the extra pair of hands. One night, it was freezing cold even though the home had been fitted with a hot-water-boiler heating system.

'Blimey, it's bloody freezing in here!' I remarked to the auxiliary as we turned the sheets over on a patient's bed.

'Didn't you stoke the boiler?' she asked, a little startled.

I looked up at her blankly.

'The boiler. We have to stoke it every few hours to keep it going so that it doesn't burn out,' she said.

I ran downstairs to the basement and threw some coke on it to try to fire it back into life.

The following morning, after spending the night caring for twenty-four elderly patients, my work still wasn't done because I had to cook everyone's breakfast. I'd started at 8 o'clock the evening before but I couldn't leave or go to bed until 8 o'clock the following morning, when the day-shift workers arrived. It was such gruelling work that I felt less like a nurse and more like Cinderella, locked away in the kitchen.

Shortly afterwards, we had a death in the nursing home. I tried to ring the doctor to come and certify death, but he was already out on his emergency calls and I couldn't get hold of anyone else. With a dead body and no doctor, the auxiliary nurse and I had to lift the poor deceased woman and wrap her inside a canvas sheet. We laid her on a table in the garage, which was used as a makeshift mortuary, until 9 o'clock the following morning when the doctor finally arrived to certify death. I began to hate the nursing home with a passion. Strangely, I didn't mind the long hours – it felt good to keep busy because when I was busy I didn't think about Peter or our marriage. But I hated the fact that they used me as nothing more than a qualified skivvy.

One day, my sister, Ann, called for me. By this time, Ann was training to become a hairdresser. She had no money so she'd walked 2 miles to reach me. I was summoned downstairs by another member of staff, who tapped on my bedroom door.

'Your sister is waiting in reception for you.'

I was surprised but also a little worried. I'd been invited over to Dad's house for dinner later that evening because it was my night off, so I worried what was so important that it couldn't wait. I walked downstairs and, as soon as I saw her standing in reception I ran over to give her a hug. I beckoned her to follow me through to the front-room reception, where she sat down on one of the old, worn leather armchairs. But Ann looked uncomfortable – a little troubled, as though there was something on her mind.

'Ann,' I said, cutting straight to the point, 'whatever's the matter?'

Ann's face crumpled as she turned to face me. Something was wrong, I could just tell.

'Dad says I'm not supposed to tell you in case you don't come home later, but Peter's at our house and he's looking for you.'

My heart leapt inside my chest. I'd left London less than a fortnight before, but Peter was here and now he wanted to speak to me and sort things out. I felt a small glimmer of hope. I asked Ann to wait while I nipped upstairs to get my bag so we could leave. As soon as I approached the front gate at home, my family spotted me through the window and made a sharp exit. It would've been comical if it hadn't been such a serious situation.

Dad came outside. He patted me lightly on the arm and muttered something in a low voice.

'I've had a talk with him. He knows what's going on here and he understands. Now it's your turn,' he said, giving me a gentle nudge towards the back door.

As soon as I walked into the house, Peter stood up. He came over, took me in his arms and gave me a hug and a kiss. As he pulled away I gazed into his face – he looked broken. I felt a pang of guilt because I knew I'd done it to him. But I'd been so unhappy, and sometimes desperate situations call for desperate measures. We sat and talked all afternoon. We spoke about our situation in London, living above my mother and the general interference from both sides.

'Your mother is as bad as mine,' I eventually sighed. 'Neither of them wants us to be together.'

Peter agreed.

'So I can't go back there,' I insisted.

Peter nodded. 'I know. I've been speaking to your dad. He says you've lived in my world long enough so it's time I came to live in yours, here in Yorkshire.'

I smiled to myself. *Good old Dad.*

'He even said he'd get me a job,' Peter continued, breaking my thoughts. 'Reckons he could fix me up with something at the pit.'

'Oh, Peter, that's brilliant!'

And it was, because it meant Peter and I could be together and far away from our two meddling mothers. The decision had been made; Peter would leave London and move to Doncaster.

'I've missed you so much,' I wept.

'Me too,' he said, wrapping his arms around me. 'Your mother has been such a cow to me. It's been horrible without you, Joan. I just want to make you happy – I want us both to be happy.'

We spoke long into the afternoon and then he told me something quite unexpected.

'You do know your mother came to Doncaster looking for you after you'd left London, don't you?'

I was astounded.

'Yes,' he continued, 'she scoured all the hospitals in the area but no one had a record of a Joan Hart, so in the end she came back to London.'

Somehow, the fact that both Mum and Peter had come looking for me filled me with hope. I thought no one would have even noticed that I'd gone, but I'd been wrong.

'I love you with all my heart,' I said, taking his hand in mine.

'Me too, Joan, me too.'

Dad was relieved when we told him we'd made up. But first, Peter had to return down south to serve his notice. In a way it made things easier because it gave me time to find us a suitable house to live in.

'I think I can help you there,' Harry, my step-brother, said.

Harry was Polly's eldest son. He was a successful businessman who owned four busy shops, so he mixed in high circles. One of his acquaintances was a flying officer in the RAF who owned a house he was looking to rent out in a place called Balby, situated on the outskirts of Doncaster. The house, on Stanley Street, sounded charming by description, but if I'd imagined a palatial home then I was sorely mistaken. The two up, two down was a complete tip! To make matters worse, the walls rattled every time a train went past on the main line, which ran along the bottom of the garden right beside the outside loo! Still, with little else available, we took it – beggars can't be choosers. Thankfully, Tony and Ann offered to help clean it.

'Don't worry, Joan. We'll soon have it sorted!' Ann said breezily, rolling up her sleeves. I admired her optimism.

There were so many empty beer bottles stashed under the sink and in various hidey-holes around the house that, by the time we'd collected and returned them all to the off-licence – or beeroff, as we called it – we'd earned ourselves £5! The previous tenant, it seemed, had been partial to a drink or three. The house was freezing cold, but thankfully it had a fireplace in the living room, which doubled up as the dining room. Ann would cart huge carrier bags of coal over to me from home, travelling all the way on the bus from Woodlands, because Dad got it for free. It was a good 8 miles away, so her arms always felt a little longer by the time she arrived. I couldn't have cleaned it without her and Tony because it was the dirtiest place I'd ever seen – even Elsie would have flinched. We discovered some strange things, but the strangest and most interesting find came right at the end, when we tackled the basement.

'Here, look what I've found,' Tony called as I squinted in the dim light. I could just make him out – he was holding something in the air, high up above his head. He started clacking them with his fingers. At first I thought they were a pair of castanets, but as Ann and I got closer we realised it was a pair of false teeth! Ann screamed the house down, but I fell about laughing and so did Tony. It was nice to laugh; otherwise I think I might have cried. Still, we did what we could with the rest of the house. Ann and I bought metres of red gingham checked material from Doncaster market so that we could make curtains. We hung them up in the kitchen window, and strung them on a piece of elastic in a 'skirt' around the bottom of the big white butler's sink.

Peter visited whenever he could to help out, but without a car he had to catch the train. It was such a long journey that half the weekend was taken up by travel alone. Peter also needed to find himself a job. True to his word, Dad had heard of a position at Brodsworth Colliery. He put Peter's name forward and helped set him on his way.

'It's hard graft, mind you,' he said, sizing Peter up. I could tell he was wondering if my southern husband was up to the job.

Peter took it, but four weeks later Dad's north–south prejudice was confirmed when Peter was laid off sick with a sprained back. He was a highly skilled plumber, so he wasn't used to digging or hard labour to earn a living.

With a house to move into, I gave my notice at the nursing home and secured a better position as Deputy Matron at a day nursery that cared for babies and children aged from a few months old up to two years. The nursery was different to others in the area in that it was used by a lot of one-parent families, which was something I identified with. The matron was an unmarried mother with a little boy who attended the same nursery. I admired her because this was a time when many mothers were so shamed by having a baby out of wedlock that they'd simply abandon them or give them up for adoption, but not this lady. She was incredible, and I had nothing but the utmost respect for how she loved and cared for her little boy.

The working hours were almost as gruelling as the nursing home. When I arrived at 6 a.m., I'd find half a dozen prams already lined up and waiting outside the main door. The parents would've gone, usually straight off to work. There was no worry or concern back then that someone might steal a baby, because everyone did the same thing. Mind you, it was also a blissful time when you could leave your front door unlocked without fear of being burgled or murdered in your bed. If I was shocked by the babies being left in the morning, then I was even more surprised when the same parents forgot to pick them up at night. More often than not there was usually a mix-up or breakdown in communication. One parent would presume a friend or relative was picking the child up and vice versa. A lot of the parents were bus drivers or conductors working long shifts, so I'd have to ring Doncaster police station to get them to trace the missing mum or dad.

'Hello, its Elmfield nursery. I'm afraid we've got another no-show,' I told the officer on the other end of the phone.

'Another one?' he gasped. 'How on earth can you forget to pick up your child?' The line went silent for a moment and I visualised the officer shaking his head in despair. 'Don't worry; someone will be along shortly.'

Whenever I had a situation like that, Peter would sit and wait with me until the police officer arrived. The officer would try to track down the parent, who always had a valid excuse, but they'd still be given a police caution.

I loved working with the children, and I often imagined myself as a mother with a brood of my own. All the same, it was nice to hand them back at the end of the day and switch off. I'd worked at the nursery for almost a year when Dad called to see me. He'd heard of a new job at Brodsworth Colliery.

'They're looking to set up a new medical centre, so they need a fully qualified nursing officer. I've put your name forward. Hope that's all right?'

It was, because by now I knew it was time to move on, although it didn't stop the nerves rising inside my stomach. I was still in my early twenties – in many ways I was still learning – yet at the pit I knew I'd be in charge of thousands of men. I'd always been confident in my own nursing world of hospitals and sterile wards, but this was a different type of nursing – this was industrial nursing, which I'd never done before. But I wasn't proud. I'd ask for help if I needed it.

Although I realised it'd be a whole different ball game, I trusted my father and his judgement. Ultimately, I knew he wouldn't have recommended me if he didn't think I was up to the job.

5

A Miner's Nurse

I was a complete first and a bit of a curiosity at Brodsworth Colliery – a female nursing officer in charge of 3,000 men – but the National Coal Board was trying to improve its safety record after the pits had been nationalised nine years previously. Now that I'd been hired, the health of the Brodsworth miners was down to me. I'd work in a preventative role as well as being there to treat the men.

Before I'd arrived, the miners relied on a bloke called Bert, a tall, slim and authoritative man in his mid-forties. He'd been at the pit for donkeys' years and was a trained first aider. He was also the man you went to in an emergency. It was 1956, and Bert was so trusted and highly respected that all the people in the village would call on him rather than use a doctor. To be honest, I didn't blame them because what Bert didn't know wasn't really worth knowing. His office was an old wooden hut situated by the shaft side. The hut was cramped and dark and as far removed from sterile hospital wards as you could get. Nevertheless, Bert, who had a mop of thick, dark, curly hair, would expertly bandage and generally patch the men up in the dim light and dusty surroundings. If it was a serious injury then he'd pack them off to the hospital, or call for one of the Coal Board doctors, but Bert was always the miners' first port of call in an emergency.

He was also very obstinate and viewed me, just 24 and a mere slip of a girl, with extreme suspicion. He resented the fact that I was heading up the brand new medical centre, because his male ego wouldn't allow him to accept orders from a young lass. The centre was being built specially but he disliked the idea so much that he refused to come out of his hut even to take a look at it. I'm sure the curiosity must have killed him, but he was a stubborn old goat and he refused to budge an inch. Despite this, I looked up to Bert because he was so knowledgeable.

I'd been brought up in Woodlands, the village attached to Brodsworth Colliery, and my father – Harry Smith to everyone else – was a senior official there. Dad was respected, and everyone knew I was his eldest daughter. By this time, my brother Tony had started at Brodsworth as a trainee cadet, so the men called me either 'Harry Smith's eldest' or 'Tony Smith's sister'. I was never called by my actual name, despite my protests. Sometimes the men couldn't even be bothered to refer to me by the family name, and instead called me 'the head girl from Woodlands school'. I'd come off the hospital wards and never done industrial nursing before, so I was also a little intimidated by the miners and my surroundings. The medical centre was still being built, so I got to choose the colour scheme.

'I think I'd like a nice canary yellow,' I said as I surveyed the plans. The man was horrified and his mouth fell open as though I'd asked him to paint it candy pink. To say the men on site were appalled by my choice of colour would be an understatement.

'Yellow!' one of the miners shrieked, shaking his head in dismay. 'But we normally have navy blue on the walls.'

I turned to face him. I was only young and I knew I was a woman working in a man's world, but I was also very determined.

'Yes,' I replied. 'And navy blue is a horrible, dark colour. I need it to be light and welcoming, so I'd like it painting yellow, please.'

I nodded my head as though that was my final word on the matter. Despite many objections, my wish was eventually granted, much to Bert's disapproval. I'd not consulted him, but I could just imagine him sitting over in his dreary dark wooden cabin, rolling his eyes in despair. As soon as the medical centre opened, I realised it was going to be hard to win the men over because, instead of coming to me, they continued to consult Bert. Now it was a battle of wills.

'Have you heard? She's only gone and painted it bloody yellow!' one of the men grumbled as he passed by my window early one morning.

I was up and running, but with no patients to treat and yellow walls to boot, I knew I had my work cut out. The medical centre held all the latest equipment, including a state-of-the-art steriliser, but try as I might, I couldn't get Bert or his team of first-aiders through the door. And then fate intervened. One day, I stretched over the autoclave – the device used to sterilise equipment to a very high temperature – when I caught my right arm against it. The burn was painful because it was deep and it had penetrated through several layers of skin. Also, because it was my right arm, it was impossible for me to dress with a bandage. With no one else to turn to, I walked across the pit yard towards Bert's hut. I tapped lightly on the door. As he opened it, I could tell he was shocked to find me standing there. He also seemed a little suspicious, as though I was trying to trick him.

'Sorry to bother you, Bert,' I began, 'but I wondered if you could take a look at my arm, please? I caught it on the autoclave. It's really painful and it's my right arm … I can't dress it properly.'

I was so busy trying to explain that I hadn't noticed that Bert had left the door ajar and had sat back down. I took it as a signal to go inside.

'Tha needs to be more careful,' he grunted as he pulled out a roll of bandage from a nearby drawer. He expertly dressed my wound as his dark curly hair flopped around his face, hiding his expression.

'I'm really grateful, Bert. I don't know what I'd have done without you.'

He looked up at me and nodded, but he was a hard man to read and I wondered if he thought I'd burned my arm on purpose. I hadn't, of course, and it was painful all the same. I winced as he tied the bandage, and he nodded to indicate that he'd finished. I wasn't quite sure what to do so I stood up and turned to leave. As I did, Bert spoke.

'It's a nasty wound, that is. Tha better come back tomorrow so I can change t'dressing.'

I turned and smiled gratefully.

'Thanks, Bert. I really appreciate it.' And I did. I also saw a chink of light. Maybe Bert wasn't such a tough nut to crack after all.

The following day I went back to have my dressing changed, and the day after, until soon I'd visited Bert for the best part of the week. Early one morning, I was told an official would be visiting the medical centre. I asked Bert if he could come over to me instead, but he wasn't keen. He'd already made it plain that he didn't approve of me or my canary-yellow walls.

'Please, Bert. I'll get into trouble if I'm over here with you and not over there,' I said, pointing at the medical centre. 'It'll only take a minute, and then you can leave.'

After much deliberation, Bert decided that he would indeed come over to dress my wound. I think a small part of him really wanted to see the inside of the centre, but his male ego wouldn't let him cross the threshold without good reason. Of course, Bert changed my dressing to his usual high standard. As he packed up to leave, I took a chance.

'While you're here I may as well show you around.'

Bert sneered until I explained that I really wanted his opinion on the equipment I already had in there. It seemed to work, because moments later I was giving him a guided tour.

'And this is the autoclave,' I explained.

Bert tried to hide it but I could tell he was impressed. He liked the new medical centre, with its sterile environment and equipment; he just didn't want to take orders from a girl. However, Bert's resolve must have melted, because hours later he returned with his three Medical Room Attendants (MRAs).

'And this is the steriliser, state of the art,' he said, demonstrating it.

I'd used my charm and womanly wiles and, sure enough, I'd eventually won him over. Only six weeks after starting at Brodsworth, Bert and his team left the freezing-cold hut and moved into the medical centre. My team of one had expanded to a team of five overnight. Soon it became a little crowded with the extra bodies, but I didn't mind because I loved the company and having Bert to call on whenever I needed advice. In return, the MRAs were so thrilled at having a sterile, warm and comfortable office to work in that they kept it absolutely spotless. In fact, they'd spend the entire week just mopping the floors until they were so clean that you could've eaten your dinner off them.

'Again?' I asked when I spotted one of them mopping the waiting-room floor for the third time that day.

He stood up, held his hands at the top of the mop and rested his chin down on them. 'Can't be too careful, Sister. Better to be safe than sorry.'

I stifled a giggle. The men certainly took pride in their work. Still, none of them accepted the fact that I was a married woman. Instead, they referred to me as either Sister or Sister Smith, using my maiden name. But it was better than 'the head girl from Woodlands school', so in many ways it was progress.

It was a good job I'd managed to get Bert on board, because only a few weeks later we were faced with a horrible situation when two workmen rushed into the medical centre with a man on a stretcher. They were still in shock as they explained how the contractor had fallen 30 feet from scaffolding against the water tower, where he was carrying out a repair. It hadn't been a straightforward fall because he had caught his head on the sharp scaffold poles on the way down and had managed to scalp himself. The patient was disorientated and thrashing around. Taking his head in my hands, I held it tight against my chest to try to compress the wound because he was losing such a frightening amount of blood. But with my legs either side of the stretcher, holding him close, I was having trouble keeping him still. I looked up at Bert, who was busy searching for a compression bandage.

'Please don't leave me,' I said, with fear trembling in my voice.

'I'm going nowhere, lass,' he replied as he held down the man.

The poor lad didn't have a clue where he was and he was clearly in agony. The medical centre didn't have Entonox (gas and air) back then, but we somehow managed to hold him for long enough to wrap a compression bandage around his scalp to try to stem the flow. Bert and I had decided that there wasn't enough time to call a doctor – the patient would've died either from shock or loss of blood while we waited – so we loaded him into the navy-blue pit ambulance. By the time we arrived at the hospital, the surgeons were waiting. The relief medical attendant had rung through from the pit switchboard. I'd held the patient's head together in my lap all the way, and I was soaked in blood. As they rushed him off to theatre, Bert turned and looked me up and down.

'Tha looks like a horror movie, lass,' he said bluntly.

'Yes,' I replied, glancing down at my uniform. 'I think I need to get scrubbed up.'

'Aye, tha does, but tha did a great job too, yer know. That lad would've died if it hadn't have been for thee.'

It was high praise indeed. Afterwards, Bert had nothing but the utmost respect for me. We were in it together now. I'd proved I wasn't just some silly little girl with canary-yellow walls and a romantic notion of caring for people; I was a qualified nurse, and someone who'd be there in times of crisis. Slowly, he began to trust me.

It was my dad who had first mentioned going underground into the pit. 'It'll help you to see where the miners work so you can get an idea of what they're faced with every day.'

I agreed. I wanted to go down the pit for the very same reason. I spoke to the Safety Department officer, but he seemed a little reluctant.

'Well, we've never really taken a woman down t'pit before, but if tha's sure tha wants to,' he said, scratching his head.

'Oh, I do,' I insisted. 'It'd be great to see their working environment and what dangers they face on a day-to-day basis – it'd be invaluable.'

In the end, he couldn't refuse, although the miners were taken aback when they saw me underground. I stood out like a sore thumb, even though I was dressed in a regulation boiler suit, because it was way too big for me. In fact, it was so big that I'd had to sew the hems of the legs up just so I could walk in it properly.

Although I felt a little out of my depth, I smiled as I was given a guided tour. The light from the lamp on my helmet danced against the pit walls, and in some quieter areas I heard, and was certain I saw, mice scuttling around in the shadows. It was noisy, humid and so dark that, without our headlamps, I couldn't see my hand in front of my face. But I didn't let my fear show because I wanted to prove I was as tough as the men. The pit continued to creak and drip as we ventured deeper. It was like being in the underbelly of a living, breathing creature, only one you couldn't control.

'Ay up, its Harry Smith's eldest,' one of the miners called as I passed by. The others stopped what they were doing, straightened up and scratched their heads in unison.

A woman. Down the pit?

They'd never seen the like before!

During the course of our visit, I checked the first-aid boxes to make sure they contained everything they needed.

'Thanks for showing me around down there,' I told the Safety Department officer as we finally stepped out of the cage onto the pit top.

He sized me up for a moment as though he didn't quite know what to make of me.

'No problem. No problem, lass.'

My second time underground followed a few months later. Dad agreed to take me down himself, so that I could do another general inspection and check the first-aid boxes. Again, it felt as though I was scrambling about in a cave. In some places it was as hot as hell, while in others it was humid and the condensation soaked into your skin.

'I'm not sure what t'men will make of it, but as long as tha does tha job tha won't go far wrong,' he said, giving me a pat on the back. He never said it directly, but I think he was proud that his daughter was becoming as tough as the miners she treated.

The third time, however, was a totally different matter. A call had come into the medical centre to say there'd been an emergency in the pit. A miner had trapped his leg between two tubs of coal and broken it. The deputy was a trained first aider, and although he'd bandaged and splinted the poor chap up I needed to examine the patient before they moved him to check he hadn't done any further damage.

'I'll not be long,' I told Bert, who agreed to staff the medical centre in case we had any more walking wounded through the door.

Once again, I pulled on my overalls, now more familiar to me than they had been before, and headed over towards the pit shaft and cage. One of the men was waiting to take me down.

'Ready, Sister?' he asked.

'Ready,' I said, nodding, as the cage descended into the dark bowels of the earth.

We located the man quickly. I gave him a thorough examination, checking him for spinal and head injuries in particular but, thankfully, apart from a fractured leg, he was fine.

'He's good to move,' I told the deputy.

Four men lifted him up and loaded the stretcher on to the seat of a waiting paddy train. They placed him flat and perched themselves either side to hold him in position. The deputy gestured for me to board the train, which I did, travelling with the patient to the pit shaft. We brought him up to the surface where the pit ambulance was waiting to take us to Doncaster Royal Infirmary. After admitting the man to hospital, I was free to leave. There was no point in me hanging around, although a few people did a double take when they saw me coming in through the hospital doors dressed in pit boots and filthy overalls. But by now I was getting used to it.

'I'm a nurse,' I told one woman. She sniffed as I passed, blackened head to toe with coal dust. She shook her head as though she didn't believe a word of it.

The miner eventually returned to work. I'm not sure how bad the fracture was so I don't know if they put him in traction or just plastered his leg, but he was off work for a good three or four months.

A few weeks later, we received another call. A miner had suffered another leg injury, only this time it was a serious underground incident. The man had bored a hole in the coalface and had tried to fire it, using shot, which is candle-shaped and similar to a stick of dynamite. Normally it'd cause the roof to crack, loosening the coal and making it easier to extract. Only this time the shot had partially fired and ricocheted back towards the miner, who was crouched at what he thought was a safe distance away. The shot had then detonated fully next to his right leg, partially blowing the top part off above the knee.

I immediately telephoned Dr Creed, one of the Coal Board doctors based at Doncaster. The disordered blast had caused coal to fall in on the patient, so he'd been trapped underground with his leg hanging on by a thread. That's when the full impact hit me – Dr Creed and I would have to travel into the pit to carry out an emergency amputation to free the man. Feeling sick with nerves, I grabbed the amputation kit and checked it over. It was pretty basic, containing artery forceps, a tourniquet, sterile saw and several sharp knives of different lengths. I knew Dr Creed was on his way with morphine, so I changed out of my nurse's outfit and pulled on my boiler suit and pit boots.

'Good luck,' Bert called as I headed towards the door.

I nodded and left him in charge of the medical centre. By the time I'd reached the pit top, Dr Creed had pulled up in his car. I'd never been more relieved to see a doctor in my whole life. He'd already changed into his overalls, so we walked over towards the shaft side. Dr Creed was a lovely middle-aged man who was very experienced, but I could tell the thought of performing an amputation in the dirt, miles underground, concerned him too. Before we entered the cage, he turned to face me.

'Are you nervous, Sister?' he asked gently.

I was absolutely terrified – my fear betrayed by my hands, which were trembling at my side. I grabbed the handle of the amputation kit for courage.

'Yes, I'm frightened to death,' I admitted.

Dr Creed turned away and fumbled around inside his bag. Moments later he pulled something out – a silver hip flask. He unscrewed the top and held it out towards me.

'Here, have a nip of this, Sister,' he insisted, pushing the bottle into my hands. I looked up at him, wondering if it was a test.

Surely drinking on the job wasn't allowed?

Then I thought of the poor man waiting for us, and the gruesome amputation. I grabbed the bottle and took a quick gulp. The brandy warmed my mouth and throat as I swallowed. I gave the hip flask back to Dr Creed, expecting him to replace the cap – only he didn't. Instead, he held it aloft and took a quick swig too! He inhaled a huge breath of air, replaced the lid and turned to face me.

'Better?' he asked.

'Better.'

And I felt it. We were just about to step into the cage when Bert came running over to find us. He'd received a call to say the miner had been freed and rescued from the rubble. His leg was barely attached but the first-aid team underground had tied a tourniquet around his thigh and strapped his legs together to keep the damaged leg stable. When the injured miner – a man called John – was brought back up to the surface, Dr Creed administered a maximum dose of morphine, and John was loaded by stretcher into the pit ambulance. I travelled with him to hospital, where I handed him over to the doctors who'd been waiting for his arrival. With nothing else to do, I travelled home, both physically and emotionally spent. I felt helpless and began to sob. I'd been taken on to care for these men but I wasn't God and I couldn't perform miracles.

'It was just so awful,' I wept. Peter wrapped his arms around me and tried his best to comfort me. 'I just felt so helpless.'

I refused to shed a tear at work. Instead, I stored it all up inside so I could release it later at home where no one could see or hear me. I couldn't let the men see me upset because I needed to be strong for them. I couldn't let them see my tears because by now they trusted me to do the right thing, even when faced with a life-or-death situation. But the truth was that the responsibility often weighed me down.

John was eventually stabilised, and later that evening the hospital surgeons amputated his right leg. He was still a little woozy when I called to visit him in hospital the following morning, but he was also very accepting in spite of losing a limb.

'I'll be honest wi' yer, I'd rather it hadn't happened, Sister, but at least I'm alive, so I've that to be grateful for,' he reasoned. His bravery made me want to let go of my resolve and cry.

It'd been a horrendous accident, made worse by the fact that John had initially been trapped underground, miles away from the nearest hospital. But that was the importance of my job. I was there to keep the men safe, and not only to try to help prevent accidents, but also to treat them accordingly should one occur. I was their first port of call, and together with Bert we had a responsibility to our men. There was such camaraderie among the miners that within 24 hours of John's accident the afternoon shift had collected enough money for a state-of-the-art wheelchair. They'd collected even more to pay his wife's wages so she could stay with him at his hospital bedside. I loved that about working at a pit – the miners were a family. The men looked out for one another in a way that most people would for their own blood. During my time as a pit nurse I became stronger because I realised I'd always have that same support too.

The automation of the pits made the mines more productive than with a man armed with just a pick and shovel. The latest machinery brought with it fewer accidents, but more danger and risk of amputation. After John's accident, I tended to men who'd had their fingers ripped off. At first, I found it difficult because the patients would be filthy from working underground when they came to see me – hardly perfect conditions when trying to keep infection at bay. I knew I always had Bert, and a Coal Board doctor was only a phone call away, but ultimately I had to learn to trust my judgement and make the right decision.

At first I was over-cautious. If a man had a foreign object in his eye, I'd send him to hospital. Chest pains were another direct route and a ride in the pit ambulance to A&E. You could never tell if a pain in the chest was the start of a heart attack or something less sinister. I didn't take any chances and packed them off all the same. However, there were a few miners who knew the system and tried to play me like a fiddle. Doncaster Rovers were playing a vital home game when I received a call an hour or so before kick-off, to say a man was being carried to the medical centre on a stretcher. He'd complained of severe stomach pains, and at first I'd been a little concerned. However, my father, who was the afternoon gaffer, knew the miner well. He also knew that he was an avid fan who became ill every time Rovers played at home.

'Watch him, Joan. He's trying to pull t'wool over yer eyes to get off work so he can go and watch t'game. He's known for it – we all call him Sick Note.'

Sure enough, I was presented with a man who had absolutely nothing wrong with him other than a burning desire to watch his home team.

'Where does it hurt?' I asked as I proceeded to examine his stomach. I placed my hands flat against it, feeling for tenseness. Patients with severe stomach pains, as he professed to have, automatically tense their muscles because the last thing they want is to be examined. His stomach was soft and relaxed. I smelt a rat. The more I examined him, the more the pain seemed to move around and change direction.

'No, Nurse, it's more over this side,' he wailed dramatically.

'That's funny. I thought you said it was over there a minute ago.'

The man stopped his crying and looked directly at me.

'It is, I mean, it's over there as well,' he said, resuming his play-acting. 'Oooh, it hurts so much, I think I need to go home to me bed.'

I knew I was being taken for a fool so I decided to give him a taste of his own medicine, or more directly, some of my own.

'Here,' I said, spooning out a foul concoction – a special mixture of peppermint, sal volatile (smelling salts) and kaolin. It was one I used specially on time-wasters.

The medicine was thick and white, and it tasted disgusting. I knew it wouldn't do him any harm, only make him feel a little queasy. If he hadn't felt sick before, he certainly would now. It seemed to do the trick because he never came to see me with stomach pains ever again.

Dad was a great source of information whenever I was in doubt. I knew I was lucky to have him there. My father was wise, firm – but fair – and he didn't suffer fools gladly. Also, he'd never, ever ask his men to do anything he wouldn't do himself. The miners knew this, so they respected him, and in turn they came to respect me.

One day, my father was complaining he couldn't hear very well.

'Must be old age,' he grumbled, putting his index finger inside his ear, ringing it around in frustration.

'Come over to the medical centre so I can have a proper look,' I shouted back at him. It was true; he'd slowly become as deaf as a post.

Once inside the medical centre, I took out my auroscope – I knew what this was by now after my embarrassing newspaper débâcle – and had a proper look. I immediately knew what was wrong.

'You're not going deaf, Dad. It's your ears – they're full of coal dust. You just need to have them syringed.'

But the thought of me sticking a big needle into his ears made him reel back in his chair.

'Whaaaat?'

I stifled a giggle.

'Don't worry. It's not as painful as it sounds. I just need to pop some olive oil inside your ears for a week, and when you come back I'll syringe it out.'

'Will it help with my hearing?' he asked dubiously.

'Absolutely. When I'm done, you'll have ears like a bat!' I grinned, before grabbing a small bottle of olive oil and some pads of cotton wool to start the procedure.

Sure enough, he was back in the chair a week later as I syringed the muck from his ears. As soon as I'd finished a wide smile broke across his face.

'Bluddy 'ell, Joan, it's a miracle! I can hear everything. Tha' sounds as clear as a bell!'

I tried not to laugh. Secretly, I was delighted my father had allowed me to treat him. But not as delighted as he'd been, because he told everyone about me and my miracle cure for deafness. At first the men had been suspicious of me and my fancy new ways, but now my father was living proof that I knew exactly what I was doing. I could and would work wonders for them too. Soon I had a queue of men at my door, all waiting for my 'miracle treatment'.

'I'd like you all to go and see your doctor first, get him to check your ears, ask for a note and then come back to see me.'

I needed a doctor to check the men first to ensure that they didn't have any underlying conditions. Days later, hordes of big burly miners dropped in one by one clutching their consent forms. A week later, when the first batch of men had been successfully syringed, they told their colleagues, and so word began to spread. One day, I arrived at the medical centre to find more than twenty miners queued up outside the door. Soon there was so much demand that I had to hold a special Saturday clinic to keep up with it. I didn't mind coming in for a few hours on my day off. The fact that I was slowly winning the trust of the men was more important to me. But it wasn't just ears I treated. One day, I was syringing a man's ears when he mentioned that he also had a bad back.

'It's all the bending and crouching underground, Sister. It doesn't half set me back off,' Bob complained, giving it a rub.

'Well, you could always come in here and try out the heat lamp,' I suggested.

He looked a little wary.

'Will it hurt?'

I smiled and shook my head.

'No, not at all. The heat will help ease the aches and pains inside the muscles in your back.'

I must've convinced old Bob because, sure enough, just days later he was back, knocking on my door.

'Er, I think I'd like to give that heat lamp of yours a go. It's me back, yer see, it's killing me.'

'Come in,' I said, closing the door behind him.

I set the heat lamp up and told Bob to lie down on the bed. After a while, I popped my head around the door to see how he was getting on. I found him lying spreadeagled, as though he was on a day out at the beach.

'Is it helping? Does it feel any better?'

Bob opened his eyes, blinked and smiled as though he was in heaven.

'Ooh, it's lovely, Sister. It's like having me very own bit o' sunshine.'

After that, word spread, and soon I had men queuing up for a go on the heat lamp too.

With Peter still off sick, I was the only breadwinner so money was extremely tight. Polly helped out, bringing us butter, loose tea and other essentials. We carried on this way for the best part of a year, until Peter received some dreadful news – his father had passed away.

'I need to go back down to London. It's Mum – she needs me.'

Although I'd never seen eye to eye with his mother, I knew he had to go. His mum needed the help and support of all her sons, including Peter. But when we travelled back for the funeral, it was clear that she wanted more than a little support.

'I need you back here with me,' she insisted. 'I need you close, not hundreds of miles away from home.'

Peter felt torn: he wanted to do the best for his mother, but he also had me, his wife, to consider.

'I can't do right for doing wrong,' he fretted.

Something had to give, so I agreed to leave Yorkshire and move back to London with my husband. After our previous separation and the heartache that had gone with it, I knew I never, ever wanted to be parted from Peter again. I'd put my relationship at risk before but we'd come such a long way that I knew I'd never do it again.

'It's all right. We can move back,' I agreed.

Peter was relieved but, despite living in a five-bedroom house, his mother made it clear that Peter, and Peter alone, was the only one allowed to move in with her.

'Your mother is impossible!' I huffed. 'She doesn't like me and she's trying her best to split us up!'

In the end, it was Peter's grandmother who came to our rescue, offering us a couple of rooms in her house.

'It's not much, but it should be enough to see you through,' Granny Baker said gently, patting my hand. She was a lovely, kind woman – the complete opposite of her daughter.

To my father's dismay, I handed my notice in at the pit and asked for a transfer back to Hammersmith Hospital.

'We're going to miss you,' Dad said sadly as I packed up the last of my things into a cardboard box, 'and not just me. All the men will miss you. You've made quite a difference; you've really turned the place around.'

A lump formed in the back of my throat. The reality was that, although the dirt and the men had been difficult in the beginning, I'd come to love my job at the colliery. I didn't relish the thought of working back on sterile wards as a staff nurse, because at Brodsworth I'd been my own boss and, despite everything, I'd done well and had gained the men's trust. It'd been tough, but now I was leaving. I was doing so with a heavy heart because I knew this was the type of nursing I loved – to be on the front line and to make that difference. All too soon it was time to leave, and I bid a sad farewell to Bert and the rest of the team. Bert looked solemn. We'd had our differences, but a year on a mutual respect had formed between us, although it had never been spoken of until now.

'I'm going to miss yer, Sister,' Bert blinked, looking up at me from his chair.

He'd been a tough old character, but once I'd managed to dig beneath that gritty, old-fashioned male ego, I'd discovered that he was as loyal as a lion but as soft as a kitten.

'Me too, Bert. Me too,' I said, choking back emotion.

'I know we didn't always see eye to eye, but,' his voice broke off as he shifted his eyes away and looked down awkwardly at his hands in his lap. 'Well, I've learned a lot from thee, if truth be told, and it's been a real pleasure working alongside yer. I know it all sounds a bit soppy, but I'm really gonna miss yer, Sister.'

I choked my tears back and wished Bert and his team well. I knew it wouldn't be goodbye for ever – just a fond farewell, until it was time to return again.

6

Cuddles and Infertility

I transferred back to Hammersmith Hospital in London in 1957, where I became a staff nurse working in the radiotherapy unit on a 40-hour week, but in reality my working hours were often much longer.

After a few months of living in rooms at Granny Baker's house, Peter managed to secure us a two-bedroom flat on Uxbridge Road, Shepherd's Bush. The flat was situated inside a grand Edwardian house above a barber's shop, so the rooms were huge, particularly the sitting room, which doubled up as a dining room. The kitchen was so spacious that it boasted its very own bath. When we weren't bathing, we'd cover it up with a worktop to provide seating around the kitchen table, which was ideal for dinner parties and entertaining. It was hardly glamorous London living, but you managed with what you had then.

I loved working on the unit but I often found myself yearning for my days as a pit nurse. I missed the men with their old-fashioned ways and good-natured banter. I even missed Bert, but most of all I missed the friendship and the unique bond the men shared. Still, I was determined to succeed at Hammersmith so I worked hard and, a year or so later, I was given the post of Acting Departmental Sister. Back then, the unit treated a whole host of different patients, including adults, but a large majority were children suffering from leukaemia or Hodgkin lymphoma – a cancer of the lymphatic system. These patients were aged from 2 to 12 years old, and their stories were heartbreaking. We were called Cancer Research nurses yet, despite our professional titles, we couldn't help but get attached to our younger patients. They'd grow up with us as we regularly treated and monitored them throughout their often very short lives. We never saw them as dying patients because we always treated them as children.

There was one young lad in particular, called Jonathan, who had battled for most of his life against leukaemia. He was given good news as a child, only to relapse years later. Jonathan underwent treatment time and time again, and at one point we thought he was winning his fight. He eventually grew into a fine young man. At 18 years old he met a girl and got married, and soon she was pregnant. Although his wife knew he'd suffered from cancer as a child, when it returned a few years later, bringing with it a grim prognosis, she promptly left. Jonathan was heartbroken and felt as though his life was over. Desperate to see his young wife, he marched over to his mother-in-law's house, where he smashed down her front door. The police were called, and he was charged with criminal damage. Shortly afterwards, he was having treatment at the unit when he broke down and told me what had happened. It was upsetting to see him distraught, so I spoke to the registrar, who agreed that something needed to be done. We telephoned the police and asked them to call in at the hospital.

'The thing is, Jonathan only has three or four years left to live, so Sister Hart and I feel it is totally unnecessary to charge him with this offence,' the doctor explained.

The police officers looked a little shocked, but I pressed further.

'The poor lad has lost everything – his wife, his unborn child – and soon he'll lose his life. Please don't add to that by taking his freedom too. As soon as she discovered he wouldn't live long, she upped and left, saying he'd never see their child. Right now, Jonathan has got nothing left to live for.'

The senior officer nodded his head grimly.

'Well, Sister. This sheds a whole new light on the situation, and if this lad has only got a short time left on this earth then I don't feel a punishment is entirely appropriate. I think we'll let him off with a caution instead.'

The anxious breath I'd been holding inside came rushing out as a sigh of relief.

'Thank you, Officer. Jonathan's already been through so much. I think he deserves a little kindness.'

The officer agreed, shook our hands and thanked us for our time. Common sense had prevailed and Jonathan was let off with a simple slap on the wrist. He died a few years later. He was just 26 years old and he never got to meet or even hold his baby.

At the unit, our patients' conditions ranged from disfiguring birthmarks to full-blown skin cancers. Those who had been hospitalised came to the unit for treatment before being taken back to their wards to rest, while others we saw were visiting outpatients or follow-up assessments. The children were mostly treated as outpatients unless they were particularly frail or unwell. The hospital had three radiotherapy wards, which housed patients with cancer. They were kept separate to patients on surgical wards because their immune systems were weak and more prone to infection. But poorly children were always kept on the children's ward. Naturally, their parents would be anxious and upset once a diagnosis had been made, but many supported their children throughout long and often gruelling bouts of radiotherapy. A cancer diagnosis for anyone, child or adult, is hard to accept, and often we'd find parents would go into denial. If they could pretend it wasn't happening, then somehow it would make it not real. Obviously their children were very ill, but more than often, I found, it was the mothers who went into denial rather than the fathers. Even though the natural female instinct is to care and protect, some mothers found the thought of a critically ill child just too much to bear, so it would be the fathers who'd bring them to the hospital. I never judged anyone because I didn't have children of my own, so I could only imagine what these poor women were going through, never mind their children. But the choices some parents made were simply unforgivable.

On one such occasion, a four-year-old boy had been referred to the unit suffering from leukaemia. He was desperately ill and needed an immediate blood transfusion, but because his parents were Jehovah's Witnesses they refused. They argued that a transfusion went against their beliefs. Back then, the medical profession had no legal power, so we were unable to go against the parents' wishes, even in a life-and-death situation. Less than a week later, the poor mite died. He was so ill that he'd passed away silently and unseen by the other parents, in a side room adjacent to the children's ward. It made me question everything.

Today, that same child would be made a 'ward of court', but back then the parents were left to choose, rightly or wrongly, the fate of their own child. I'd never been particularly religious, but it made me question how a parent could put his or her religion before the life of their child. I'd seen a similar situation some years earlier as a student nurse. A little boy, aged five, had been admitted to the children's ward. He had something seriously wrong with his throat and was quite literally choking to death.

The doctors had pleaded with his parents to allow the operation, which required a blood transfusion, to go ahead, but they refused point blank. I'll never forget sitting with him during those final few days, holding his tiny hand as his life ebbed away. I was so distraught that the doctor dipped his head around the curtain and beckoned me outside to have a word.

'You leave now, Nurse,' he said.

'But the little boy …' I replied, pointing back to my young patient.

'Nurse, you shouldn't have to witness that,' he said. 'It is their decision, not yours. It is a decision that will cost their child his life. We are here to save lives, not to watch them be taken. It is far too upsetting for you, so I'd like you to carry on with your other duties. It will be the parents who will sit and watch their child die.'

The parents had effectively condemned their son to death. As medical professionals we were there to treat and preserve life, not watch it be taken away, be it through religion or any other means. But also we were not there to judge, and we had to remain impartial and professional at all times, however hard that may be. Sadly, a day or so later the poor little boy lost his fight for life. I have never forgotten him to this day, or the choice his parents made.

Although I tried my best to be a nurse first and foremost, it was hard not to get too attached to my young patients. Back then, radiation was a very frightening word. Members of the hospital management didn't venture too close to the unit for fear of it, so we were pretty much left to our own devices, which suited me. With no one to bark orders, I tried to make the hospital experience as much fun as possible for the children. I'd book half a day off work and take three children at a time to visit London Zoo, just so they could forget about hospitals and cancer for one day. I always paid with my own money, but I didn't mind – the joy on their faces made it worthwhile.

A young patient was referred to us called Michael. Michael was very ill indeed. He was only two years old, but his spleen was so enlarged that he couldn't stand up without toppling over. He had chronic myeloid leukaemia. Michael's spleen had become so enlarged that it had all but disabled him. He had unnaturally long hair for a boy and his clothes were threadbare. I soon found out why. His father had brought him in for radiotherapy but there was no sign of his mother. I wondered if she'd gone into denial like so many of the others, but then I discovered that as soon as Michael had been diagnosed with cancer she'd simply upped and left. Michael was such a beautiful little lad, with long blond hair and big blue eyes, that it broke my heart to think of his mother abandoning him. I knew what that felt like.

'I try to look after the children, but I have to work. Now Michael's ill, so I have to be here. To be honest, Sister, some days I don't know if I'm coming or going,' his father admitted.

Michael's cancer meant that his dad had taken so much time off work that money was scarce. It certainly explained the child's threadbare clothes and long hair. I knew I shouldn't have got involved, but I couldn't help myself.

'Don't you worry. We'll try our best to get him better, and any time you get stuck you come and see me.'

Michael's father was grateful, and after that day I made it my mission to help out wherever I could.

'You should see him,' I told Peter later that evening as we sat down at the kitchen table to eat. 'He's only a baby and his father is trying his best to keep a roof over their heads. I hate to see them struggle; there must be something I can do?'

Peter paused and then said, 'It's hard not to get involved, and I know what you're like, you'll do anything you can to help.'

It was at moments like these that I really valued Peter because, whatever I decided, I knew he'd always be there, right beside me.

It took three years, but Michael responded well to treatment and finally he grew stronger. The swelling in his spleen subsided until he was not only able to stand, but also to run too. For the first time he was able to play like a regular little boy. During his treatment, Michael's father and I often talked about his son and his remarkable progress.

'You've worked wonders on him,' he remarked as we watched Michael bomb around the ward. 'At one point I really thought I'd lose him.'

I rested my hand down on top of his and left it there.

'But you haven't. Look, he's a happy and delightful little boy. He's responded so well to the treatment, better than we could've ever hoped. You should be proud of yourself,' I insisted, patting his hand gently, 'and everything you've done for him.'

'Thank you, Sister Hart,' he replied, dipping his head so I wouldn't see the tears welling up in his eyes.

For a moment there was a comfortable silence, as we both contemplated how far Michael had come and just how hard he'd fought to stay alive.

'I'll tell you what, though,' I said, breaking the silence. 'What he really needs is a haircut!'

Michael's dad shook his head in dismay.

'I know. I keep telling him, but he won't listen to me. What that boy needs is a woman's touch, because he won't let me cut it with a pair of scissors.'

'Won't he?' I said, standing up. 'Well, just you watch this.'

I walked across the ward and called out his name. Michael stopped in his tracks and wandered over towards me. The scissors were already in my hand. 'What you need is a haircut, young man!'

Michael spotted the scissors and backed away warily.

'No, I don't want it cut,' he protested. 'I like it like this,' he said, running his fingers through his shoulder-length curly locks. In truth, he had the hair of an angel, which is exactly what he was.

I sighed and knelt down on the ground so that we were face to face.

'You're a little boy, but with long hair like that,' I said, twisting his curls in between my fingers, 'you look like a little girl. And you don't want to look like a little girl now, do you?'

Michael shrugged his shoulders, looked down and shook his head.

'So, can I cut it, then? Your hair, shall I cut it so that you can look like all the other little boys?'

Michael's eyes darted from his father's and back to mine. He dipped to the side to check if the scissors were still in my hand. They were, but I didn't want to frighten him, so I let him decide. His face clouded over for a moment as he thought.

'It won't hurt, will it?'

'No, of course not, Michael. It won't hurt a bit, I promise.'

'Promise?' he asked, crossing his fingers across his heart.

'Promise.'

With that, he sat down in a chair and let me cut his hair to a more manageable length. His father was amazed.

'I can't believe he's let you do that,' he said, shaking his head in disbelief. 'I've been trying to get it cut for ages but he wouldn't let me anywhere near him.'

I knew why Michael had let me. He hadn't said it, but he hadn't needed to. He missed his mum, just as I had done. I knew he was still hurting. I wasn't his mother, but I vowed to be there for him whenever he needed me. As he grew, Michael became a part of the unit. He visited us every three months for a check-up, and I came to love him as a son. One day, when he was seven or eight years old, I decided to take him on a visit to the zoo with some of the other children. As we walked around the animal enclosures I noticed that he was limping. Alarm bells rang and my heart raced with uncertainty.

'Michael, are you well?' I asked, pulling him gently to one side.

He looked up at me. 'Yes, I'm fine, Sister Joan.'

'Does it hurt anywhere?' I asked. 'It's just that I've noticed something. You seem to be limping.'

Michael looked down at his feet and then up at me. A grin spread across his face.

'No, Sister Joan. It's my shoes, you see, they're really hurting me. They're not mine. They're my brother's, but they're too tight.'

I was flummoxed.

'So why did you put them on, then, if they're too tight for you?'

Michael shrugged. 'Because they were the smartest shoes we had and I wanted to look my very best for you, Sister Joan.'

I put a hand to my chest and tried to stop the tears welling up in my eyes.

'Come here,' I said, pulling him close. 'You daft brush! I don't care what you wear; you don't have to look smart for me. As long as you're well, that's all I care about.'

To be honest, I was just so relieved it wasn't anything sinister causing Michael to limp. I also couldn't bear to watch him suffer, so I took the children to a shoe shop and bought him some shoes that actually fitted. They only cost me 2 shillings, but you'd have thought I'd given him the world.

'Are they mine?' he asked, twisting his feet to admire them. 'Are they all mine, to keep?'

'They are, Michael. They are.'

'Wow! Thanks, Sister Joan,' he said, running into my arms.

After our day out at the zoo, I took Michael and two other children back to my flat to wait for their parents to pick them up. Michael was the last one to be collected because his father was running late from work, so he was still sitting there when Peter came in. Michael's face lit up as soon as he saw him – he'd met Peter before and the pair had got on famously.

'Hello, Michael,' Peter said, hanging his coat up on a peg inside the doorway. 'How was your day at the zoo?'

Michael's eyes were wide with excitement as he told him all about the monkeys, elephants, tigers and lions we'd seen.

'So, you had a good time then?'

'Yes, and Sister Joan even got me these,' he said, holding his snazzy new footwear aloft.

Peter looked at me and smiled.

'Wow, you're quite the little gent in those,' he said as Michael sat up proudly in his chair. Peter then pulled something out of his pocket – it was a gift for Michael.

'Are you sure?' Michael asked, taking it from the palm of his hand.

Peter nodded and glanced over at me to check that it was okay. It was.

'Do I have to do anything for it, any chores or anything?' the little boy asked, clutching the 10-shilling note in his hand.

'No, it's yours to keep. It's a present, from us,' I insisted.

Later, after his dad had picked him up, I turned to Peter. 'That was a kind thing to do,' I said, planting a kiss on his lips.

'He's a good kid. Besides, it was worth it just to see the smile on his face.'

And it was. Back then, ten bob was quite a sum, and to Michael it was as though Peter had given him the crown jewels.

But Michael was one of my favourite patients. In many ways, I identified with him and what his family had gone through. Even though I wasn't supposed to get too involved, when it came to birthdays I made sure every child was given a party. With no management to interfere, I'd allow cake, balloons and party games – anything to put a smile back on the children's faces so they could forget about being ill, if only for a few hours.

It was strictly against the rules, but if a child was particularly sick or anxious I'd allow their parents to bring in the family pets to help calm them. Over the years, we welcomed everything from dogs to goldfish; in fact, any creature (within reason) that we thought would lift a child's spirits. Animals have a unique ability to bring joy and a quiet calm even to the most stressful situations. Besides, what harm could it actually do? I'd seen the pleasure those simple days out at the zoo had given them, so bringing the odd pet into the unit, however forbidden, seemed a natural progression.

As well as birthday parties, we also held Christmas parties. The nurses would turn their capes inside out so the scarlet lining was visible. We'd stand and sing Christmas carols along with the patients as the surgeon popped in to carve the turkey. Back in the radiotherapy unit, we'd make a fuss of the younger patients. Every year, we'd arrange for one of the male members of staff to dress up as Father Christmas and deliver a sack of presents individually labelled for each patient. It was wonderful to see their little faces light up as we handed them out.

'Oh, look. He remembered, Sister Joan,' a little boy gasped. It melted my heart.

I dealt with many patients from different walks of life, but none were more dashing than Colonel James Johnson. Colonel Johnson was tall, dark and handsome. He was attached to the American Air Force, and he was also a terrible flirt. I always knew when the colonel was in for treatment because all the nurses would blush and go weak at the knees. I had five staff nurses working in the unit, but for some reason, even though I was happily married, the colonel decided to make a play for me.

'So,' he asked one day as he waited for treatment, 'when are you going to let me take you out, Sister Hart?'

The colonel flashed me a megawatt smile and, in spite of myself, I felt my face flush like a silly schoolgirl. I hadn't realised it until that moment, but it seemed that I was as taken with the handsome American pilot as the other girls.

'Don't be daft – you know I'm married.'

'Okay. As a friend, then. When will you let me take you out to say thank you for all the care you've given me? You know how grateful I am.'

I blushed a little more.

'All right. I'll go for a drink with you,' I agreed, imagining the look on the other girls' faces when I told them the heartthrob had 'asked me out'.

'Great! Lunch, then? At the American Officers' Club?'

I felt my heart flip. It sounded fantastic.

'Yes, I'll go,' I replied, a little too quickly.

And so our 'date' was set. It was never really a date, just a thank you from a charming and grateful officer, who also happened to be drop-dead gorgeous. The others were pea-green with envy when I told them.

'Oh, you lucky thing! I wish he'd asked me. I'd have gone as quick as that!' one said with a click of her fingers.

'Me too,' sighed another.

'What dress are you going to wear, Joan? I bet it's really fancy there.'

And that's when it struck me; I didn't have a clue what to wear.

'Something smart,' one of the girls suggested. 'You've got to look your best if you're on the arm of Colonel Johnson.'

The three of them sighed in unison. 'Love-struck' had never seemed a more appropriate expression than at that moment.

On the actual day, I wore a grey tailored suit with a skirt, white blouse and black court shoes. I never wore trousers because they were deemed to be too masculine. True to his word, Colonel Johnson was a gentleman and the date was purely platonic, not that I ever told Peter about it. Sometimes there are certain things best left unsaid. The American Officers' Club was amazing. Colonel Johnson led me into the grand dining room, which was filled with small tables, with five or six people seated at each one. I was impressed with the food – a prawn cocktail starter, which at the time seemed very cosmopolitan. It was followed by a huge steak and washed down with a large glass of white wine.

'This is the wonderful Sister Hart,' he said, introducing me to the other pilots. 'She not only helped save my life, but my flying career too!'

I waved my hand as though it'd been nothing. Besides, I could hardly take the credit. It'd been the team that had got him back on his feet, not just me. If truth be told, his life had been improved with regular bouts of radiotherapy treatment. The colonel had suffered from a condition called polycythaemia rubra vera (PRV). It is caused by a rare abnormality in a gene, which causes the bone marrow cells to multiply and produce too many red blood cells. Essentially, the condition makes the blood thick and less able to circulate to organs in the body. Symptoms include confusion, headaches, chest pains and blurred vision, which meant he wasn't able to fly without suitable and regular treatment. We used radiation to kill off the extra blood cells over a period of three months to get him back on his feet, but then he almost knocked me off mine with his charm, good looks and constant supply of amusing anecdotes. Despite the date being entirely honourable, I soon found myself falling for the delightful Colonel Johnson. However, that particular bubble burst only a few days later, when I was asked by one of the consultants to pop something inside his medical records. That's when I saw it – a list of three previous wives in almost as many years. Needless to say, my schoolgirl infatuation with the dashing colonel ended in a heartbeat.

'So, are you going out for lunch with the colonel again?' one of my colleagues asked with a knowing wink.

'Er, I don't think he's quite my type. Besides, I told you, I'm a happily married woman.'

She looked at me as though I was nuts, but I could hardly tell her the real reason.

During my time at Hammersmith, we were asked to give radiation treatment to a 40-year-old kidney patient who was also a doctor. He was to undergo one of the first kidney transplants ever carried out, with the kidney being taken from a dead donor. This was in the days before anti-rejection drugs, so, instead, before his operation he was blasted with radiation to kill off any bugs or bacteria in his body. Following his operation, the patient came back down to the unit where he was given more radiation to stop his body from rejecting the donor kidney. At the time it all seemed very cutting edge and sci-fi – the same operation today is routine by comparison – but it was great to have played a small part in it and to have been at the forefront of pioneering new treatment.

There wasn't then a book on radiotherapy nursing, and we were already in the process of writing our own when we heard a whisper that the Royal Marsden Hospital had decided to bring one out. We worked around the clock to bring ours out first; it was published as *Guide to Radiotherapy Nursing*, and I was named as co-author. It was a very proud moment in my life.

As Acting Departmental Sister I was required to stock up on supplies. I also had to attend regular sisters' meetings, although I didn't tell them about the impromptu birthday parties or visits from family pets. I never informed them that I often allowed exhausted parents to stay over at our flat. I didn't tell anyone about the extra services I'd provided because I knew they'd be stopped and all the joy in our young patients' lives would be lost for ever. It seemed that as long as we did our job and got good results, which we did, the management would leave us alone.

Peter often visited patients who didn't have any family. Hospital can be a very lonely place to be if you're all alone in the world. As nurses, we'd constantly be rushing around, trying to care for our patients, when all some really wanted was a friendly face and a listening ear, and that's what Peter provided. Many were grateful just to have someone to chat to during the long afternoons.

Peter and I were desperately trying for a child of our own, without success. I convinced myself it would happen with the passage of time, but it never did. I couldn't work out what the problem could be. Back in those days, you certainly didn't discuss fertility problems with anyone, let alone doctors I knew well, so I just put it down to fate. Back in the unit, we'd treat lots of children with disfiguring birthmarks that were often on their faces, heads or necks. Sometimes these marks would be on their torsos or backs, and I'd hold distraught children on my lap to comfort them so that radiation treatment could be given. I was supposed to wear a lead apron, but when faced with a crying or frightened toddler the last thing I'd think of would be myself. It was wrong, but I broke the rules and cuddled and held the children as they underwent their radiotherapy.

Looking back, I often wonder if it was those extra cuddles that had robbed me of the chance of ever having children of my own. It is something I will never, ever know.

7

Babies and Bicycles

During my time working on the radiation unit, I decided to go for the position of Departmental Sister. I'd done the job for quite a while anyway, if not strictly by title. But in order to become one, I first had to pass part 1 of my midwifery exam. It was the mid-60s, and the Beatles were riding high in the charts. I'd not sat any exams for over 10 years, so reading my test papers was like trying to absorb a storybook. I knew it was something I'd never need in my area of nursing, but I had to have it to achieve the post of my dreams. However, back then, pupil midwives were treated like dirt. This became apparent on my first day as a student when the professor stood at the front of the class.

'As pupil midwives, remember this,' he began, his voice as clear as a bell as it carried across the lecture theatre, 'you are the lowest thing to crawl out from underneath a stone.' He peered at us over the top of his spectacles. It was downhill from that moment on.

I realised that this was because pupil midwives were seen by many as silly little girls whose life ambition was to deliver and cuddle babies. But the harsh reality was nothing like that. My first birth was a huge 9-pound baby boy. I don't know how, but his poor mother somehow managed to deliver him and he emerged, squashed-faced and wailing, into the world. I cried with him – as I did at every birth I attended.

'Oh God, Joan,' the midwife muttered, turning to face me. 'You're not crying, are you?'

'I'm sorry,' I blubbed. 'It's just so beautiful.'

The mother smiled. 'If he'd been a girl, I would've called him Joan, after you,' she said, nestling him in her arms as I cooed overhead. 'But, as he's a boy, I'm going to call him Johnny.'

'Oh,' I said, beginning to weep even more. 'That's a beautiful name for a boy.'

The pattern continued, with me sobbing at each and every birth. To make matters worse, I'd trained most of the midwives as nurses so they all knew me. But now I was back on the bottom rung of the ladder. To be honest, I would have made a useless midwife anyway. You could always tell which babies I'd delivered because I'd cut their umbilical cords so long that they'd hang between their legs. I was too frightened to cut them high in case I hurt the baby. I remained permanently petrified, and I would drag my feet whenever I was called to a delivery. I knew that if I delayed long enough, I'd miss it. After a while, my colleagues cottoned on to my plan and began calling me hours in advance to make sure I was there.

One day, a consultant beckoned me over.

'I'd like you to examine this lady, Nurse,' he asked, taking a step away.

I approached the woman's hospital bed, which was sectioned off behind a curtain, and began to palpate her abdomen. But the more I checked, the more I could feel. I pulled my hands away in horror and urged the doctor to follow me outside to have a word.

'Is everything all right?' he asked.

My face clouded over as I tried to find the right words to explain what I'd discovered. I took a deep breath.

'Doctor, does the mother know her baby has two heads?'

The consultant looked at me, shook his head and snorted with laughter.

'I should hope so, Nurse. She's expecting twins!'

Unsurprisingly, after six months in training I failed my first midwifery exam. The stress took its toll as I worked extra hours so that I could take it again. I lost a dreadful amount of weight while slogging away on 12-hour shifts covering both the labour and postnatal wards. Back then, all the babies would be taken from their mothers during the night to allow the mum some time to rest. The babies would be placed inside a nursery, where they would be fed breast milk, labelled from mother to child. In total, there were 24 babies in the nursery and, although there were three staff – a sister and two pupil midwives – we'd be flat out because it was non-stop trying to change and feed each child. With my retakes looming, I studied both night and day. Peter tested me so much that I'm sure he could have delivered a baby too!

Thankfully, the second time around I passed with flying colours, and my stint as a midwife ended there, or so I thought. On a rare weekend off, I visited home. My brother Tony was working as a rep for a mining supplies company based in Cheshire, and his wife, Joyce, was heavily pregnant, so I went to stay with them. I was sat having a cup of tea when Joyce's midwife called by.

'I believe you're now a midwife,' she said by way of conversation. I nodded, although I'd no intention of taking that particular career path any further.

'I'll tell you what, I'll leave a midwifery pack here, just in case,' she suggested as she packed away her things and left.

Hours later, Joyce had ventured upstairs when she shouted down to me in a panic: 'Joan, quick! The baby's on its way!'

I felt my mouth go dry and my stomach clench as I ran up the stairs.

'I want to go to the toilet!' Joyce wailed. It was obvious she'd gone into labour.

'No,' I insisted, 'lie back down and I'll help you.' My voice sounded calm even though I felt anything but.

I started to open the midwifery pack, but as I looked up I realised that the baby's head was already presenting.

'Call the midwife!' I screamed downstairs to Tony. His new job paid a good wage so they rented their own home telephone.

I did what I could but, thankfully, the doctor and midwife arrived soon afterwards.

'Thank goodness you're here,' I gasped as the midwife unbuttoned her coat.

Tony was so nervous that he couldn't bear to be in the house; he wandered up to his allotment where he stayed for the next four hours until his beautiful baby daughter had been born. Joyce called her Joanna – a combination of both my sister Ann's and my name.

'Oh, Joyce,' I said, beginning to weep, 'she's absolutely beautiful and you popped her out like a tiny pea!'

Soon everyone was laughing, everyone apart from Tony and me. We were standing in the corner, crying at the wonder of it all.

I returned to the radiotherapy unit having taken the first steps towards being a Departmental Sister, but then the hospital decided to combine us with the general outpatients department. A senior sister was drafted in to head up my department so that she could raise her status in the hospital. We immediately clashed. I disliked her because she brought with her sudden overnight changes. Luckily, I worked with a good team of nurses who supported me. I became friends with one in particular – her name was Jean and she was a beautiful nurse from Ghana. Jean had a smile that could light up a whole room. We were similar because Jean also had a wicked sense of humour, and so together we became a bit of a double act. One day, I complained that I needed to buy a tailor's dummy, because I made all my own clothes.

'But they're so expensive, Jean. I wish I could afford one because it'd make life so much easier.'

Jean sympathised but we were both on nurses' wages so neither of us had any savings to speak of. Then I hit on a fabulous idea. In fact, it was so fabulous that I couldn't believe anyone else hadn't thought of it first. I shared it with Jean and asked if she'd help. Later that evening, I stripped off to my underwear as Jean soaked and wrapped a series of plaster-of-Paris bandages around my torso. The bandages had to be tight enough to replicate my figure. The plan was that when they were dry we'd cut them off and I'd be left with the perfect dummy, with my exact measurements.

'I can't believe I didn't think of this before,' I crowed as the chalky water streamed down my legs into the empty bath below.

Jean slowly wound bandages from my thighs towards my shoulders and neck; however, as soon as they started to dry I felt them crushing my ribcage.

'Joan, are you all right?' Jean asked.

But the bandages had started to set and now I was taking quick, shallow breaths.

'Yes, I'm fine,' I gasped. 'It's a little tight but we're almost there.'

Jean wasn't convinced but I begged her to continue. I wasn't going to have gone through it all for nothing! Soon, the pressure on my chest became too much and then I needed a wee!

'Jean, I think you're going to have to cut me out. I can't breathe properly,' I cried.

'No problem' she said, putting the bandages down at the side of the bath. 'Where did you put the cutters?'

'But I thought you'd brought them?'

'No, you said you would.'

A hand shot to my mouth as the horrid truth dawned on me.

'Oh no, I've forgotten the cutters. Pete, Peter!' I wailed as the plaster of Paris continued to dry, squeezing the life out of me.

Peter came running in as Jean and I explained my predicament.

'What the hell …' he exclaimed as soon as he spotted me togged up like a live mummy.

'Hang on,' he called as he emptied out the bathroom cabinet. Seconds later, the metal edge of a razor glinted between his fingers. 'This should do it,' he said, holding it up triumphantly.

'Hurry up!' I wailed as the body cast became more restrictive.

Between them, Peter and Jean managed to cut through the plaster until I was able to breathe. Peter had instructed me to hold up my arms so that he could cut it underneath my armpit. But when he finally removed me from my cast, the proportions were all wrong because, with an arm raised in the air, one breast had set higher than the other! To make matters worse, as soon as they released me, my knickers and bra fell promptly to my ankles! In a panic, Peter had sliced right through the sides of them. Jean couldn't stop laughing, and then Peter joined in until soon the three of us were doubled up in hysterics.

'Joan, you're crazy!' Jean howled, clutching at her sides.

'That's why I married her!' Peter quipped.

Jean was my best friend and I loved her with all my heart, although by now it was 1970 and racism was rife. But woe betide anyone who mentioned the colour of her skin because I'd be the first to shoot them down. A few weeks later, Jean invited us to a party at her house. Peter and I were the only white people there but we were welcomed like old friends. Living in London, I was used to mixing with people from countries all over the world. Different cultures fascinated me, and although times were changing they were moving far too slowly for my liking. Many British people were predominantly racist and small-minded. I loathed it because I couldn't understand why the colour of someone's skin should define who they were. If anything, I dug my heels in even more and, on my days off, I'd dress in beautiful Indian saris because I found them more attractive and comfortable than the high-street fashions.

One day, Bill told me that Mum had suffered a nasty fall at home. I called to see her but it was obvious she was having trouble breathing. I rang the doctor and asked if he could do a home visit. He arrived soon afterwards but he was useless. It soon became apparent that he didn't have a clue what he was doing, so after he'd left I telephoned for an ambulance.

'I'm fine,' Mum panted. But my instinct told me something was wrong.

I travelled with her to the A&E department at Hammersmith, where one of the consultants sent her for an X-ray to check that she hadn't broken a rib in the fall. As we waited for the results, the consultant, who I knew well, beckoned me over.

'I'm afraid it's not a normal fracture – it's a pathological one.'

My heart plummeted because I knew what it meant: something was underlying.

'I think its bone cancer,' he concluded. 'She'll need more tests but I think that's what we're looking at.'

In a strange way, the news didn't come as a shock because my mother had undergone a radical mastectomy for breast cancer in the early 1950s, and I was certain the bone cancer was secondary. It was a hard thing to do but I knew it was up to me to try to deliver the news to her.

'But they told me it was a tumour in my breast; they didn't say anything about breast cancer,' she gasped.

Like many people, she was unable to connect the words tumour and cancer together because cancer wasn't spoken of then as it is today.

I tried to explain that she'd need to visit my radiotherapy unit to receive testosterone injections, which was the treatment at that time.

'All right,' she said. 'But I'll only have them if you do it.'

In the end, it was agreed that Mum would be an outpatient in my department, where I would administer the painful and deep injections. When faced with a second cancer diagnosis, most people would've given up, but not my mum. Instead, she turned her regular appointments into a jolly day out and would even bring in homemade sandwiches for the consultant. She'd always use home-baked bread, the finest butter and the leanest ham she could find.

'Now,' she said, putting the carrier bag down on the doctor's desk. 'I bet you've not had your lunch yet, have you?'

'But Mum, I don't think Dr …' I tried to interrupt, but she held up her hand to quieten me.

'Nonsense, Joan, I've just seen him walk over from the eye hospital. Anyway, I've made you some lovely ham sandwiches. They're in here somewhere,' she said, rummaging around inside her bag.

I wanted the ground to swallow me whole, but the consultant seemed delighted that one of his patients had made him lunch.

'It's good ham, that,' Mum insisted, pointing at the meat as he bit into it. 'I've even cut off all the fatty bits.'

From then on, my mother brought his lunch along to every visit.

''Ere, I've put some of that mustard on that you like,' she grinned one afternoon as she handed over a brown paper bag.

I was mortified because the senior sister had made it clear that she didn't approve of Mum's over-familiarity with the consultant. She didn't say anything, but she didn't have to – the look she gave me was enough.

'Go and get the man a glass of milk, Nurse,' Mum barked at one of my colleagues. 'He can't eat his sandwich with nothing to wash it down, now, can he?'

Mum continued with her treatment, although I realised it wouldn't save her life, just slow down the cancer growth.

The new Departmental Sister continued to implement changes. She altered clinics even though they'd run like clockwork before she'd arrived. She also changed our working hours, and put a ban on all pets in the unit. It wasn't long before I found work impossible. Before, the radiotherapy unit had been a happy ship, but suddenly it felt as though we were drowning in red tape, rules and regulations. I went to see Matron to protest, but she made it clear that I was no longer in charge. So, after 19 years at Hammersmith Hospital, including my year out at Brodsworth pit, I handed in my resignation. I knew I'd miss my patients and colleagues, and Jean in particular, but I also knew it was time to leave. However, first I needed to say goodbye to my favourite patient, Michael. He was 12 years old, and he'd been one of the luckier ones to survive cancer.

'I'll miss you, Sister Joan,' he said, wrapping his arms tight around me.

'Me too, Michael. Me too.'

After that day I never saw him again, but I expect and hope he went on to live a full and happy life.

I was wondering where life would lead me next when my old tutor mentioned she was looking for a district nurse to cover an area of London. On her word, I went to see the sister in charge of Kensington borough, who gave me the job on the spot. On my first day, I shadowed a nurse who was leaving to get married. As we whizzed through London in her red Mini, I thought what fun it was to be a district nurse. A few days later she left and I was on my own. I didn't drive, so I was handed a black bag and a large, heavy iron bicycle.

My 'area' covered Portobello Road, South Kensington and Ladbroke Grove. The only problem was that I had absolutely no sense of direction. On my first day solo, I finished work over three hours late because I'd got lost so many times. It was 1971, and there were riots across London, so I was assigned a police officer to escort me. However, he'd presumed I was in a car and so zoomed off, leaving me for dust on my antique bike. Peter tried his best to help. He drew a map and even drove me along my route the night before. But cycling through London when you haven't got a clue where you're going is a complete nightmare.

One winter's day, I was cycling behind a car when it came to a sudden halt without indicating. I slammed on my brakes to try to stop myself from crashing into the back of it. Tutting loudly, I huffed, readjusted my twisted front wheel and cycled around it, only for the motorist to then swing his door open. How I didn't come off and fall into the heavy traffic, I'll never know. After a bit of a wobble, I managed to regain my balance, but by now a fury had boiled inside me and there was no turning back. I threw the blasted bike against the kerb and banged loudly on the front of his car bonnet with both fists. The man looked up at me, startled.

'Go on then, have another go! Run me over, see if I care!' I screamed.

'Er, I don't know what you mean.'

He looked sheepish and, if I'm honest, a tad scared of me. But I didn't care because by now I was in full flow. I continued to scold him as passers-by stopped in their tracks to stare and listen.

'Yes, you do know what I mean,' I hissed, holding my arms out like a demented woman. 'I almost went into the back of you because you didn't signal. Then you opened the door and almost took me out! So go on, get back in your car and run me over because you seem intent on doing so!'

The man looked so frightened that I lowered my arms. Huffing loudly, I straightened my coat, picked up my bike and climbed back on. I cycled away into the busy London traffic, cursing him as I went. As much as I hated the bike, I missed it when it was gone. A few weeks later, I was working down Portobello Road, so I chained it to a set of railings. Shortly afterwards, I emerged to find that not only had the wheels gone, but the handlebars had been stolen too.

'Unbelievable!' I cried as I marched off to a phone box. I searched for coins in my purse and rang Peter to ask if he'd come and collect me.

'I think I've had enough of this district nursing lark,' I moaned as I slid into the passenger seat. 'I just don't think it's for me.'

It wasn't. After a year of cycling the streets of London, I handed in my notice and took up a position as an industrial nurse working for British Petroleum at its headquarters in Moorgate, London. The salary was incredible. It was February 1972 – exactly a year after decimalisation – and my starting wage was £1,722 per annum. It seemed like a small fortune compared to the £705 I'd risen to at Hammersmith. For the first time in my life, I felt like the richest woman on earth, and, more importantly, I was back doing industrial nursing – the job I loved best.

8

A Heartbeat from Death

I adored my job at BP. Peter had left his old job, working as a plumber at the council, and secured a position working as a buyer for Trusthouse Forte. It wasn't long before he'd moved up the ranks. In many ways our lives were on the up, and, for the first time ever, we had money to spend. We loved to socialise and would often be found in bars with his colleagues, drinking cocktails and spirits into the early hours. After my time working down the pit, I liked to keep up with the boys, and so, despite being a nurse, I enjoyed the odd cigar or two, usually King Edwards. But this was back in the days when smoking was considered glamorous and everyone did it. My special trick was to try to keep the ash on the end of the cigar for as long as I could.

'I think I'll call you Ginger,' one of Peter's colleagues said, alluding to my distinctive red hair. After that, all his friends called me 'Ginger', even Peter, although he shortened it to 'Ginge'.

While I was working at BP, another nurse called Deirdre and I were offered the chance to set up a medical centre in Saudi Arabia. It all sounded very glamorous, until we discovered that we'd be expected to perform minor surgery, including appendectomies. Unsurprisingly, we turned it down. BP housed a state-of-the-art operating theatre. It was permanently on standby in case of IRA bomb attacks, which were on the increase at that time. But, other than give injections and deal with general injuries, I wasn't called on to do anything too extreme and so I came to expect the humdrum. One day, I was sitting in the medical centre when I received a call to say someone on one of the top floors had cut their hand.

'No problem, I'll be right up,' I said, searching inside the first-aid box for plasters and a piece of gauze.

I took the lift up, but as soon as I stepped out of it the office was in complete pandemonium.

'Over here, Sister,' a man cried. That's when I spotted it – blood splattered all over the ceiling, walls and floor. It looked like a scene from a horror movie.

I dashed over, cursing the pathetic plasters in my hand.

'What on earth have you done?' I asked the injured man, who was slumped against the floor. He was pale and looked in danger of passing out. As I uncurled his hand I realised why. He had such deep lacerations that he'd almost severed three of his fingers.

'He went to close the window,' his colleague explained, 'when the wind blew it shut. His hand went through the glass but he pulled it out again.'

I shook my head. Offices aren't usually dangerous places but the first rule of nursing is to always expect the unexpected. Thankfully, I knew what to do and I began by deploying his work colleagues.

'You,' I said, pointing towards the first man. 'You run back downstairs and fetch the other sister. Ask her to bring up some morphine, a blanket and a set of bandages.' The man nodded and ran off in the direction of the medical room.

'You,' I said, pointing to another. 'Call an ambulance. I want you to go straight outside and wait at the front of the building for it. When it arrives, bring them straight up here because we haven't got time for them to get lost inside the building.'

I held the injured man's hand upwards, clasped in both of mine. His blood was pumping furiously and I could feel it dripping down the side of my wrist. I applied pressure using a cotton-wool pad and tightened a tourniquet to stem the flow.

'What do you want us to do, Sister?' two other men asked.

They looked almost as ashen and shaken as their injured colleague.

'Nothing. I want you to stay here with me. And whatever you do, don't leave me.'

My words did little to comfort them. If anything, they looked even more terrified.

Moments later, Deirdre appeared along with the first man. She'd brought bandages and immediately began to wrap the patient's hand while I administered morphine to kill some of his pain. He'd gone into shock and had started to shake, so we wrapped him up in the blanket. Two ambulance men emerged from the lift and came dashing over to help. They checked him as I relayed what had happened and what his injuries were. They loaded him up onto a stretcher and whisked him off to St Bartholomew's Hospital, where surgeons had been alerted. Amazingly, despite his blood loss, the man was extremely lucky and managed to keep all three fingers. It was nothing short of a miracle, although I expect he was a little more careful shutting the window after that.

During my time at BP, I did a crash course in industrial nursing, flying up to Dundee University for specialised training. Peter's job with the hotel chain meant he was able to wangle a few days up in Scotland. Like me, he was always dashing around, so when he started complaining of chest pains I put it down to indigestion. But I became concerned because Peter had gradually become very overweight. Working for a hotel chain often meant long, boozy lunches, which quickly thickened his waistline, yet, despite my worries, he insisted it was nothing. Peter headed back to London, and, a few weeks later, I finished my course at Dundee. I'd learned all about preventative medicine, law, legislation and health and safety in the working environment. I loved the fact that industrial nursing meant it was always down to you to make the decision and trust your own judgement, which came in useful when Peter's chest pains continued.

'You need to see the doctor,' I nagged.

Peter was headstrong but he realised I was right. He agreed to see a GP, who referred him for an X-ray. It revealed that he'd suffered a mild heart attack. Not only that, but his heart was enlarged. The doctor had seemed largely unconcerned, but I was worried so I had a word with one of the consultants at BP, who agreed to examine Peter and take further X-rays. BP had its very own X-ray room, so Peter underwent more tests, which confirmed his heart was enlarged. The consultant recommended a heart specialist, so we paid privately to see him at his consultation rooms in central London. His office was very grand. I couldn't take my eyes off the glass-topped desk in front of him, which was both unusual and expensive at the time.

I sat down as he proceeded to examine Peter and read through his medical notes. Finally, he showed him back to his chair, sat down and gave us his damning verdict.

'It's like this,' he said, clasping his hands together in front of him. 'Your heart is clapped out, like an old motor.'

I glanced at Peter, who looked shocked and frightened.

'Now, how did you both get here?' the doctor continued, breaking my thoughts.

'Er, we caught a taxi,' Peter began, but the consultant cut him off mid-sentence with a wave of his hand.

'Well, you need to go straight to hospital to be treated. There's not a minute to waste, so you'd better get yourselves over there right now.' He scribbled something down on a piece of paper and handed it to us. 'Now, here's where you need to go. They'll have a bed waiting for you, so I'll see you when I get over there.'

We walked out of his office in a complete daze. We were totally shell-shocked.

'Right,' I said, trying to gather my thoughts outside on the busy London street. 'We'd better catch a cab.'

I held out my arm but Peter raised his hand to stop me.

'Let's just pop in and get some lunch first, eh? If I'm going to be stuck inside a hospital the food will be awful, so allow me at least one last good meal,' he said, sounding like a condemned man.

I agreed. I could tell the news had hit him hard and he needed time to think and process everything. We both did.

'No problem. Where shall we go?' I replied, brightening up a little.

'Somewhere that serves champagne and oysters!'

We caught a cab and stopped off at George's restaurant in central London for a slap-up meal. Several hours later, we stumbled, giggling and a little unsteady on our feet, into Charing Cross Hospital. When the ward sister spotted us through beady eyes I could tell she wasn't impressed.

'Mr Hart,' she called from the other end of the ward. 'Where on earth have you been? Your bed has been ready for hours.'

I looked up at Peter, but he didn't seem to care.

'We had a little trouble getting a taxi,' he lied.

The sister nodded, although it was obvious she didn't believe him. She looked down at her paper and ticked him off her list before asking which name he preferred.

'Shall we call you Peter, or do you prefer Mr Hart?' she enquired.

'Sir will do,' he replied, quick as a flash. 'You can call me sir.'

Even though the champagne had loosened my inhibitions, I wanted the ground to swallow me whole. I was a nurse and, although Peter was only joking, I also knew what it was like to deal with a difficult patient – and one who was also a little bit tipsy.

'Right,' she snapped, her face a picture. She dropped her patients' list down onto the desk with a clatter and looked at Peter with steely determination. 'Mr Hart it is, then.'

She led him over towards a bed situated next to the main door.

'This is your bed, Mr Hart,' she announced.

'Oh, I'm not having that one.'

Although I'd sobered up, I could still hear Peter slurring ever so slightly.

The sister glanced up at him sternly.

'Why ever not?' she asked, her patience wearing thin.

'Because it's near the door, and those,' he said with absolute conviction, 'are usually the first patients to die.'

After a bit of a kerfuffle, Peter got his wish and managed to secure a bed next to the window and, more importantly, away from the door.

'Happy now, Mr Hart?' Sister enquired as she tucked the bed sheet in beneath him.

'Yes,' he grinned, resting his head back against the pillows.

Once he'd settled, I left to fetch his pyjamas and a dressing gown from home.

Later that evening we saw the same consultant, although his new and revolutionary techniques didn't fill me with much hope. His belief was that the heart was a muscle, so in order to get it working correctly you had to rest it and slowly build it back up again. In Peter's case, this involved sedating him until his heart had slowed and almost stopped beating. It was then steadily worked, using physiotherapy, in a bid to strengthen it. However, all it seemed to do was make poor Peter even more desperately ill. If anything, I believed the new technique was actually dangerous. Peter remained in bed for almost a month, in which time he lost so much weight that he became skeletal. He was eventually discharged but, just two weeks later, he suffered a second heart attack. He was admitted to hospital and then had several more heart attacks in quick succession. I was so terrified I'd lose him that I lived at his bedside. I stopped eating, and watched him day and night, praying that he'd get better. I was extremely doubtful of the consultant's technique, so I spoke to a registrar friend. I could tell by the shocked look on his face that he agreed with me.

'Joan, if you don't get Peter out of London, he'll be dead within the next six months,' he said. I'd suspected as much, but he'd just confirmed my worst fears.

'Surely there must be somewhere or someone else we can go to?'

He shook his head. 'Look, Peter is his patient and, knowing this consultant, he'll not only refuse heart surgery, he won't let you hand him over to another doctor. If you don't get him out of here, your husband will be dead. The best thing you can do is leave London, for Peter's sake.'

So that's what we did. I applied for five jobs back up north and, thankfully, I got them all. But there was only one job I wanted, and that was to work for the National Coal Board as a pit nurse. Dad had told me about two nursing officer positions based in Doncaster. One was at Hatfield and the other was at Rossington pit. I accepted the job at Hatfield and moved in to a spare bedroom at my brother Tony's house. By now, Tony and Joyce had three children, so there was barely enough space for me, never mind Peter. But with Peter now too sick to work, I had to take the job to bring in an income. Meanwhile, he stayed on at our old flat in London, which we still had a lease on. I tried not to worry because I knew his family would be on hand to help out should he ever need them. It would mean we'd be apart for a few months, but I also knew it'd be temporary. I needed the job to build a better future for us. I was going back home, but more importantly, I was returning to the miners and the pits – the place where my heart belonged.

9

At the Coalface

I started as the nursing officer at Hatfield pit in June 1974. Although I'd worked in the same position at Brodsworth pit years earlier, things had changed. The nurses at the other pits had also been trained in occupational health. My first few weeks at Hatfield were hectic because I had so many people to meet. Despite being up north and away from London, my wages rose once again to a respectable £1,833 per annum. For this I had to travel to different pits in the Doncaster area to carry out medicals on new cadets, usually boys aged 16 who had followed their fathers and grandfathers down the mine. I also had to carry out medicals on men who'd been off on long-term sick leave but who were returning to work. They had to have a clean bill of health to return to a job that was so physically demanding.

After a fortnight in my new position, I was called to Leeds to be measured up for my navy-blue sisters' uniform. Up until that point, I'd been wearing my own clothes – a smart grey suit and white blouse – but I soon realised a tailored suit wasn't the best attire for working at a filthy colliery. Also, when I arrived I'd sensed there was a bit of an atmosphere. The sister who'd interviewed me for the position was retiring, and it soon became apparent that I had more nursing qualifications than she did. To say this got up her nose would be an understatement. Instead, she'd warned the men I was 'posh' because I'd come from London and spoke with a slight southern twang. They'd also been told I was a bit 'bossy' too and that I intended to make sweeping changes, which was absolute nonsense – although she'd been right about the bossy bit.

When I first saw the medical centre I was aghast because it needed a good lick of paint throughout. The walls were a cold, dark colour. They were not only depressing but unwelcoming too. Recalling my days at Brodsworth, I knew exactly what needed to be done.

'No, it won't do. It's much too dark – it needs to be decorated,' I decided.

Bill, the man showing me around, was one of the older Medical Room Assistants (MRAs). I could tell that he didn't like me very much, and he was suspicious of me with my so-called fancy 'southern' ways. Bill was in his fifties, tall and slim with greying dark hair. He wore a pair of traditional thick-rimmed glasses that made him look a bit like Eric Morecambe, only without the sense of humour. As soon as I mentioned changing the colour scheme his face dropped.

'But we've always had navy-blue walls here,' he gasped. 'We keep 'em dark so they don't show t'blood or muck.'

'Yes, and it's such a horrible colour. Creams, pale greens and yellows are much more inviting, so I think I'd like it painting yellow,' I said, glancing around.

'Yellow!' Bill shrieked as though I'd gone mad.

'Yes, yellow,' I insisted as I turned to survey the rest of the room. 'Now, about this table …'

He gave me the same look the men had given me when I'd painted the waiting room at Brodsworth. Despite Bill's misgivings, I got my way and the walls were indeed painted daffodil yellow – a happy, sunshine colour. I also felt a personal victory when my office was later decorated a pale fern green. In the middle of the treatment room there was a very large table that dominated the room. It was the same size and height as a table-tennis table, and the chairs, which were used for dressing wounds and examining eyes, had been shoved right at the back of the room behind it. They were so far away from the nearest window that all natural light was lost. I shook my head. It was worse than I'd thought.

'This table,' I said, tapping the top of it with my hand. 'It'll have to go.'

'No,' Bill said, shaking his head vehemently. 'We need it.'

I looked over at him. 'But what's it for? What do you use it for?'

Bill waved his hands around as though it should be obvious. 'To put bodies on, of course!'

I stifled a gasp. 'Bodies? Good Lord, how many bodies do you get here?'

He looked a bit shifty. 'Well, not that many,' he admitted. 'But it's useful for lots of other things too.'

I shook my head. 'Well, I'm sorry, but it has to go. We need to reorganise it in here to make the work easier for everyone. We'll use the stretcher trestles in future.'

I could tell Bill didn't think it was a good idea, but my mind was made up. I went to see the pit manager to ask if I could get rid of the table.

'Will it interfere with the production of coal?' he asked, looking up from a pile of papers scattered across his desk.

'No, not at all.'

'Well, in that case, do as you want,' he said, with a wave of his hand.

Bill sulked in a corner while I grabbed a biro and a piece of paper and wrote a note.

Table – Free to a Good Home, it read.

I pinned the notice up outside the time office and called in at the workshops to tell the lads it was up for grabs.

'If you can use it, it's yours.'

It must have been a very special table indeed because, to my delight, within the hour it had gone, freeing up the whole of the medical centre. Bill wasn't happy, of course, but I hoped that, with the passage of time, he'd eventually see sense. The space its loss had created was wonderful. The centre was manned by three MRAs – Bill, Frank and Andy – who had all been specially trained for the job. Bill and Frank had served alongside the previous sister and had been at the pit for a good 20 years, while Andy, who was in his late twenties, had only just qualified. However, Andy was a lovely lad who was popular with the men and very keen to learn. The MRAs covered the centre in three shifts so it was manned 24 hours a day, with either me or a sister from another pit on call. I was also backed by three underground first-aid men, who were attached to both the safety department and the medical centre. They were required to work to cover holidays or unexpected sick leave. I asked the MRAs to write down any suggestions they thought would help improve their working conditions. Initially, this was met with a fair bit of suspicion because it was clear they didn't believe that I, a woman, could alter or change things for the better in a pit full of men.

'What do you want us to write?' one asked suspiciously.

'Anything. Listen, you lot work here all the time, but sometimes I'll be out at clinics and meetings, so I won't always be around. If you have any sensible suggestions then I'm willing to consider them, as long as they are sensible.'

The MRAs looked at me and then at one another. One by one, they nodded their heads and began to make small lists. I was finally getting through to them, albeit slowly. They did, however, come up with some good suggestions. The main desk was moved closer to the entrance and the chairs were placed underneath the window to ensure better light. With the table gone, it seemed as though we suddenly had acres of room. In the days that followed, the men began to realise that I was there to help and support them, not hinder. If I was a little bossy, then it was only for their own good and to make their lives easier in the long run. However, the dreaded table came back to haunt me only a week later when a man collapsed underground from a fatal heart attack. Four miners carried him out on a stretcher into the medical centre. I could see by the look on their faces that I was under scrutiny, because the 'dead body table' was missing and they had nowhere to put him.

'What will she do?' I heard one whisper as they watched and waited to see if I knew the correct procedure.

Thankfully, I did. I instructed the men to leave the deceased miner on the stretcher, held up by the trestle table, and then I telephoned a local GP and asked him to come to the pit to certify the man's death. In the case of a death, the body has to be formally identified and the police coroner informed. Thankfully, the local GP, Dr Walters, arrived quickly. But as soon as he entered the medical centre, he looked over at me and did a double take.

'You're not Sister Brown,' he said, stating the obvious.

'No, I'm Sister Hart. The man is through here if you'd like to follow me, Doctor,' I replied, calmly leading the way.

He looked back over his shoulder and took me to one side.

'Do you know what to do, Sister?' he whispered gently. I was grateful for his concern because I was new and he realised the men were uncertain about me.

'Yes,' I replied, clearing my throat, speaking loud enough so the others would hear. 'You need to certify death and then we need to notify the police and the coroner.'

'That is correct, Sister,' he nodded, before going over to examine the man.

The National Union of Miners (NUM) representative was duly dispatched not only to deliver the grim news to the miner's wife, but also to bring her back so that she could identify her husband. I washed his face so she would be able to recognise him – a gesture of both necessity and respect. A short while later, the rep returned with the miner's wife. She was clearly shaken and suffering from shock. To lose a man to a heart attack is often quick and distressing because there is nothing to be done. But to then have to go to the miner's wife to tell her that the man she waved off to work that morning, fit and well, wasn't coming home that night, was doubly harrowing. The man had neither been old nor ill. His sudden death had come as a shock to everyone.

'He didn't suffer,' I insisted, patting the woman's arm gently. I hoped it would bring her a small crumb of comfort in the days, months and years that would follow.

In many ways, I understood how she felt. Peter was back in London, living with his own time bomb of a failing heart. During the past three years he'd suffered six heart attacks; he was living miles away, where I knew I'd never be able to reach him in time. I knew it was only temporary, but I couldn't wait for him to finally move up north and be with me for good.

After witnessing the wife's shock and grief, I made a pledge that, in future, whenever possible, I'd go down the pit to the injured or collapsed man and bring him out myself. I also wanted to be present when loved ones were told, in the hope that I could shed a little more light and perhaps comfort them in some way.

My hours of work were decided by the colliery manager, Mr Bumstead, but generally they were from 8 a.m. to 4 p.m., five days a week. The nursing sisters were also 'on call' 24 hours a day for their own pit and for two others. My other 'on call' pits were Bentley Colliery, which was 9 miles away, and Markham Main in Armthorpe, which was 5 miles down the road. However, I was told that, in an emergency, I could expect to be called out to any of 10 pits in the Doncaster area.

I was still staying with Tony and Joyce, in Scawthorpe, Doncaster. As I didn't drive, the pit van would come and pick me up in the morning and I'd travel home later that evening by bus. My sister, Ann, her husband, John, and their boys took me out in a little van so we could scour the area local to Hatfield for a suitable property to buy. After two months of searching, we finally found one, a bungalow in a village called Barnby Dun, which was 4 miles from Hatfield pit. It was exactly what we needed because Peter had limited mobility and I knew he'd struggle to climb a set of stairs. He was finding it increasingly difficult back at the flat, but at least I knew that was only for the short-term. I had to choose our future home wisely, because it would be somewhere we would live for the rest of our lives.

The bungalow was pricey at £7,500 – a small fortune back then – so I waited a few weeks until he was able to travel up north to view it. Thankfully, Peter fell in love with it too, so we sorted out a mortgage and asked his brother Terry to help us move. A month later, Peter left London and came to live with me. It was lovely to finally own our own home and, more importantly, it was a relief to have my husband back by my side where I could keep an eye on him and his health.

For Peter, it all seemed very quiet in comparison to living in a flat on a busy main road in Shepherd's Bush. With his health growing steadily worse, I feared for the future, and just three months later those fears came true when he suffered another heart attack. We'd been drinking in a local pub when he began to feel clammy and sick. I got him home and rang for the doctor. But he wasn't happy and I called for an ambulance. On the way to hospital, Peter's left arm numbed and then he started to have chest pains. He was taken to Doncaster Royal Infirmary where he was admitted to the Coronary Care Unit. Peter was eventually referred to Dr Dore, who continued to monitor him as an outpatient for the following three months. He was referred again and, in 1975, he visited the Northern General Hospital in Sheffield, where he was placed under a brilliant surgeon called Mr Smith. The only problem was that, because he was such a fantastic surgeon, Mr Smith had a long waiting list of patients.

'You need a triple bypass operation, Mr Hart. Tell me, why wasn't this done in London?'

Peter told him all about the heart consultant and his pioneering new techniques.

'Well, you shall be having one here, that's for sure,' he said, pulling Peter's top back down following the examination. 'Now, I have a waiting list, which is approximately three to four months long, but I'll try to get you in as soon as possible.'

Peter was a young patient at only 43 years old. He faced a major operation but his age also meant that he had a better chance of recovery. I felt encouraged by Mr Smith, and I was certain my husband was in good hands. True to his word, Peter was called back just three weeks later for surgery. It was a red-hot summer's day when they took him down to theatre. I was such a nervous wreck that, despite my medical training, or perhaps because of it, I was petrified that something would go wrong. As the hours ticked by, I convinced myself that something had gone terribly wrong.

'Is there any news yet?' I asked a nurse, but she shook her head.

Major heart operations were relatively new at that time. The longer it took, the more convinced I became that Peter had died. Each hour that passed seemed like a lifetime. In the end, poor Peter was in theatre for an astonishing eight hours. When they finally brought him back up to recovery, I was so relieved that I cried.

Mr Smith emerged, exhausted but hopeful. 'The operation was more complicated than we first anticipated because, instead of taking one vein from his leg, we had to take two to help his heart pump properly. We also discovered that the muscle at the back of his heart wasn't working.'

The surgeon explained that Peter had coronary heart failure, but the operation had been a success. I hoped and prayed it'd bought him a second chance at life. When I was finally allowed in to see him I stole an anxious breath. He'd been placed on a ventilator and put into a drug-induced coma to allow his body time to recover. I slept at the hospital for the following three days. The other nursing sisters, working at adjacent pits, were fantastic and covered not only my daily work, but my 'calls' too. Three days after his op, the nurse on the ward came in to do her regular checks.

'If he manages to breathe unaided when we take the ventilator off, then you can go home and get some rest,' she said, placing a hand gently on my shoulder.

I felt so grateful to her and all the wonderful medical staff who had saved my husband's life. I realised then the difference nurses make and just how vital our role is when dealing with the loved ones of patients.

I'm certain that the operation saved Peter's life, and without it he would've died prematurely. His father died at just 60 from a heart attack. Looking back now, I'm convinced it was a genetic problem in his family.

The nurse removed the ventilator and Peter was able to breathe unaided, although he looked absolutely ghastly. His skin was both pale and grey.

'How do you feel?' I asked as he blinked open his eyes.

'Bloody awful,' he croaked. 'And sore. I feel really, really sore.'

I put a finger to his lips to quieten him because I didn't want him to over-exert himself.

'Hush, don't try to talk too much. Everything went really well and it's worked. The doctors are really pleased with you,' I whispered.

But the truth was that he looked absolutely terrible. Although his heart was pumping properly, my nursing instincts told me he would never be the same again. A few days later, the physiotherapist appeared and, in a bid to get Peter moving, she manoeuvred him towards the edge of the bed so he could begin some simple exercises. He complained, but I took it as a good sign that he was slowly on the road to recovery.

I visited Peter in Sheffield every day while holding down my job at Hatfield. My fellow nursing sisters continued to be amazingly helpful, and some even offered me lifts to the hospital. Peter wasn't a good patient because he hated being stuck on a hospital ward, but a month later he was allowed back home where I was able to care and nurse him in between going to work. To be honest, I ran myself ragged, trying to win the support of the miners and care for a sick husband. But my colleagues were so supportive that I honestly don't know what I would've done without them. If I was needed during an emergency, management would send a van out to collect me. Slowly but surely, I'd begun to feel accepted as part of the wonderful mining community.

10

Nurse in Pit Boots

With Peter home and finally on the mend, I decided to throw myself back into work. I needed to fulfil the pledge I'd made to myself – to go underground to tend to the injured. But first I had to get permission from both management and the Safety Department.

'Will it interfere with coal production?' asked Mr Bumstead, the pit manager.

'No, I just need to understand where the injured man is coming from to enable me to treat him correctly. I need to know how wet or hot his working environment is. I need to see how they lift an injured miner out of the pit. But I can't do any of these things if I'm stuck over there in the medical centre,' I said, pointing towards it.

He shook his head doubtfully.

'But what can you do underground? I mean, the men already get the injured miners out as quickly as possible. How would having you down there help?'

'Because I can check they've done everything that can possibly be done. I can check the man over before they bring him up to the surface.'

Although Mr Bumstead was a little sceptical, I could tell he trusted my judgement. The more we spoke, the more interested he seemed in my medical expertise.

'You'll have to be accompanied by one of the men from the Safety Department. You must never go down there alone,' he said.

'Absolutely, whatever you say,' I agreed, before he could finish his sentence or change his mind.

He looked at me, put down his pen and leaned back in his chair.

'Okay, run it past the Safety Department first. If they're happy, then so am I.'

'Great! You won't regret it.'

But the three men in the Safety Department were a little more reticent.

'What did t'manager say?' they asked.

'He says he's happy for me to do it, but I just need to run it past you,' I said, bending the truth a little.

'Well, you can't go down on yer own,' the senior one insisted. 'You'll have to have one of us with yer.'

'Yes, I understand.'

'But,' he said, scratching the point of his bristly chin between his fingers, 'that depends if we can spare someone. Also, you'll have to wear t'right gear. You can't go down dressed like that.'

I looked at my navy-blue nurses' uniform. He was right about my clothes.

'Don't worry. I'll get something sorted.'

'Well, if t'manager's 'appy then I suppose we'll have to sort summat out and find someone to take thee underground.'

In the end, the Safety Department had a meeting with the manager and, a week later, my wish was granted.

'As long as you get permission from t'under-manager and overman of t'area you wanna go to before yer visit,' the safety lads insisted.

'And as long as it doesn't interfere with the production of coal,' Mr Bumstead stressed once more, pointing his fountain pen in my direction.

While I waited for my first visit underground, I was issued with a pair of regulation pit wellies.

'Are these the smallest size you've got?' I asked, sizing them up in my hands. They looked absolutely enormous.

'You're lucky to have 'em. Those are a size 7 – they're only little,' the man handing them to me replied in a gruff voice.

'But I'm only a size 5!'

He shrugged his shoulders as though it wasn't his problem.

'They're smallest ones we've got. Take 'em or leave 'em.'

I took them. The yard was extremely muddy, especially in bad weather, so I wore them to protect my 'indoor' nurses' shoes. A day or so later, I was crossing the yard with one of the men, and the blasted wellies were so big that I was barely able to walk. I shuffled along, trying to keep up with him.

'Is tha having problems walking, Sister?' my companion asked, a little bemused.

'It's these wellies,' I complained. 'They're far too big for me.' I twisted one to show him, although my movement was restricted.

The miner looked down at my ankles and started to howl with laughter. He laughed for so long that I looked around to see what was so funny. But there wasn't anyone else in the yard, only us. The more he laughed, the more annoyed I became.

'What's so funny?' I demanded.

Only he wasn't listening; instead, he'd dipped his head behind me and dissolved into fits of laughter.

'Come on then, share the joke!' I huffed, with both hands on my hips.

'It's t'boots,' he began, wiping tears of mirth from his eyes. 'No wonder tha can't walk in 'em. They're tied together at t'back with a piece o' string. Gie 'em here.'

He bent down and grabbed the length of string between his fingers. I twisted awkwardly so that I could see the tops of my boots.

'But … but I thought that's what you hung them up with. That's why I didn't cut it.'

He wasn't listening; he was doubled up, clutching his sides.

'Aw, stop it, Sister. I'm gonna wet mesen!' he howled.

I'd done it again. I'd buggered up, and I'd only just started!

The miners worked at Hatfield around the clock in three shifts. Each man would start his shift by calling in at the time office to collect his 'checks'. Checks were brass discs with the man's unique number and NCB (National Coal Board) stamped on them. The shape of the check varied from pit to pit to help identify which one it was from, but Hatfield Colliery issued eight-sided checks, which were slightly larger than a 50-pence piece. The miner would be given two metal checks. He'd hand one to the banksman (the man in charge of the pit top, who controlled the access of men into the cage) on his descent into the pit, while the second check would be given to the onsetter (equivalent of the banksman at the pit bottom) when he came back out. At the end of his shift, the onsetter would hang them all on the relevant nails in the 'checks room', so that it was possible to identify which men were still underground. If they were, only one check would be hanging on the nail. It was a simple system but it worked.

When the man collected his checks for the day, he'd move to the canteen to await his shift time. It was then that most men enjoyed a cup of tea and a cigarette. Some would buy tobacco or snuff and fill their water bottle up for the day to keep the dry coal dust at bay. The miner would walk to his locker, situated at the 'clean' end of the showers, and undress, removing his clean clothes, which he'd store away in his locker. He'd then move to the 'dirty' end and dress in an overall, pit boots and helmet. The man's next stop would be across the yard, which was usually where he'd enjoy his last cigarette. He'd collect his headlamp and battery pack from the lamp cabin, along with his self-rescuer – a small metal canister containing a portable short-term oxygen source – and walk to the shaft side to go down in the cage. At the end of his shift, the procedure would be reversed, and the miner would take off his dirty overalls and shower, changing into his clean clothes before he went home. The medical centre was situated slap, bang between the two areas, which gave the miners direct access before they went down the pit or as soon as they came out. This was vital because it encouraged the men to seek medical attention as soon as possible.

A few weeks later, I was told that a Safety Department officer was available to take me down the pit so I could carry out an inspection of the first-aid and stretcher boxes. But first I had to find the right gear to wear. Without it, I knew that I wouldn't be allowed to set foot underground. I scoured the area for a suitable boiler suit.

'Reckon we need to measure tha up for one of those orange overalls, Sister,' one of the men suggested. But I thought it'd take too long.

'No, I'm not bothered,' I told him. 'I'll sort something out.' Although I didn't have a clue what I'd get or where I'd find it.

In the end, my prayers were answered by the manager's secretary.

'Sister Hart,' she called to me across the yard one morning.

I walked over to her.

'I think I might have just the thing you're looking for,' she said, beckoning me inside. She pointed towards a metal cupboard. 'There's a blue overall in there. It doesn't look very big, although you still might have to alter it.'

I pulled the pale blue cloth out of the cupboard, unravelled it and held it up against myself. It completely drowned me length-wise.

'Well,' I said, turning the hems up by almost half a foot, 'it's nothing a good needle and thread won't sort out.'

The secretary laughed. She knew I was determined, if nothing else. Later that evening, Peter found me on my hands and knees in the bottom of the wardrobe.

'Joan, what are you looking for?' he asked as I emptied the wardrobe of one shoe after another.

'My walking boots,' I replied in a muffled voice. I emerged triumphant, clutching them both in my hands.

'Here they are. Look, they're perfect!'

'For walking?'

'No, for going down the pit.'

Peter went back to watching TV while I busied myself cutting and sewing up the legs of my boiler suit by hand. I pulled it on to check the trouser length, which was spot on.

'Well, what do you think?' I asked, giving him a twirl in the front room.

'You look like one of the men,' he said, laughing.

It was exactly the look I'd been aiming for.

I collected an old brown hard hat, a headlamp and battery pack from the lamp office and my metal checks, and with Pat Swords, a member of the Safety Department, as my guide, I finally ventured underground at Hatfield, as I'd done many years before at Brodsworth Colliery. I inspected the first-aid and stretcher boxes to make sure they had everything they needed and that they were in good condition and easily accessible.

The pit bottom reminded me of an Underground railway station with its whitewashed walls. It was well lit but incredibly dirty. Despite my love of yellow walls, I thought it odd that they'd chosen to whitewash the walls in such a filthy environment, but I soon realised that the walls had been painted stark white to reflect the fluorescent lighting. It made sense, but it also made the rest of the pit seem darker by comparison. Once the electric strip lighting ran out, the pit was black. Without the dim glow of my headlamp, it was impossible to see my own hand in front of my face. In some areas it was so quiet and still that you could have heard a pin drop. It was also very warm, much warmer than I'd anticipated. I understood why some of the men rolled down their overalls and worked in their bare skin. The blackness allowed me to conjure up images from stories my father had once told me of pit men holding onto the tails of pit ponies when their lamps had gone out, in a bid to find their way back.

I was a little apprehensive about what the miners would say or think of me, but Peter had set me straight the night before my visit.

'You don't have to prove yourself, Joan. You're a trained nurse, but these men have been at the pit all their lives. They see it as their domain, not yours. You can't change that. Just be there for them – it's all you can do.'

Naturally, some of the men were a little curious, but after Peter's words I'd gone down well prepared.

'I've brought some boiled sweets, if anyone wants one?' I called out to a group of miners.

'Aw, ta, Sister.' The men smiled, digging their filthy hands into the white paper bag. I made a mental note to bring down individually wrapped sweets next time.

'What's tha doing down 'ere then, Sister?' one asked in the darkness. As I turned, his face was immediately bathed in a circle of golden light, which only highlighted how filthy it actually was. His teeth were the only things that looked clean as he grinned back at me.

'I'm inspecting the first-aid boxes, checking that they've got everything they need.'

'Right,' he nodded. 'And has tha only brought sweets?' he asked cheekily.

'Oh, no,' I said, fumbling around in my pocket, 'I've brought a bit of chewing tobacco too, and a bit of snuff.'

'Ooh, gie us some, Sister. I'm parched!'

After that, the miners looked forward to my underground inspections because, like little boys, they always knew I had a pocketful of treats stashed away.

'Thanks for taking me down today,' I said to Pat as we stepped back into the cage and began our ascent to the pit top.

'No worries, Sister. But there is one thing,' he said, looking downwards.

'What's that?'

'It's them boots. They'll have to go. They're not regulation, you see, and I'll get shot if I'm caught bringing you down wearing 'em again cos they haven't got steel toe-caps.'

'Right, I see.'

'It's not me,' Pat insisted, shifting uneasily from one foot to the other. 'Them's the rules – that's all.'

I knew Pat, and if he said I had to wear steel-toe-capped boots then so be it. But where on earth would I find a pair small enough to fit me? We'd just had a new intake of cadets, so I knew all the smaller sizes would have already been taken. My answer came only a few days later. As soon as I spotted him walking across the yard I knew he'd be perfect, so I waited until I saw him cross again.

'Can I have a word?' I called, beckoning the young lad over towards me and into the medical centre.

'Is everything all right, Sister?' he asked.

I knew Tony well. He was one of the fresh-faced cadets, only 16 years old. He was also very small for his age, which suited me perfectly.

'I've been meaning to ask you for ages, Tony. Are your legs okay?'

Tony looked a little baffled. He looked down towards his legs and back up at me.

'Yeah, I think so. Why?' he replied, a little puzzled.

'Well, it's just I've been watching you, you know, walking across the yard,' I said, gesturing out of the window, 'and it's just that, well, you seem to be walking with a bit of a limp.'

Tony's eyes widened. 'A limp?'

'Yes.'

Tony shook his head in bewilderment. 'Well, I feel okay, and my legs,' he said, patting them for reassurance, 'well, I reckon they're okay too …'

'If it's not your legs then maybe it's your feet?' I said, casting my eyes downwards. 'Or, more importantly, maybe it's your boots. Perhaps they're too tight for you?'

Tony lifted up his right leg to check the shoe size stamped on the underneath of his sole.

'What size are you, Tony?'

'Size 5, Sister.'

'And what size are you wearing?'

'These, they're a 5,' he said, checking again.

'Ah, you see, that's your problem. These pit boots, well, they come up a bit small, so what you need to do is to go along and get yourself a pair of size 6.'

Tony looked up from his boots at me again.

'But I'm a 5.'

'Yes, I know, but you're limping so you need a size 6. You don't want to damage your feet now, do you?'

'No, Sister,' Tony agreed. 'I've always been a 5, but if you reckon I'd be better off wi' a 6 then …'

'Yes, I do,' I said, cutting him short. 'Now, why don't you go and get yourself sorted with a size 6, and tell them I sent you. I bet you'll find you can walk so much better in them. Also, it'll get rid of your limp.'

I sat back in my chair and smiled reassuringly at him.

'Rightio, Sister,' he said, getting up and heading over towards the door.

'And Tony,' I called. He stopped in his tracks and turned to face me. 'When you get yourself sorted, be a good lad and bring your old boots back in here.'

Tony nodded as if obeying a schoolmistress. He opened the door and closed it quietly behind him. I watched through the window as he stood outside the medical centre and self-consciously checked the sole of each boot once again. After a few moments, he straightened up and headed over the yard to source a larger pair. Sure enough, the following day his boots reappeared. He'd popped them just inside the main door where they were waiting for me. From that moment on I made them my own. Dressed in my snazzy new regulation steel-toe-capped boots, I'd been allowed back underground without concern or complaint, with Pat Sword as my trusty guide.

'Nice boots,' he commented as we descended down the pit shaft.

'Thanks,' I grinned.

As usual, as soon as we stepped away from the fluorescent lighting the pit was pitch black and we only had the dim beam from our headlamps to guide us. We spotted the overman talking to a few men, and we approached him.

'By, tha's a bonny-looking lad,' the short-sighted overman remarked as soon as he saw me.

I waited for the punchline, only there wasn't one.

'No,' Pat explained, realising the old man's obvious gaffe. 'This is Sister Hart.'

Unfortunately, as well as bad eyes, the overman was a little hard of hearing.

'Well, Mr 'Art, tha smells lovely too.'

All the miners fell about laughing, so I was grateful of the surrounding darkness to prevent them seeing my scarlet face. Afterwards, I asked one of the men if I could change my brown helmet to a white hard hat.

'And could you paint the words SISTER HART across the front of it too, in big letters?' I added.

'Is capitals okay, Sister?'

'Perfect,' I replied. If I needed to advertise who I was, then so be it.

'There,' he said, handing the freshly painted helmet back to me. 'There'll be no mistaking tha for a lad now.'

The sister before me had been at Hatfield for many years but, unlike me, she'd never been on regular inspections underground. However, all the men trusted her, mainly because she'd known them since they were boys. One day, one of the lads asked a strange question.

'Are you going to be smacking our bottoms in the shower then, Sister?' he added with a knowing wink.

I didn't have a clue what he was talking about. He cleared his throat and decided to elaborate.

'She was a right 'un, that last sister 'ere.'

'Was she?' I replied. I was desperate to know, but I didn't want to ask and look like a gossip.

'Yeah,' he continued, a grin breaking out across his face. 'You know t'shortcut from 'ere through t'canteen?'

I shook my head.

'What shortcut?'

'Through t'shower block, there's a shortcut. Anyroad, she used to walk through there, smacking all t'men's bums as she went!' With that he began to chortle.

I was shocked, but I tried my best to keep a straight face.

'So, Sister,' he asked, 'are you gonna be taking t'shortcut through t'showers too?'

I stood up and fixed him with a stern glare.

'Not on your Nelly, young man!'

Even though he'd insisted he'd been telling the truth, it wasn't long before I realised that the pit was full of practical jokers.

11

Practical Jokers and Perfume

We had two pit shafts at Hatfield Colliery. Coal was wound up the main No. 1 shaft from the Barnsley seam in two 10-tonne capacity skips. Each skip carried a man-riding deck, which was capable of transporting up to 18 men. The fresh air intake into the pit was also down No. 1 shaft. Once the air had circulated around the pit it was extracted through pipes out of No. 2 shaft, which meant No. 1 shaft was dirty and always very cold.

Our Chief Medical Officer, Dr Macdonald, had decided that nursing officers should be involved in all aspects of the pit surface, and underground too. He suggested that any sister interested should ask permission from their pit manager to allow them to examine the pit shaft from the top of the cage, or 'chair', as it was also called. Our cages were double-decker, and carried 20 men in the top and up to 25 in the lower cage. Of course, the doctor's suggestion had been music to my ears, and I was first in the queue. I chose shaft No. 2, which took the men and equipment down into the pit, so I made an appointment and went to speak to the new pit manager, Ken Deeming. He'd replaced Mr Bumstead, who had retired through ill health. Mr Deeming was lovely and also a bit of a joker on the quiet.

'I wish to examine a shaft,' I told him.

A huge grin broke out across his face as I realised I hadn't worded my request well at all.

'Whose shaft?' he teased.

I blushed. 'Not yours! The pit shaft. Shaft No. 2, preferably.'

I'd always found management to be very helpful and support-ive, but also total wind-up merchants, and they were always trying to shock or embarrass me.

'Okay,' he nodded, 'but you need to get permission from the surveyors who will tell you what time you can go down. You'll also need to go to the blacksmith's shop to be fitted with a safety harness.'

'Thanks.'

Only, the surveyors weren't quite so enthusiastic about my request. It was their job to survey the pit shaft and I could tell that they didn't want me, a 'silly little woman', delaying their examination. Despite their reticence, I won them over and was duly dispatched to the blacksmith's shop to be fitted with my very own harness. The harness was a leather contraption, which threaded between the legs and across the chest. It had lots of heavy safety chains to keep you in place in the event of an accident. There was only one problem. The chains were usually used to stretch across the frame of a strapping 6-foot-tall miner, not a petite weakling like me, so adjustments had to be made. This caused quite a commotion in the blacksmith's shop; the men went into a huddle to discuss what needed to be done.

'I'll do it,' one said, his hand shooting straight into the air.

'No, I will. Tha always gets to have all the fun,' another argued.

I stifled a giggle as they discussed who was going to measure me up and how.

'No, it's my turn to do t'kitting up. Besides, I'm much better looking than thee, aren't I, Sister?' a lad called Billy cried, giving me a cheeky wink.

'Yes, Billy,' I sighed. 'Listen, I don't care who does it, just get it done otherwise I'll never get to do the inspection.'

The men laughed and Billy was indeed granted the unusual job of 'kitting me up'.

But the chains were much heavier than I'd thought. I could hear the men's laughter echoing in my ears as I dragged them across the pit yard like Jacob Marley in *A Christmas Carol*. The chains were for my own safety. They were needed to secure me to the top of the cage so I didn't fall off. If you fell from the top of the cage, it was a long way down – over 600 metres – to a certain death.

'Blimey, they're heavy, aren't they?' I remarked to the two surveyors dressed in a similar manner. They were my guides, along with the shaftsman.

'Aye, but you get used to 'em after a while, Sister.'

As soon as we reached the pit top, one of the surveyors turned to speak.

'Now we're going to lower the cage, then I want you to hop on top of it. That's when I'll fasten yer chains t'winding gear. They might be heavy, but they'll keep tha safe if tha should slip.'

I gulped and climbed up, holding on for dear life.

'Tha can walk about a bit, you know,' he explained.

'Er, thanks,' I replied, my voice high-pitched, although I had no ambition to do so. He climbed in next to me, budging me up alongside the others. There was plenty of room, but it was pitch black apart from the glow coming from our headlamps. Thankfully, the cage travelled very slowly, descending inch by inch. I tried not to show it, but I was frightened to death.

'Isn't it neat? And clean. I'd never expected it to be so clean,' I remarked, trying to hide my nerves.

'S'ppose. I've never really thought about it,' one of the surveyors grunted. 'Now then, if tha walks over t'edge, Sister, tha can see ascending cage coming up.'

I wasn't keen because it felt as though I was dangling over a cliff edge. At the same time, I didn't want to make a fuss or show fear because I wanted to be allowed to go down the pit again. I dipped my head a smidge over, until I could see the top of the other chair approaching. We couldn't see inside the other cage because it crossed at such speed; in contrast, we travelled down the shaft slowly, at 5 feet per second, instead of the cage's usual 35. We did this until both surveyors were happy with all the relevant piping and wires.

During an inspection, the only way to communicate with the banksman on the surface and be moved up or down slowly is to send signals. This was done by banging a 2-pound hammer against a metal slab. It was one tap to stop, two to lower, three to be brought to the surface and four to move upwards steadily. The piece of metal looked exactly like a flat shovel, but when the surveyor hit it, it made enough noise for the banksman to hear. The roof of the cage felt weird – akin to standing on top of a lift in an office or high-street department store. I'd expected it to be messy, but I was amazed at just how intricate and neatly fitted the electrical wires, pipes and tubing were. When they'd checked it all, the surveyor banged the metal three times and we were lifted again, only this time to the surface. I felt relieved when I finally planted both feet back on solid ground.

'Thanks for taking me,' I said, adjusting the chains around me.

'Nay problem, lass.' The shaftsman grinned. 'If truth be told, I thought tha were quite brave doing it.'

'Really?'

'Yeah. Not many men would've done what tha just did.'

My chest swelled with pride, but only after I'd got the blasted chains off.

'So, you gonna be doing it again, Sister?' Billy in the black-smith's shop asked as I handed my safety gear in.

'Er, I think I'll give it a while.'

Billy laughed and nodded knowingly. I soon realised why.

'Tha did what?' Dad exclaimed as soon as he heard.

'I rode on top of the chair. Why?'

'Because even I haven't done that and I've worked down t'pit all me life. Tha needs to be careful, Joan. Tha could've been killed,' he said, scolding me as though I was still a child.

Later that night, my father visited the working men's club and boasted how his daughter had ridden on top of the chair. He told the same story for weeks, but he made a point never to tell me how proud he was just in case I decided to do it again!

A fortnight later, I'd just sat down to do some paperwork when the treatment-room bell rang. Unusually, I was alone because Bill had just left to talk to some men across the yard. I put down my pen, opened the door to the waiting room and that's when I spotted him – a very large man who seemed to be clutching his eye.

'How can I help?' I asked, leading him into the treatment room and sitting him down in the examination chair.

'It's me eye,' he began. 'I've got summat in it and it's giving me a bit of jip.'

'Not to worry,' I said, grabbing the treatment book so I could record his name.

'And what is it you do at the colliery?'

'I'm a crane driver, but I work 'ere on contract, like,' he said with a nod.

I wrote it down and told him to lean back against the chair's headrest. As soon as he tilted his head backwards I spotted a large foreign body right next to his lower lid. He was obviously in a lot of pain. Although he was a burly bloke, every time my hand went near him he flinched, so I decided to administer a little local anaesthetic.

'I'll just wait a few moments for that to work and then I'll have another look,' I explained.

The man relaxed and began to chat about the weather.

'Looks like rain again,' he remarked, nodding towards the window.

'Yes, it's been freezing lately, though, hasn't it?'

I didn't hang about when it came to eye treatments because you only have two eyes, and if I messed up my patient would be left with just the one.

'There,' I said, checking the clock on the treatment-room wall. 'That should have numbed it a bit. Let me see if I can get it out.'

This time I did, with ease.

'Better?' I asked as he began to blink his eye.

'Ooh, loads better. It felt like a bloody great big brick in there!'

'Good. Now, I'll just rinse the eye out and test for any abrasion.'

I poured some solution into an eye bath and tipped his head back. The solution was a weak pale yellow, but if there were ulcers or a scratched cornea I knew it'd stain deep orange. Thankfully, it remained clear, indicating there was no further damage. Satisfied he was okay, I went to fetch a clean eye pad to dress it with.

'Right, you'll have to wear this eye pad for a little while because you won't be able to feel anything if another bit of dirt goes in your eye. It'll still be numb, you see.'

But the man was horrified and backed away from the eye pad, shaking his head.

'Oh, I can't do that, Sister. You can't cover me eye!'

'Why ever not?' I asked, a little puzzled.

'Because t'other one,' he said, pointing at his remaining eye, 'is made of glass, and I won't be able to see owt at all!'

I looked at him in astonishment and then back at my patient notes.

'But I thought you said you were a crane driver?'

'Aye, I am, but if tha covers up me good 'un I won't be able to see a chuffing thing!'

I wasn't listening because I was still in shock that he was driving a crane with just one eye. I was unsure what to do because he wasn't employed by the National Coal Board. After much deliberation, I decided to telephone the Safety Department to ask if I could loan a pair of safety goggles, which would enclose the damaged eye and enable him to finish his shift safely without further incident. It had been a lesson learned. Afterwards, I decided I'd always ask the patient if both eyes were fully functional before commencing treatment.

If I thought it was going to be my only bizarre experience, I was wrong. A few weeks later, another one followed. Once again, Bill had left the medical centre, to go to the main office to collect the post.

'Won't be long,' he called as he closed the door behind him.

'Okay.'

He'd only been gone a matter of minutes when I heard someone come in and ring the bell. I opened the door to an ordinary-looking man, in his mid forties, who was rake thin and medium height. I showed him into the treatment room and told him to take a seat, before asking what the problem was.

He shifted about in his seat a bit and looked me directly in the eye.

'Is tha a proper nurse?' he asked, a little suspiciously.

I tried not to laugh or feel offended because I knew some of the men were still getting used to having me on site instead of Sister Brown.

'Yes,' I nodded. 'Now, what seems to be the problem?'

'So you've worked in hospital, like? On the men's wards and everything?'

I began to wonder where this was leading.

'Yes.'

He looked at me oddly, and suddenly I began to feel uneasy in his presence. Although very little actually frightened me, his particular line of questioning had started to put me on edge.

'So have tha seen a man wi' no clothes on?' he leered. A sickly smirk spread across his face, revealing tiny crooked teeth, which made him look a bit like a rodent.

I looked over towards the door and prayed that Bill would return soon. I didn't want the man to sense my fear, so I cleared my throat and adopted a no-nonsense tone.

'Of course I've seen a man with no clothes on; I'm a nurse and a married woman.'

'Well,' he said, standing up and unzipping his trousers in front of me. 'What do you reckon to that, then?' He gestured downwards, grabbed his manhood and waggled it around. He grinned as he waited for my reaction. I decided not to show fear, knowing it would only fuel his perversion more.

'Oh,' I replied, a little disappointed. 'It's rather small, isn't it?' My voice was both flat and deadpan, as the man shrank in more ways than one. 'It looks as though it's rubbing on your trousers. I tell you what, I'll get you a plaster.'

I got up and walked through to the other room to fetch the

smallest plaster I could find. By the time I returned, the man had scarpered, no doubt a little red-faced.

Moments later, Bill returned. He looked behind him as he walked into the office.

'What did he want?' he asked, gesturing back at the missing patient he'd passed en route.

'Nothing. Just a plaster,' I muttered.

'Good,' he said, placing the letters down on the desk.

'Why?'

'Because he's a right funny bugger, him.'

I was touched by Bill's concern, but I never told him what had happened because I knew I'd dealt with it and I'd never see the miner or his manhood again. Although it was clear he'd targeted me because I was a woman, I refused to give up my feminine ways. While my hair was kept short for practical reasons, I always wore my smart nurses' uniform when I was on duty – unless I was called to an inspection, a visit or to deal with an emergency down the pit.

It was hard working in an all-male environment, especially being the only female nurse for miles. However, I decided that the men would accept and respect me just as much if I kept up a 'female approach', namely wearing perfume. I loved perfume and my favourite scent was Helena Rubinstein's 'Apple Blossom', which carried a light and pleasant fragrance. Soon it became my trademark. The men always knew when Sister Hart was around, often just by scent alone.

Early one morning, I was asked to visit 72 district. Every area in the pit had a different number, and 72 district, in particular, was a long way out – around 4 miles away – which meant a paddy train ride and lots of walking. As usual, earlier that morning I'd sprayed a little of my favourite scent onto my neck and wrist. It was a particularly dark and cold winter's morning, so I thought a spot of perfume would be just the thing to lift my spirits. I changed into my regulation boiler suit, acquired pit boots and customised helmet, and joined the men at the shaft side to wait for the cage. As it surfaced, we turned off our headlamps and stepped inside, ready to go down.

'Right, lads, no farting this morning because t'Sister's on board,' a voice called out in the darkness.

'How do you know?' a miner replied.

'Because I smelt her.'

'Oh, why? Has she farted already?'

'No, stupid! She's got that bluddy perfume on!'

A roar of laughter erupted and we all fell about. I couldn't see the face of my colleagues clearly, but I could certainly hear them. Even though it was dark, wet and miserable, the men never lost their sense of humour. It made working alongside them an absolute joy.

Afterwards, word got around and the perfume became my calling card. Whenever Apple Blossom lingered in the air, the bad language would cease because Sister Hart was in the area.

12

Birthday down the Pit

It was my birthday and Peter was taking me out for a lovely Italian meal. Smoothing down my hair, I pulled on my stockings and looked around for my silky trousers. I'd had a long soak after a particularly hard shift at work and was really looking forward to our night out. I wrinkled my stockings up between my fingers and slid them from my toes up over my legs, making sure not to snag them with my nails, and carefully clipping them onto my suspender belt.

Peter was pottering in the other room, waiting for me as usual.

'Won't be long,' I called to him through the open bedroom door.

'Okay,' he replied as I grabbed my blouse, and then I heard the phone go.

'I'll get it,' he called as he picked it up in the hallway.

I was rooting through my underwear drawer for a pair of knickers when I heard Peter's voice. It sounded panicked and urgent.

'When? How many? Of course, we'll be there in 10 minutes,' he said, putting the receiver down.

Moments later, he was standing in the doorway.

'Joan, there's an emergency at the pit. Don't get dressed up, love. They want you at Hatfield. There are three men buried.'

I gasped, threw my silky trousers and blouse on the bed, and grabbed a pair of jeans and a T-shirt. There was no need for posh clothes now.

This was my worst nightmare. *What could I do when there were men buried?*

Peter's car dashed along the rain-soaked road as I looked out of the window at the blackened night, wondering what would face me when I arrived at the scene. Living only a few miles away from the colliery had its benefits: I could be on the scene within minutes if there was an emergency, and this certainly was that.

Ken Deeming, the pit manager, spotted the headlights of Peter's car and came over towards us. His face was flushed and worried.

'How many?' I asked as soon as I jumped out of the passenger seat. 'How many men are trapped underground?'

'There were three, but the rescue team has managed to get two out. But there's still one lad trapped, deep underground.'

I began to run towards the offices to get changed, but Mr Deeming called after me.

'Sister Hart, we think he's in a bad way.'

My stomach twisted with fear. That poor man, trapped underground with heaven knows what injuries. Bill greeted me as soon as I entered the room. Bill and Peter had become good friends. They'd often sit and chat as Peter waited for me to finish work and take me home in the car. Bill knew I was worried and tried his best to make me feel better.

'Dr Macdonald's on his way,' he explained, 'but he said you're to go ahead with oxygen, Entonox, intravenous-giving set … and the surgical kit.'

Bill didn't have to say any more because I knew exactly what he meant. I'd need the surgical kit in case an urgent amputation was required.

At that moment, Mr Deeming ran in after me.

'Get in your underground gear,' he ordered.

I wasn't offended by his gruff tone and I didn't take it person-ally. This was an emergency; there was no time for niceties or small talk. As Bill collected the essential equipment together I went into my office to get changed into my blue boiler suit, helmet and pit boots. But as I pulled off my jeans and looked down I got quite a shock. I was wearing my stockings from our abandoned night out but, in my rush, I'd forgotten to put on a pair of knickers! My heart sank to my knees as I looked at my stockings with dismay – they were made of nylon and were extremely flammable so I couldn't wear them underground! With no time to spare, I pulled on my overalls and prayed that there weren't any splits in the seams. The boiler suit was baggy, with big open legs, so I tucked the hems deep into the top of my boots. Even though I'd drastically altered it with needle and thread, the NCB issued them to fit big, burly miners, not a petite woman like me!

With no time to lose, Mr Deeming and his deputy picked up the heaviest equipment while I grabbed the saline and intrave-nous drip. I kissed Pete goodbye as we headed towards the pit shaft.

'You go home and I'll ring you when I get out,' I insisted.

'No way,' he replied, shaking his head. 'I'll wait in your office and help the other lads.'

Deep down, I'd have preferred it if Peter had gone back home because I knew it was going to be a long night. But he respected all the men at the pit and he liked Bill in particular, so I knew he'd be okay.

Together with the manager and deputy, I marched across the yard to the lamp cabin to collect our lamps, batteries and checks, which we'd need underground. We arrived at the shaft side where the banksman was waiting by his wooden hut to send us into the pit. He secured the gates and pulled a lever, sending the cage down. Normally, we'd have had a laugh and a bit of banter, but tonight was different. With a man trapped underground the atmosphere was sombre – everyone was subdued and quiet. The onsetter at the pit bottom had the paddy train ready to take us inbye to the district.

'Were you off out tonight, then?' Mr Deeming asked as we travelled along in the darkness. The lights from our helmets lit the way dimly as we ventured deeper and deeper into the mine.

'Yes,' I replied. 'It's my birthday. Peter and I were planning to go out for a meal, but we never made it.'

'Oh,' he said, his face changing.

Without warning, his hand shot down into his pocket. I watched as his fingers fumbled awkwardly for something until finally they located whatever it was he was looking for. After a few moments he triumphantly pulled it out into the light.

'Want one of these, then?' he smiled, holding up a packet of Polo mints.

I chuckled as I took one. He turned to his deputy and offered him a Polo too before they both turned back to face me.

'Happy birthday, Sister Hart!' they chorused as we trundled along in the paddy train towards the trapped miner.

I felt apprehensive as we neared the scene, but suddenly I spotted three shadowy figures sitting at the entrance to the collapse. It was the two men who had escaped, along with the first aider. I quickly examined them and was relieved when I found no bleeding or obvious fractures. The first-aid man filled me in on what had been happening.

'We got 'em out quickly, Sister. They're both fine, just a little shocked.'

I told him to escort the men to the bottom of the pit and to get the ambulance driver to take them to Doncaster Royal Infirmary.

'But make sure the ambulance returns for the other man,' I called after him.

'Rightio, Sister,' he shouted as the men disappeared off into the darkness.

I got to work. The man had been buried for well over an hour under heavy rubble in stifling heat underground. It was dark and difficult to see, but his colleagues had erected a temporary shield to protect him from more rock falls. As I neared him in the darkness I fumbled around in the limited space I had. Thankfully, I realised that they'd managed to free his head and face, and pull an air pipe to allow him to breathe and keep cool. Surprisingly, he was not only conscious, but quite cheerful too.

'Ay up, Sister,' he gasped as soon as he saw me, a half smile playing on his lips.

'You owe me a meal for this, Charlie,' I joked as I stretched down, trying to reach him.

Charlie looked up, a little confused. I could tell he was totally exhausted but relieved to see a friendly face.

'Meal, Sister? Why?' he asked.

'Because I was just going out.'

'It's her birthday,' Mr Deeming called from behind me.

Charlie grinned and, without warning, the men burst into song with a rendition of 'Happy Birthday'. I stifled a laugh because I had work to do, but the camaraderie and goodwill among the mining fraternity never ceased to amaze me, especially at a time like this.

'Okay,' said Mr Deeming, bringing the song to a halt. 'Let's get on with it. You can kiss her when she's freed you! Now, Sister, we have to assess his condition.' Mr Deeming sucked thoughtfully on his Polo mint and, before long, a decision was made.

'Right,' he said, pointing at me. 'You're the smallest, so the two deputies will hold your ankles and lower you down. You must try to examine his damage and position.'

I nodded in agreement. I was the smallest so it made perfect sense. But as I prepared to be dangled I remembered one thing and one thing only – I wasn't wearing any knickers! However, there was no time for modesty, and just moments later, there I was, hanging by my ankles as two burly miners lowered me upside down into the confined space.

Please don't let there be any splits in the seams of this overall! I prayed silently.

'Right, Charlie,' I said, getting closer towards the trapped miner. 'What position were you in when the fall occurred? Were you sitting, standing or kneeling?'

'I was sitting, Sister,' he said, gasping for air.

'Right, then. I need to feel your legs.'

I heard the men laugh from up above.

'Lucky sod!' one called down. 'You watch her, Charlie; just shout if yer need any help!'

I ignored him and felt around through the rubble to see what I could find. It was hard trying to treat a patient in the dark, miles below the earth's surface, upside down and wearing no knickers, but finally my hand brushed against something – his legs.

'Right, I've found his knees,' I called back up. 'Could someone pass me a Stanley knife?'

There was a hush from up above until a lone voice broke the silence.

'Oh, Christ! She's going to cut his bloody legs off!'

I tried not to laugh because, if I did, I knew they might drop me, and then I'd be trapped alongside poor Charlie.

'No' I said, shaking my head, 'not his legs, just his knee pads – they're too tight!'

I glanced upwards just in time to see one of the men put a hand on his chest to calm his pounding heart.

'Well, thank God for that,' he sighed as his mate passed me the knife.

After a bit of a struggle I somehow managed to cut the straps around Charlie's knees. I called for them to lift me back up and pull me out of the hole. The blood had rushed to my brain and I was feeling quite light-headed by the time my feet were planted back on the ground. They were all waiting for my assessment.

'He's having a lot of pain in his arm but his legs aren't trapped, so you're going to have to try to yank him out,' I said. 'I think you should remove a bit more rubble and then get him out. Just mind his arm, though, won't you? That needs attention. But we can't leave him much longer; if we do he'll go into shock.'

'How about giving him a shot of morphine for the pain?' one of the deputies suggested.

I shook my head.

'We can't do that because he's under a lot of rubble and I can't rule out head injury. But I'll give him Entonox when you get him out.'

It took another 10 minutes or so before Charlie was finally pulled free from the rubble and laid on a waiting stretcher. By this time the first aider had returned, so he examined him below the waist while I did his chest and arms. Charlie had suffered a complicated fracture of his radius and ulna (two large bones in the forearm) but, thankfully, there were no other obvious fractures.

'His ankles are swollen but, other than that, I can't find owt else,' the first aider reported.

With no head injury to treat, I was able to administer Entonox while we splinted his arm to help ease the pain. It was decided that we'd transport Charlie directly on the belt to get him out of the pit quickly. The conveyor belt was usually used to take coal from the face to the pit bottom, but in Charlie's case it became his very own underground ambulance. I hated riding on the belt because you had to be able to get off quickly when it was moving, which I always found to be quite a challenge. But Charlie's needs were greater than mine, so I hopped on with Mr Deeming and his deputy. We told the four men carrying the stretcher to load Charlie onto the belt and to jump on. We'd travelled quite a way when we suddenly spotted Dr Macdonald and the NUM representative heading towards us. We stopped the belt as Dr Macdonald glanced all around us with a puzzled look on his face.

'Where's the patient, Sister Hart?'

I gestured behind me but Charlie wasn't there, and there was no sign of the stretcher or the four men who'd been carrying it. Fearing the worst, the managers, the doctor, the union rep and I ran back down the pit like the Keystone cops, trying to find Charlie. The stretcher-bearers had decided that the belt was far too dangerous to load Charlie onto, so they'd agreed to carry him. There were lumps of coal on the belt and the men were worried that they'd knock against him, so they'd carried Charlie out the rest of the way. Dr Macdonald examined the patient and decided that he needed an intravenous drip. I was terrified because I'd never helped put up an intravenous drip in the pitch black before. The doctor spoke to Charlie and explained that he needed to put a needle in his arm.

'Is that okay?' the doctor asked gently, patting him lightly on his good arm.

'You can shove it up me arse, Doc, as long as you get me out of t'bloody pit!' he whined.

The other men laughed and so did I. Charlie spotted me and apologised.

'Excuse me language, Sister Hart,' he grinned weakly.

Charlie was exhausted, his body had gone into shock and his veins were collapsing, so it wasn't easy, but somehow Dr Mac got the needle in. Meanwhile, I made a better splint from a cardboard box.

'Just hold the drip bottle up, Sister,' Dr Mac ordered, so I did as I was told.

By this time, the deputies realised that Charlie was in good hands and left us to it. When we finally reached the top of the shaft the pit ambulance was waiting. I was still holding the drip bottle up as we loaded Charlie in, and I remained that way, with my hand high in the air, as we travelled to hospital. By the time we eventually arrived my arm was killing me, although not as much as Charlie's. Thankfully, the staff at A&E had been notified and there were a couple of doctors waiting as the ambulance pulled up outside. They took over immediately and whisked Charlie away. I decided to go and check on the other two men who'd been brought in earlier. They'd been seen, X-rayed and discharged with no major injuries. I asked the ambulance driver to take them back to the pit so they could shower and clean themselves up.

'I'll stay here and wait to see how Charlie is, but could you come back in a bit?' I asked as I slammed the ambulance door.

'Okay, Sister Hart,' the driver called out through the half-opened window. He pulled away and headed back towards the colliery.

It was nearly midnight and I was tired and filthy, sitting inside a sterile hospital dressed in a helmet, overalls and pit boots. I glanced down at my hands; they were blackened, and my fingernails ruined – so much for my glamorous night out.

Suddenly, the casualty officer burst out into the corridor shouting my name.

'I'm looking for a Sister Hart?' he called. 'I need her to speak to the pit manager …' he said, glancing around at everyone but me.

'That's me!' I said, sticking my hand up in the air like a schoolgirl.

He took one look at me and turned up his nose. But as he took me in, from my filthy feet to the top of my head, he spotted the name SISTER HART sprayed on the front of my helmet.

'Yes,' he said, the disdain obvious in his voice. 'So I see.'

I knew I wasn't exactly his idea of how a nurse should look, and I also realised he didn't appreciate my pit boots and overalls messing up his pristine corridor, but Charlie was my main concern and as long as he was all right then I'd done my job.

'The patient is, er, being admitted,' he informed me. He rubbed his fingertips against his white coat as though my coal dust was catching.

'Right, I see. And is he going to be all right?'

'Yes, but he will have to be admitted and taken to theatre to have a plate to repair the fracture.'

'Okay,' I nodded. 'We'd better inform the mines inspector, then.'

The man took one last look down his nose at me, turned on his heels and disappeared off through a set of double doors.

Half an hour later, the pit ambulance returned and I climbed in and headed back to Hatfield Colliery.

'Let's just call in at Charlie's house on the way back so I can let his wife know he's okay,' I said.

The driver nodded and we headed over there to deliver the good news. Thankfully, Mr Deeming had already notified her that her husband had been involved in an accident, but she seemed grateful for the latest update from me.

'My son's just on his way so we're heading t'hospital right now,' she said as soon she answered the door.

Moments later, as she passed, she grabbed one of my filthy hands in hers and gave it a tight squeeze.

'Thank you, Sister Hart. Thanks for coming to see me.'

And then she was gone. I returned to the pit, showered the grime away and reported to Mr Deeming. It had been a birthday to remember, but I was delighted when I saw that Pete was still there, waiting to take me home – the most understanding and patient husband in the world.

'Sorry about the meal,' I said, giving him a hug, my eyes filled with tears of relief.

'Never mind. There's always another day. At least Charlie's all right,' Peter said, hugging me back.

Charlie was taken to theatre. My makeshift cardboard splint was removed and a plate was inserted into his arm to correct the fracture. He was off work for a while, but as soon as he returned he came to the medical centre to see me.

'You gave me quite a scare there, Charlie,' I teased as soon as I saw him.

'Thanks for everything,' he said, and made to leave before stopping. 'Oh, and I forgot to say, like …'

'Yes, Charlie,' I replied, glancing up from my desk.

'Happy Birthday, Sister Hart.' He grinned.

I smiled, but as I did he winked at me and said something quite unexpected.

'I bet those lads got quite an eyeful when they dangled you down by the ankles. Let's hope you had your best underwear on, Sister!'

With that, Charlie left the medical centre, but I could still hear his laughter in the yard outside as he walked away.

My mouth fell open and I felt my face flush a deep shade of scarlet. I still can't be sure, even to this day, if Charlie knew about my knickerless secret or if he was just winding me up, but from that day on I made sure I always had an emergency pair of knickers in the office, just in case.

13

Medical Emergencies and Marriage Guidance

One morning, I decided to carry out another pit inspection. By now, I was inspecting the first-aid boxes at least once a month. I wanted to check that the morphine had been safely locked away. This was kept separate to the first-aid box and was accessed using a key held by the underground first-aid team, with a copy of it held by me. I also needed to make sure that the stretchers and blankets were in good order. These were kept at regular intervals in the pit in case of an emergency. They were held inside 6-foot-long cylinders, which were fixed onto the wall with brackets. The stretcher and accompanying blanket would be folded into it, but they weren't locked and had a lid that could be opened by anyone. At one end there was a smaller box, which also contained bandages and slings, in case of emergency.

As my visits had become more frequent, the Safety Department had decided that they couldn't keep sparing someone to guide me underground, so I was told to use one of my three first-aid men. I was with one of the first aiders that morning as we followed lots of miners about to start their morning shift to the shaft side. It was a dark, cold morning, and it was busy with lads chatting and putting out their last smoke in the yard as they headed towards the cage. By the time we'd reached it, the banksman was in a bad mood. He was usually such a chatty bloke, but that morning he was gruff and seemed a little stressed.

'Right, you lot, line up so I can check you,' he barked.

The men groaned but did as they were told, so I took my place towards the back of the queue, behind a miner but in front of my guide. Slowly, the banksman worked his way along the line, checking each and every man for contraband cigarettes. It was strictly forbidden for the men to smoke underground because of possible leaks of natural gas, so it was important that no one tried to sneak any ciggies down.

'Next,' he called as the man two in front of me stepped forward. He frisked him expertly, checking his pockets before declaring him okay to travel.

'Next,' he called again, without even looking up.

When it came to my turn, I expected him to just wave me through as he'd done many times before, but today he seemed determined and frisked me as thoroughly as the rest of the miners. Without warning, he put a hand around my chest and near the front of my pelvis, checking for hidden pockets.

Whoa, careful, sunshine! I thought as I fixed him with a hard stare, but he didn't even look up as my body stiffened beneath his touch. I'd never been frisked like that before, so I was a little dumbstruck, to say the least. As I glanced around, I noticed the men looked surprised too. Nevertheless, I was checked and sent on my way with the rest of the group. As I travelled down in the cage, I thought how odd it'd been.

Maybe he suspected me too? I wondered.

I put the thought to the back of my mind and busied myself, checking the first-aid boxes and blankets. To my surprise, a few blankets were missing, four in total. I decided to replace them, although, underneath my calm nursing exterior, I was fuming.

'I can't believe it,' I remarked to Stewart, one of the first aiders and my guide for the day. He was equally disgusted by the 'theft'.

'How bad is that?' he said, shaking his head in despair.

I was still muttering away about it as the cage approached ground level and I stepped out into the yard. As I did, the red-faced banksman was waiting to greet me.

'Er, Sister, can I have a word, please?' he asked a little sheep-ishly, beckoning me away from the men.

I followed him over.

'I think I owe you an apology,' he began, looking awkward. He fixed his eyes downwards on the tips of his steel-capped pit boots.

'Why?' I asked, my mind still full of the missing blankets.

'Because I frisked you. I mean, I frisked you, like the men. I'm sorry, Sister, but I was stressed out, and I didn't realise it was you. I thought you were one of t'lads.'

I smiled as I remembered earlier. Of course, he'd mixed me up with the miners. It all made sense now. But the more I thought about it, the more I wasn't sure whether to thank him or slap him! I had my name written across the front of my helmet in bloody big capital letters – wasn't it clear I was a woman?

'It's okay, no harm done,' I said, smiling graciously through gritted teeth.

'It's not that, Sister. It's just I have to watch these buggers. They're sods for trying to sneak stuff down there, so I have to keep me wits about me. There's 10 men after me job and, if I don't watch it, one of the sneaky buggers will set me up to fail,' he said, his face colouring.

'Don't worry, it's forgotten,' I insisted.

As soon as I reached the confines of the medical centre I began to see the funny side and started to laugh. The banksman had been mortified by his actions, but I was beginning to get used to the miners and their funny ways of doing things.

I replaced the missing blankets but, a month later, when I carried out my next routine check, I found they were missing again. It made my blood boil because this wasn't someone being sloppy and not putting them back – we actually had a thief on our hands. The blankets were vital in the case of emergency, especially if we had a stretcher case or if a miner had suffered shock. The blanket thief must have been pretty desperate to steal the very thing that could make the world of difference to themselves or one of their colleagues in the event of an accident. As I wondered what to do, the door of the medical centre opened and Bill walked in.

'You'll never guess what,' I began.

Bill shook his head. 'What?'

'Someone's only gone and stolen the emergency blankets again.'

Bill's mouth fell open. 'Yer joking me?' he gasped. Bill had worked there for years and he thought he'd seen it all, but this was a new low.

'I'm not. And, if I catch who's done it, I'll … I'll …'

To be honest, I wasn't sure what I'd do because I was so angry that a miner could put his colleagues in danger. Instead, I decided to put pen to paper and write the thief a note:

To Whom It May Concern,

I am concerned about the stretcher blankets, which have been going missing. If any man thinks he is more entitled to a blanket than a man who has been seriously injured, then he should call in at the medical centre where I will give him a blanket for free, so he will leave the blankets in their rightful place – the stretcher container.

Sister Hart

I put down my pen and read it back to myself.

'Do you think it's a bit strong?' I asked Bill.

He took the note from my hand and read it.

'No, gie o'er. It says exactly what it needs to say. It's bang on, that,' Bill said, prodding the note with his finger. 'Let's just hope it pricks someone's conscience.'

I took the notice, copied it out two more times, and pinned one up in the lamp cabin, the checks office and finally on the wall at the dirty end of the showers. I needed to ensure that every miner read it. A few days later, Bill had some news.

'I've just been in t'waiting room and guess what I've found.'

I looked up from the paperwork on my desk. 'Go on, surprise me.'

'Four stretcher blankets, all clean and neatly folded. Someone's left 'em in there, just inside t'door.'

'Never!'

Bill nodded. 'It's true! Come on, come and have a look if you don't believe me.'

I got up from my chair and wandered over towards the door. Bill was right.

'So, the note, it worked then?' I said.

'Looks like it, Sister.'

The blankets had been returned to their rightful place. I realised then that all the miners looked out for one another, and when the thief, whoever he was, realised the knock-on effect his actions would have on his colleagues, his conscience got the better of him. I felt satisfied that the note had appealed to his better nature.

A couple of weeks later, I was in the medical centre when one of the pit deputies knocked at the door.

'Hi, what can I do for you?' I asked, showing him through to the treatment room.

'It's me finger, Sister,' he said, holding up the offending digit to show me. 'I've trapped it and got mesen a black nail.'

Black nails were a common injury down the pit as miners were always getting their fingers caught and trapped in the dark.

'No problem,' I told him. 'We'll soon have you sorted.'

Normally, a black fingernail is caused by the build-up of blood behind the nail. They look terrible and are extremely painful. Usually, I'd ease the pressure by heating up a paperclip and popping the nail to release the blood and pressure. But I'd just taken delivery of a new and better tool to do the job – a small, sharp drill.

'I've got just the thing. I've been dying to use it. It's brand new, so you'll be the first to try it,' I said, taking the new equipment out of its sterile packaging, the enthusiasm rising in my voice.

'Erm …' the deputy said, wincing as soon as he saw it. 'Actually, it's not too bad, Sister. It's not that painful. I think I'll just …'

He turned towards the door.

'Nonsense. It'll only take a mo, and we'll soon have you sorted. Now,' I said, grabbing his hand in mine, 'just put your finger on the table and hold still.'

The miner was standing to the side of me as I positioned his index finger flat on top of the work surface.

'Just put your hand on there like that,' I said, holding it still as I started up the drill. It immediately fired into life, making a shrill, whizzing noise, similar to the sound heard in a dentist's surgery.

I was so busy looking at the deputy's finger that when I felt his weight slouch against me, I became annoyed.

'Could you stop leaning on me?'

But the more I drilled, the more he leaned, until soon I could feel his whole body weight against me. The deputy was a big man, standing around 6 feet tall and weighing 13 stone, so his weight was knocking the accuracy of my drilling. In fact, the more I drilled, the more I felt him, until he'd almost knocked me off my feet.

'For goodness' sake, will you stop leaning against me!' I snapped. 'It's hard enough as it is without you …'

As I let go of his hand and turned to face him, he slid straight to the floor, as delicate and as graceful as a ballet dancer. He'd passed out, but only for a matter of minutes.

Bill, who'd been using the toilet next door, heard the commotion and came running in. He saw the deputy lifeless on the floor, and for a moment he looked at me as though I'd killed him!

'He's passed out!' I exclaimed, putting the drill down on the side. 'Here, help me sit him up.' I hooked my arm under the deputy's armpit for leverage.

Once we'd checked him over to make sure it had been nothing more sinister, we propped him against the wall where he finally started to come around.

'What happened?' he asked, dazed and slightly confused.

'You passed out.'

He looked up, blinked and, for a moment, took in his surroundings, trying to register where he was. He rubbed his eyes but flinched as he remembered the pain in his finger. He held out his right hand and looked down anxiously at his fingernail.

'It's all right, I've finished the drilling,' I reassured him. 'I think it was the noise that set you off.'

The deputy shook his head. 'Bluddy 'ell, I feel such a fool.'

'Don't. You're not a fool. If anyone's a fool here, it's me. I thought you were leaning on me!'

His eyes widened as I explained what had happened, and then his face slowly began to colour with humiliation. Despite our protests, the mortified deputy clambered to his feet, but he staggered as his big, heavy frame tried to regain its balance.

'You won't, er, tell anyone, will you?' he begged.

Bill and I looked at one another. 'Course not,' I replied. 'But what I would like you to do is to sit back down so that I can check your blood pressure.'

After a normal reading, I asked him to sit and wait for five minutes longer before leaving the medical centre.

'How's the finger?' I asked as he finally got up to leave.

'It's much better, Sister. Ta very much.'

True to our word, Bill and I never told a soul. The deputy was in charge of 1,000 or so men. Miners are a tough breed, and he knew he couldn't run the risk of them finding out; otherwise, his image would've been shot to pieces.

If I'd thought I'd seen everything then I was wrong. A month or so later, I had a phone call to say the first aiders were bringing a miner out on a stretcher.

'What's wrong with him?' I asked the deputy in charge.

'Well, I don't really know what to say …' he began, sounding a little flustered.

'Listen, I'm a nurse,' I said, shaking my head in frustration. 'There's nothing you can say that will shock me, so you might as well just tell me straight.'

I heard the deputy clear his throat and then he spoke. 'Okay, I'll tell you as it's been told to me. The man has got, er, well, he's got three balls,' he said. There was a pause as he waited for my reaction.

'Three what?' I exclaimed, thinking I'd misheard him.

'Er, um, he's got three balls. That's it. I don't know any more, Sister, so don't ask me. Anyroad, they'll be there with you soon.'

And with that he hung up, leaving me with the dial tone. I turned the telephone receiver in my hand, looking at it as though it had just bitten me, before dropping it back in its cradle.

Three balls? Had he really just said that? Surely I'd misheard him. I'd been a nurse for years. I had lots of experience in different hospital wards but I'd never, in my whole nursing career, seen a man with three testicles before!

Moments later, I heard the sound of footsteps. I stood up and waited for the patient as four stretcher-bearers brought him in.

'Put him over there,' I said, indicating towards the trestle legs. I knew I needed to examine him. I looked at his face, which was contorted with pain while his whole body writhed. I washed my hands – we didn't wear rubber gloves at that time – and as I turned around I noticed that the stretcher-bearers were still standing there.

'Is everything all right?' I asked, half expecting them to furnish me with more medical information.

No one spoke. Instead, they all looked a bit shifty, although it was clear that they had no intention of leaving.

'You can go now,' I instructed. No one moved, so I repeated myself: 'I said you can go.'

One of them glanced across at the others with an awkward look on his face.

'Er, it's just we've never seen a fella with three balls before, Sister, and we really wanted to see it,' he mumbled.

I shook my head in annoyance. 'Well, you're not going to, either. So just go,' I said, raising my voice and pointing towards the exit.

I shooed them out of the medical centre, slamming the door behind them before beginning my examination. It transpired that the miner had recently undergone a vasectomy but had returned to work too soon after the operation, so he was still carrying a lot of excess fluid in his testicles. Not only were they causing him great pain, they were also extremely swollen, giving the appearance of three, not two, 'balls', as the deputy had put it. Other than administer painkillers, I wasn't sure what to do, so I telephoned the village doctor, who also happened to be the miner's GP.

'Hello, it's Sister Hart from Hatfield pit. I wonder if you could look at a patient as an urgent case for me. The ambulance will bring him over to you.'

'Yes, of course, Sister,' the doctor replied. 'Now, what seems to be the problem?'

I scratched my head and looked at the telephone receiver in my hand. *Where should I start?* I remembered the awkwardness of the deputy and decided to take my lead from him.

'Well, it's like this. I'll tell you exactly as it was told to me. I have a patient here who has three testicles …'

Thankfully, the doctor realised that the man's discomfort had been related to his vasectomy and signed him off work for a long time.

Afterwards, I made it my mission to introduce myself to all the doctors in the surrounding area, should I ever need to speak to them about any miners who were their patients. Also, I wanted to let them know that I was able to perform nursing tasks. With the GPs' permission, this included everything from syringing ears and taking out stitches to checking blood pressure, changing dressings and giving out diet advice. It not only eased the burden on the doctors' waiting lists, it also saved the miner taking valuable time off work and allowed him to keep his wage packet full.

There was a main practice in Hatfield village, which had six doctors, and another single practitioner in the village of

Stainforth. However, my first port of call in an emergency was Dr Macdonald, the Chief Medical Officer with the National Coal Board, who was based at Doncaster, although the doctor who usually came was Dr Walters. He was based at Hatfield surgery and knew all the men at the pit.

But there were some things doctors couldn't help with. By now the men were used to seeing me, as my inspections and underground visits had increased to once a fortnight. I'd often venture underground to collect water samples to test its purity to ensure the men weren't exposed to anything that might cause a nasty skin rash. If a miner did develop a reaction working underground, I'd send samples off to be tested to see what we were dealing with so that he could be treated accordingly. Once we were infested by a plague of red mites, which had travelled underground in a pile of timber. The mites became a nuisance when they crawled into the men's socks and bit them on their ankles, leaving them both swollen and sore. In the end, they became such a problem that we had to call in pest control.

Hatfield pit stretched all the way underground to Thorne, a village situated 4 miles away. Thorne was our egress, or escape route, if ever needed. I walked over there a few times, taking a series of tunnels and walkways, some of which ran underneath the canal. It was strange that hundreds of feet above daily life continued, with canal boats and barges sailing tranquilly over our heads. I tried not to think of them or all the water the canal held.

As soon as the men smelled my perfume lingering in the dank air, they'd put on their clothes and mind their language, but by now I was used to them and they to me.

'Oh, fucking 'ell,' a man cursed one afternoon when I was out and about on my usual inspection. He turned and, to his horror, spotted me lurking in the background.

'Sorry, Sister Hart. I didn't see yer there,' he apologised.

I could tell the miner was mortified but there really was no need.

'Listen, you don't have to apologise and, as much as I appreciate it, I'm the visitor here. I'm in your world; you're not in mine, okay?' I said.

The miner and his colleagues looked astonished and nodded their heads respectfully as I passed by and carried on further down into the pit.

Some of the men had suffered heart attacks while working underground. Whenever I was presented with someone suffering from chest pains, I'd err on the side of caution and send them straight to the hospital. However, when a man struggled to breathe underground, if it wasn't a heart attack, it was usually one of two things – an asthma or panic attack. Most panic attacks occurred among the young trainees, who'd followed their fathers and grandfathers down the pit. Often, the panic attacks would lessen with the passage of time as they got used to their working environment, but often, even with all the will in the world, some couldn't overcome their deep-rooted fears. There was one young cadet in particular, called Jim, who had a panic attack every time he went underground. The noise and dirt were bad enough, but the cold, damp earth and general claustrophobia of working in such a confined space were enough to set him off. After it had happened several times, I realised what was wrong. Jim came to me because he was frightened, but he was even more terrified of telling his father.

'You're scared, aren't you?' I said, after I'd carried out a routine examination on him.

'No, I'm not,' Jim replied, a little too defensively. I knew that being scared wasn't in a miner's vocabulary, and Jim realised he had the good family name to uphold.

'It's okay to be scared,' I said gently. 'This kind of work isn't suited to everyone – there's no shame in it.'

As Jim glanced down at his feet, I realised I'd hit the nail on the head.

'I'll tell you what. Why don't I come down with you and see how you get on? That way I'll know for sure if it's what we call a panic attack, or not.'

Jim agreed. To be honest, I think he was just relieved to have someone with him. But as soon as we entered the cage his whole body tensed up and his breathing became shallow and erratic. By the time we reached the bottom he'd managed to calm himself down, but once we got to the spot where he was to work panic rose once more.

'How much longer have I got, Sister?'

I glanced at my watch in the beam of my headlamp.

'Another 20 minutes yet, Jim,' I replied. As soon as he heard, his breathing became erratic and his body tensed. The thought of spending 20 more minutes down there was too much for the poor lad.

'How much longer?' he asked moments later as he began to gasp for air.

'I'll tell you what, Jim. I reckon I should take you back up now, don't you?'

Jim nodded – the relief evident on his face. It was clear that this cadet was quite unsuitable to work underground. He was not only a danger to himself, but to others around him. As soon as we stepped back into the cage, Jim calmed down and his breathing slowed to a normal pace.

'Go and get yourself changed, while I have a word with the manager,' I said.

Jim did as he was told and I went to look for Eddie Smith, the personnel manager.

'The poor lad's having panic attacks underground,' I explained in Eddie's office. 'You need to find him a job on the pit top.'

Eddie listened and agreed to set Jim on as a trainee electrician. When I later told him the good news, Jim was over the moon.

'Thanks, Sister Hart – you're a diamond!'

Jim thrived in his new job and, to my knowledge, he never suffered another panic attack at work again. Despite his initial worries, even his dad took the news well. As long as Jim was okay, that was all that mattered.

After a while, I started to notice a breakthrough. While the pit and its miners were known for their tough stance and no-nonsense male attitude, there were certain things that needed a delicate touch – namely female advice. Despite having so many doctors on call, there were some things no amount of medicine could ever hope to cure, and soon I was holding impromptu meetings underground – a kind of pit marriage-guidance service. One day, I was walking around underground when a miner approached me in the darkness. The small white dot of light on his helmet grew bigger as he got nearer. Soon he was so close that I could see the blackness of coal dust against his skin marking out the whites of his eyes.

'Er, could I have a word, if you've got a minute, Sister?'

I ushered the miner to one side, away from his colleagues.

'It's the wife,' he began, trying to find the right words. 'We've been falling out, see. She's fed up of me working these long hours. We've been having some almighty rows, and she says if I can't sort out me shift patterns, then …' His voice trailed off to a whisper as he checked behind his shoulder to make sure that no one was listening. 'It's just … I reckon she's gonna leave us if I don't get something sorted, and I don't know what to do. I mean, I have to work, otherwise she'd be complaining we didn't have enough money,' he mumbled as he picked at his fingernails.

'I see,' I told him, and I did.

The pressures on the miners were great. Not only was the work physically demanding, it also needed nerves of steel to do it, day in, day out. On top of this, they also had to balance some kind of family life, which often added to the pressure.

'Listen,' I suggested. 'I'm not sure what I can do, but I'll have a word. See if I can get you on a decent shift pattern for the next few months. Leave it with me and I promise I'll try my best.'

I spoke to management and got the miner's shift patterns changed so that he could spend more time at home. Word must have spread because, after that, other miners came to speak with me underground. We would speak underneath the chocks (hydraulic roof supports), where the gob (waste) had been thrown; it was noisy here, so no one was able to hear. This seemed to relax the men. They felt more comfortable in their own environment, as though the cloak of darkness protected them from any awkwardness they might feel outside on the pit top.

In the blackness, they spoke to me about marital problems and other worries. This counselling pattern continued as more miners sought my advice. The more night shifts a man worked, the more he fretted about his wife straying or having an affair. Most of the time, it didn't happen, but on a few occasions I like to think that my interaction helped save a few marriages. I'd ask if the worried miner would be able to work day shifts instead. The miners came to trust me because they knew everything would be treated in the strictest confidence.

One day, an older man called Arthur approached. I could tell that something was on his mind, and I knew he'd already been marked out by management because he'd taken so much time off work. They were baffled because his record had always been exemplary, with not a day off sick. Something in his personal circumstances had changed and I needed to find out what was wrong. In the end, Arthur came to see me because he'd reached breaking point.

'Can I have a word, please?' Arthur asked.

'Of course, come over here,' I said, ushering him to the side, away from the others. 'What's wrong?'

He looked uncomfortable. 'Well, it's kind of private,' he said.

'That's not a problem because everything you tell me is confidential.'

Arthur wrung his hands together for comfort as he spoke. 'I'm in trouble, see, for taking so much time off work. But it's not me, it's the wife. I mean, she's sick. She's got cancer, and, well ...' he said, casting his face downwards, 'the truth is, I'm really struggling to cope wi' it all.'

My heart went out to Arthur. He looked broken. He'd been getting it in the neck from his deputy, when the only reason he'd been missing his shifts was because he was trying to help nurse a sick wife.

'Oh, Arthur,' I said, placing a gentle hand on his arm.

He blinked back his emotions, trying to keep them in check.

'Its breast cancer, Sister Hart. I'm frightened to leave her at home on her own and come to work, but, at the same time, I'm worried about taking more time off work cos I can't afford to lose me job, either.'

I nodded. I understood completely.

'You need some support, Arthur,' I said. 'You need specialist help. Leave it with me and I'll see what I can do.'

Arthur looked up at me, his face and body a bundle of stress and worry.

'Would you really do that, for me?' he asked.

'Of course I would,' I replied. 'Now, give me your wife's name, and your home address, and I'll see what I can do to help.'

With Arthur's blessing, I spoke to the personnel manager and asked that his shifts be arranged to accommodate his wife's hospital appointments. Arthur and his wife, Jane, lived 6 miles away from Hatfield, so I rang his doctor's surgery and spoke with the practice nurse. I organised for a nurse to go in on a regular basis to visit Jane while she underwent both chemo- and radio-therapy. I left a note pinned to Arthur's pit lamp, asking him to call in at the medical centre to see me so that I could tell him what I'd arranged.

'Really?' Arthur gasped. 'You've done all that?'

'Yes,' I said. 'The surgery will be in touch to arrange suitable times when they can come in and check on Jane, which should take some of the pressure off. You see, I can do something about this. I hate seeing you struggle on your own, and it's daft because you don't have to. That's what I'm here for. Now, if there's anything else, all you have to do is come and see me. My door is always open.'

'Thank you, Sister Hart,' Arthur replied. I noticed that he had tears in his eyes but he blinked them away because crying wasn't something a miner did, not even in front of a nurse.

Jane was only in her forties, and the couple had a young daughter. The chemotherapy had robbed her of her hair, but Jane retained her fighting spirit. Even though she wasn't on my official list, I often travelled over to their house to check on her.

'I don't know what I'd have done wi'out you, Sister Hart. You're an angel, d'you know that?' she said, clutching my hand in hers as we sat sharing a cup of tea at the kitchen table.

By now, Jane wasn't so much a patient as she was a friend, and just because she didn't work at the pit, it didn't make a jot of difference. The nurse in me had just answered their call for help and I like to think that I made their lives just that little bit easier. So, two years later, when Jane sadly passed away, I felt the pain because I'd lost a good friend. I attended her funeral with Eddie, the personnel manager. I didn't see Arthur very much after that, as he tried to rebuild his life and bring up his child single-handedly, but I was told he left the pit and moved with his daughter back to his native North East.

Shortly after Arthur left, another miner who'd also lost his wife to cancer and had a young daughter arrived at the medical centre. His name was Fred and he had a favour to ask.

'What is it, Fred?' I said, looking up from my desk. He looked so upset and worried that I wondered for a moment what was wrong.

'It's our Sally,' he said, referring to his only daughter.

'What's the matter? Is she unwell?' I stopped what I was doing and rested my pen down on the desk.

Fred fiddled with the cap in his hands. He circled it round and round between his fingers as he struggled to find the right words.

'No, she's very well, thank you, Sister. It's nowt like that ...'

'So what is it, Fred?'

'Well, it's just our Sally's almost 13. It's her birthday coming up soon,' he said, looking awkward. I noticed his face blush as he spoke. 'And ... well, I expect she'll be starting wi' her periods soon and ... well, erm ... I don't really know what I should tell her.'

Fred's voice crumbled as he said the word 'period'. I could tell that he was finding this conversation beyond excruciating.

'Ah, I see,' I said as the penny dropped. 'So do you want me to have a word with her?'

'Oh, would you, Sister?' Fred sighed, the relief obvious as he looked at me for the first time. 'I mean, I've got sisters and all, but the thing is, how I see it, wi' Sally not having a mum around, well, I just thought she'd be better off talking to a nurse.'

'Fred, honestly, it's fine. Just bring her to see me when you come in to collect your wages.'

Fred nodded, placed his hat upon his head and left the medical centre. He was so relieved that his footsteps seemed far lighter leaving than they'd been when he'd first walked in. Back then, lots of miners would bring their children in with them on Friday afternoon when they collected their wages, so I knew Sally wouldn't think anything of it or look out of place. Sure enough, a few days later Fred knocked at the door.

'Ah, Fred – hello. Come in. Hi, Sally,' I called when I saw her standing shyly behind her father.

'Listen, Sister, I've got a few things to sort out over there,' Fred said, giving me a knowing wink. It was so obvious that it made me cringe. 'So is it okay if I leave our Sally wi' you for a bit while I go and sort 'em out?'

'Sure, no problem,' I smiled, playing along with the ruse.

Sally was relaxed and none the wiser as we sat down and began to chat away.

'I'm sorry to hear about your mum.'

Her face crumpled a little, and for a moment I thought she might cry.

'Your dad, well, he's so proud of you, did you know that?' I said handing her a tissue, just in case.

Sally looked up from her chair and smiled.

'So, how old are you now? You're looking so grown-up.'

'I'm 12, but I'm gonna be 13 soon,' she said proudly, sitting up in her chair. 'My birthday's only a few weeks away.'

I slowly turned the conversation around and eventually asked whether she'd started her periods. Sally shook her head. She told me she'd heard of them from girls at school, but other than that, she knew very little. I began to explain what would happen to her body and what she should expect. If anything, by the time I'd finished, she seemed relieved by our chat.

'It must be difficult for you, not having anyone to talk to,' I guessed correctly.

Sally shrugged and nodded her head.

'I was once just like you. My mother wasn't around and I didn't have anyone to talk to about this kind of stuff either, so I know what you're going through. That's why, if you ever need anyone to talk to, then you know where I am.'

'Yes, Sister,' she answered. 'Thanks.'

'Anyway, I don't want you to worry about it because your aunties will help out and buy you stuff, so you won't even have to ask your dad.'

Sally smiled. 'I wanted to ask him, Sister, but I was too embarrassed, so it's been really good to talk to you.'

I could tell by the look on her face that the weight of the world had just been lifted off her young shoulders.

Moments later, there was a tap at the door. I opened it to find Fred standing there.

'Sorry about that, Sister. I got held up. Is everything all right?' he said, peering around the edge of the door.

Sally and I shared a secret smile.

'Everything's fine,' I said. 'She's been as good as gold; we've just been having a nice chat, haven't we?'

Sally nodded and grinned.

'Anyway, I'll see you soon … and Sally,' I said, calling after her. The young girl stopped in her tracks and turned to face me. 'You're welcome here any time you want, even if it's just for a chat. You know where I am. Just give me a call first to check I'm here, okay?'

'Yes,' she nodded. 'And thanks, Sister. I will.'

'No problem. Now you both mind how you go,' I said, turning my attentions to a pile of forms on my desk.

'Bye, Sister Hart,' Fred called.

'Bye.'

After the door had closed I allowed myself a little smile. I'd only done a small thing, but I knew it was something that had made a world of difference to Sally's life. It was exactly the sort of thing I'd chosen to become a nurse for.

14

Chewing Tobacco and Cursing in Casualty

'Ay up, Sister. What yer' got for us today, then?' a voice called in the darkness.

I turned and the beam of light from my hard hat illuminated his face, and then the contents in my hand.

'Ah, well, let's see, John. Boiled sweets?' I said, holding up the small, crumpled white paper bag. It was better to take down individually wrapped sweets, because of just how many filthy fingers would be dipped inside the bag later that day. 'Or,' I continued, sounding a bit like a shopkeeper, 'I've also a bit of snuff.'

'Aww, 'as tha not got any bacca?'

I searched around inside my pocket until my fingers located a soft square packet.

'Yep, here it is,' I said, holding it up to the light.

John's face lit up in more ways than one as I looked up at him. 'Champion, Sister! Gie us a bit, will yer?'

'Sure,' I smiled warmly, handing him the packet.

The tobacco wasn't to smoke, but to chew. The men used it to keep the insides of their mouths moist. Traditional chewing gum wasn't suitable, unless you wanted it ingrained with tiny particles of coal dust. However, as my father had once taught me, there was a real knack to chewing tobacco.

'Whatever tha does, don't swallow the juice,' Dad had warned years before, during my days at Brodsworth pit.

At first I did exactly as he said and, surprisingly, I found the tobacco not only moistened my mouth, but it was pleasantly refreshing, too. However, a few weeks later I forgot and accidently swallowed the juice. Shortly afterwards, I realised why you must never, ever do it.

'Ooh, I feel as sick as a dog,' I groaned as Dad shook his head in dismay.

'I told you, didn't I? Now go and lie down until you feel better,' he said.

I felt nauseous for the rest of the day. You should never swallow the juice because not only does it cause stomach upsets and sickness, it leaves you in that same state for hours. So, when the young cadets started appearing at the medical centre a little green around the gills, I knew exactly what they'd done because I'd been there and bought the T-shirt.

One day, a young lad rang the bell in the waiting room. I called him through to the treatment room, only I didn't need to ask what was wrong because it was written all over his face. I'd never seen anyone look such a sickly, pallid colour.

'It's my stomach,' he moaned, clutching it. 'It's griping me summat terrible.'

'And when did this start?' I asked, gesturing for him to take a seat.

The lad hobbled over like a little old man. He continued to rock backwards and forwards as he explained. 'It started around two hours ago, Sister,' he replied with a pitiful moan.

'And have you been sick?'

'Yeah, loads.'

'And have you eaten anything?'

'No, not a thing. I couldn't stomach owt, not even my snap [lunch]. In fact, even the thought of it makes me wanna gip,' he said, placing a hand dramatically over his mouth.

'And what about tobacco?'

The cadet swallowed hard, took a deep breath and regained his composure.

'Nope, I haven't fancied a smoke much, either.'

'No, I don't mean to smoke – I mean to chew.'

He rested his baby-faced chin between his fingers and thought for a moment.

'Yeah, I had some bacca earlier,' he recalled.

'And the juice. How about the juice? Did you swallow it when you were chewing?'

'Yeah, a bit. Well, I mean, I didn't spit it out, if that's what you're on about.'

'That's it, then,' I decided, getting to my feet. 'It'll be the tobacco juice. Do you feel a bit like you're seasick?'

'Yeah,' he answered, immediately getting my drift. 'That's exactly how I feel.'

'I knew it!'

I checked the young man over just in case, but it was obvious why he felt so poorly – he'd had a nicotine overdose, only one he'd swallowed. I sent him on his way, with strict instructions to drink plenty of water to 'flush out' his system. I told him to come back later if his symptoms got worse, but he didn't. I knew from bitter experience that the sickness only lasted a matter of hours, so he must have started to feel a little brighter. More importantly, he'd learned to only ever make that mistake once. In a way, doing the same thing had done me a huge favour – not only did I understand how my patients felt, I empathised with them too.

Boys started at the pit as cadets straight from school, usually aged between 16 and 17 years old. Most came from traditional mining families, and they remained as a cadet for around a year, until they'd decided which branch of mining they wanted to go into. Some trained as plumbers or electricians, while others became tunnellers, blacksmiths or specialist surveyors. Despite popular belief, not all cadets ended up working on the coalface; however, they all did their initial training together. In my area this meant sessions on the pit top at nearby Bentley or Markham Main collieries.

They all had to undergo a full medical before they were able to venture underground. This was usually carried out by Dr Macdonald, the Chief Medical Officer, or one of the other Coal Board doctors. They'd check the cadet's lungs, heart, testicles and ears. A cadet's hearing would be tested by asking him a series of questions and using an audiometry examination, which measured the ability to hear sounds at different levels. Then it was down to me to check their eyes, take a urine sample, measure both their weight and height, and record any relevant medical family history. I'd also administer tetanus injections as a preventative measure in case they cut themselves on site. However, my work didn't end there. I'd continue to monitor each and every lad, checking that he was coping with the pressures of being underground. I enjoyed my work and the fact that it was so hands on. Slowly, I not only got to know each and every one of them, I also discovered who was related to whom.

One morning, I was with Bill in the medical centre when the bell rang in the waiting room. I opened the door to find a 17-year-old standing there, clutching his stomach. He looked a little pale and under the weather.

'What's the matter, love?' I asked.

'Urgh, I just don't feel right, Sister,' he groaned.

'Well, come in and let me have a look at you.'

The cadet walked in and I told him to sit down. Bill was busy with some paperwork and was only half listening.

'Now, where does it hurt?' I said, even though I could hazard a guess.

'It's me stomach. I've got terrible belly ache,' he grumbled.

'And have you been sick at all?' I asked, beginning my usual line of enquiry.

He shook his head.

'Well, have you eaten anything, then?'

This time he nodded. 'Yeah, I have … and I've shit enough to fill two pans!'

He wasn't joking. I tried to keep a straight face, but it was a struggle. Then I heard Bill let out a muffled snort from behind. He put a hand up to his mouth and pretended to cough, but it was no good – he couldn't do it and had to leave the room. The lad looked up, his eyes following Bill towards the door. He watched as it closed and then he turned back to face me. I tried my best not to let Bill's infectious laughter set me off. Although he'd tried to hold it in, the poor lad must have heard Bill's chortles from outside because the window was open. I looked back at him and tried to stop the grin from twitching at the side of my mouth. Try as I might, all I could picture in my mind was this poor lad leaping from one toilet to another, filling both. As much as I wanted to giggle, I couldn't. Laughing was extremely unprofessional, and although Bill was professional at all times, even he couldn't keep a straight face.

'Well' I replied, clearing my throat. My voice was low and serious. 'You must have eaten a lot of food to do that, because it has to go in your mouth to come out the other end. So, what is it you've eaten?'

The boy slumped back in his chair and tried to remember all the culinary delights that had passed his lips since the night before.

'Well, I had some fish 'n' chips for tea, and then some crisps, I had a pack of them … cheese 'n' onion,' he recalled, counting them off one by one on his fingers. 'Then I had a burger for supper, and some toast wi' a bit of jam, a bacon butty this morning and a chicken sandwich – I love me sandwiches, see,' he insisted. 'Half a pack of biscuits – shortbread, I think they were – a piece of chocolate cake and a few boiled sweets … oh, and a bit of snap out of me snap tin. A pinch of snuff. Er, did you want me to include drinks …?'

'No, no,' I said, putting my hand up to stop him. I'd heard quite enough. 'Well, it sounds as though you have had quite a lot to eat, but let me take your temperature, just to be on the safe side.'

Unsurprisingly, it was normal. This cadet's stomach ache wasn't down to chewing tobacco; it was down to a little greed. After a brief discussion about his digestive system, I sat down and drew him a diagram to explain. Then I asked him to lie on the couch so I could examine him. His stomach felt soft (rigid abdominal muscle and tenderness usually suggest appendicitis), so I wasn't unduly concerned. Instead, I administered a dose of kaolin and morphine, and asked if he wanted to go home.

'I can't, Sister. I'm a trainee; I can't afford to take time off work!' he said.

I picked up the phone and called the training officer, explaining the lad's predicament. The officer knew the cadet would have to be close to a toilet for the rest of the day, so he found him a job working on the pit top. He left the medical centre, promising to call in on his way home after his shift to see the MRA on duty.

'But if you don't feel better, then you must go to see your GP,' I insisted.

Two-pans man nodded and closed the door behind him. Moments later, Bill appeared in the doorway, wiping away tears from his eyes.

'Has he gone?' he chuckled.

'Yes,' I said, with a grin spreading across my face.

'Two pans?' Bill squeaked.

'Don't!'

Sadly, he never did report back to us, so we never got to find out what was wrong with him, although I reckon he was just a typical young lad whose eyes were bigger than his belly.

A few weeks later, I was having a cup of tea when the phone in the medical office rang. One of the MRAs, Frank, answered, but his voice changed suddenly.

'I see,' he replied, beckoning me over.

'There's been a serious injury underground, Sister Hart,' he said, pressing his hand against the receiver. 'The first aider wants to speak to you.'

I took it and spoke to one of the underground men. His voice sounded so calm that, for a moment, I wondered if Frank had misunderstood, but he hadn't. Although the first aiders were highly trained, it never ceased to amaze me just how calm they remained, even in the most fraught situations.

'Hullo, Sister. We have a man here with a serious head injury,' he began, before explaining what had happened.

The injured miner had been standing up, about to get off the coal belt, but somehow he'd slipped and caught the side of his temple.

'What did he catch it on?' I asked.

'A corrugated metal sheet.'

I didn't show it, but inside I physically winced – I knew this was no run-of-the-mill cut or graze.

'So, what are we looking at?' I asked.

'Well, I suspect he's cut his temporal artery. I've applied a pad and digital pressure to the laceration, but his bleeding is very severe and he's losing quite a bit o' blood.'

I steeled myself. This was serious; I had to get down there fast. But the first aider hadn't finished.

'Sister, I think he's going unconscious on me.'

'Right,' I said, almost dropping the phone in my rush. 'I'm on my way.'

I wondered what I should do. I couldn't put up an intravenous drip on my own, and there wasn't enough time to call a doctor. Despite being a fully qualified nurse with years of experience under my belt, I had never lost my anxiety. In times like these, I'd try to hold it all inside, but my mouth would always feel as dry as the Sahara desert and my heart would pound thirteen to the dozen. I took my nerves as a good sign. I knew that the moment I started to feel complacent would be the moment I should give up the job, because adrenalin always pushed me to do the right thing. However, I knew I couldn't look scared or even slightly ruffled when attending an accident, even if I felt it inside, as the miners would lose confidence in me.

Come on, Joan, keep it together, I told myself as I grabbed my things.

I changed into my underground gear, while Frank called for the pit ambulance to wait at the shaft side. He also arranged for Pat Sword to accompany me underground. Pat was a trained first aider and an officer in the St John Ambulance Brigade, so I knew I'd have good back-up. As soon as I stepped outside the medical centre I spotted him waiting. I signalled over with my hand.

'I just need to nip to the lamp cabin, Pat,' I called as I dashed over the yard to collect my lamp and metal pit checks.

Although Pat was a friendly fellow, very little was said and the mood was sombre as we travelled down together in the cage to the pit bottom. We were both apprehensive about what would greet us. The injured miner had been stretchered close to the pit bottom, so thankfully we didn't have to travel far inbye to reach him. As soon as I approached, the beam from my headlamp illuminated his figure in the darkness. His head wound was extremely deep and, even with the pressure pad holding his skin together, he seemed to be oozing blood at a terrifying rate. It had covered his head, neck and body – even his clothes were soaked. The light glistened against a wet patch of liquid underneath his body, and that's when I realised that he was lying in a pool of his own blood. The miner was a man called Ray, or 'Curly' as the men nicknamed him because he didn't have a hair on his head, and he was drifting in and out of consciousness. He had almost gone into hypovolemic shock. We needed to get him to hospital as soon as possible. I glanced up at Pat, who was waiting for instructions.

'The only way to get good continual pressure to the wound is if I hold it,' I explained. 'Here, pass me that thick pad.'

Pat passed it over, and I held it firmly against the wound on Ray's head.

'Right, bandage me in,' I said.

Pat looked at me with his mouth open, as though he'd misheard.

'You want me to bandage your hand to his head, Sister?'

I nodded. 'It's the only way I can keep enough pressure applied and stop him from bleeding to death.'

Pat grabbed a clean bandage and began to wrap it around both Ray and my hand. It was awkward, walking at the side of the stretcher, into the cage and then into the ambulance with my hand attached to Ray's head by bandage, but I did it. Even with the applied pressure, the patient was still losing a considerable amount of blood, and it wasn't long before my overalls were soaked through. I took a seat in the back alongside Ray's stretcher as the ambulance doors slammed shut. We raced straight to Doncaster Royal Infirmary, with lights flashing and the siren wailing. I kept a constant check on Ray because, by now, he was unconscious. Suddenly, his colour began to change. The more I looked, the more I noticed that his face and lips had tinged blue.

I turned to Pat. 'Something's wrong.'

Pat helped me as I examined Ray's head and neck with my remaining free hand. As I felt Ray's neck, I realised that the cotton bandage, which had been originally applied underground, had tightened with the bleeding. In fact, it had become so tight that it was strangling him.

'Scissors!' I shouted. Pat passed them over.

I cut the bandage, and Ray's face changed colour as the blood began to pump again properly.

'Thank God for that! He's getting his colour back,' I said.

Frank had already telephoned ahead to the hospital, and a set of porters had been dispatched to help us with the stretcher. As we rushed en masse into A&E, a staff nurse stepped forward and stopped us in our tracks. My heart sank. I recognised her because we'd clashed on a previous occasion. Only a few months earlier I'd arrived at casualty with a miner who'd lost the tip of his finger, which had been sliced off by a machine underground.

'And did you save it?' she'd asked me at the time, pointing towards the tip of the bloodied digit.

'There was nothing to save,' I'd replied.

I could tell she hadn't been impressed. Although we were both trained nurses, she looked down her nose at me because, unlike her, I wasn't wearing a nurse's uniform.

'Well, didn't you at least try to save it?' she'd asked, implying that I didn't have a clue what I was doing.

'Well, I would have, but it was hard to see, you know, in the pitch black, among the coal dust,' I'd said.

After that, she'd taken an instant dislike to me and, unlike the other staff, whenever I arrived with a patient she'd query everything, as though she didn't believe a single word I said. I was a fully trained nurse, but because I didn't look like one she treated me as though I was inferior. It was a red rag to a bull, and on a few occasions I had demanded that the casualty officer examine my patients because I didn't think she'd appreciated just how serious their injuries were. So, as soon as she saw me walk through the door with my hand bandaged to Ray's head, she immediately went on the defensive. Deep down, I knew she had me down as a panicker – and I never panicked.

'What's the problem?' she asked, sounding unduly unconcerned.

I looked down at Ray, wondering if she could see what I could – a man with a severe head injury, bleeding heavily, with my hand strapped to him. By now, Ray was fully unconscious and I didn't have time for her petty point scoring, so I told her exactly as it was.

'The patient has lost a considerable amount of blood and is going into second-degree shock. He needs to be seen by a doctor, and then he needs to be transfused.'

But, instead of acting on my words, she looked down at me and then at Ray, and shook her head. 'Well, I think you're exaggerating,' she said, 'so I'll just take his blood pressure.'

I was soaked from head to toe in Ray's blood, yet she was treating him as though he'd cut his finger. I was absolutely livid. It was at this moment that I completely lost my temper.

'You're joking, aren't you? Just look at him, you stupid cow!' I shouted, not caring who heard. 'Just look at the bloody state of him! This man needs immediate medical attention.'

Pat turned to me with his mouth agape as I proceeded to call her a few other choice names too. It was highly unprofessional and totally out of character for me, but I'd had enough. Ray was my main concern and I was worried a delay could cost him his life. I was shouting so loud that the whole of the casualty department heard, and heads turned to look at me. But I feared that Ray would die, and nothing else mattered – me, her or what anyone thought. Ray was my priority.

'I want a casualty officer and I want one NOW!' I bellowed.

The sister heard the commotion and came rushing over. She took one glimpse at Ray and immediately beckoned one of the doctors over. As we transferred Ray from the stretcher to the bed, I was shocked at the amount of blood that had pooled underneath his body.

'I'll need his boots off, please,' the doctor ordered as he got to work.

I started to undo the laces on Ray's boots. As I unfastened them, I heard a swishing sound coming from within. It was only when I removed them that I understood why – they were full of blood. The doctor erected an intravenous drip of saline, and Ray was given an immediate blood transfusion. A few hours later, when his condition had stabilised, he was admitted to a men's ward. Pat and I remained there so that we could speak with his wife who, it transpired, was also a nurse.

'How is he?' she cried, dashing over to his bedside.

I explained what had happened and watched as her expression changed from one of concern to one of terror. Being a nurse can sometimes be a hindrance, because she immediately understood the severity of her husband's injuries. Within the hour,

Ray was surrounded by his loved ones, so we knew it was time for us to leave. As we did, his wife followed us down the corridor.

'Thanks for looking after him,' she said, gently clasping her hand against the top of my arm.

'I'm sure he'll be okay from now on,' I said, trying to reassure her. She nodded gratefully, turned and was gone – back to her husband who, despite a severe head injury, had survived.

Exhausted, I climbed back into the pit ambulance, which was parked outside in the hospital car park. It'd been quite a day, but we still needed to go back to the colliery and report the incident to the pit manager. The driver turned the key in the ignition and the vehicle fired up and juddered back into life. As we pulled away, Pat turned to face me. I could see that he really wanted to say something.

'What?' I asked.

'Nothing,' he smirked.

'What? What is it, Pat?'

'It's nowt.' He chuckled, shaking his head, but soon he could hold it in no longer. 'Well, it's just that, yer know, you certainly told that nurse where to get off, didn't you, Sister?'

My face reddened as I remembered how I'd lost my temper and called her a few choice names.

'Well, I mean, you could see how serious Ray was!' I huffed, trying to justify it.

'It's not that, it's just, well, I didn't know you could swear!' Pat smirked.

The driver swivelled towards us in his seat, his eyes half on us and half on the road ahead.

'Why, what did she say, Pat?' he asked.

'Well, I don't like to repeat it, but it was filth, pure and utter filth! I didn't even know Sister knew such words.'

I nudged against him with my elbow. 'There's a lot you don't know about me, Pat,' I said, grinning and giving him a sly wink, 'so don't you ever push your luck!'

The three of us laughed as the ambulance taxied along the road and made its way back towards the colliery yard.

Ray was off work for a long time afterwards, but as soon as he came back he popped his head around the door of the medical centre to see me. He needed to be examined and signed as fit to return to work.

'It's good to see you back. So, how are you feeling, Ray?' I asked, inviting him to sit down.

Ray did so and folded his coat across his lap. 'Oh, I'm much better, Sister. And, thanks, yer know, for everything you did for me after t'accident 'n' all.'

'No problem, Ray, although you almost didn't make it in the ambulance, you know,' I confessed.

'What's that? Why, Sister? Was I losing a lot of blood or summat?'

'Well, there was that, but no. We nearly choked you to death with a bandage.'

Ray pulled a puzzled face.

I explained how he'd nearly been strangled on top of his serious head injury. 'But don't worry,' I added. 'I'll just make sure we tie it a little looser in future.'

Ray looked down at the floor and began to laugh. It was a big, deep, hearty laugh, which made his heavy shoulders shake up and down.

'Yeah, just try not to kill us next time, eh, Sister?' he said.

'Oh, we'll try our best.'

With that we both fell about laughing. Our laughter carried through the open medical centre window and trailed across the pit yard. Ray had given us quite a scare, so it was good to see him back. Despite a nasty scar to the side of his head, he'd not only made a full recovery, but he'd also retained his sense of humour. To be honest, I think he was just glad to be alive to tell the tale. Ray, or Curly, sent me a bottle of whisky every Christmas after that as a thank you for saving his life.

15

The Mines
Rescue Service

With Peter on the mend, the next few years had passed by without incident. Peter was coping with his health on a day-to-day basis, although he became easily tired when he exerted himself and he also had terrible problems with circulation in his legs where the surgeon had removed his main veins for his heart bypass. Still, I got into a routine where I'd call home around midday, just to check he was okay. To be honest, I also telephoned because, deep down, I knew I'd be able to reach him quickly should I need to. Each morning, I started work at 8 o'clock, finishing in the afternoon around 5, when I'd either cycle home or Peter would pick me up in the car, depending on how he was feeling. Although his health had improved considerably since the operation, it didn't stop me worrying about him when I wasn't there. It'd just reached noon one day when I picked up the telephone and dialled home. I let it ring for ages, but there was no reply. It was odd because Peter was always there.

Maybe he's in the garden? I reasoned, putting the telephone receiver back down.

Over the next few hours I tried again and again, but there was still no answer. It worried me. I paced up and down the office, wondering what I should do, when Frank walked in.

'What is it, Sister?' he asked as I sat down, picked up the phone and dialled home for the umpteenth time.

'It's Peter,' I said, twisting the mouthpiece away. 'I've tried him time and time again but he's not answering.'

I started to feel a little frantic. My stomach ached with nerves as I racked my brains for a reasonable explanation.

Had Peter mentioned anything about nipping out? No, I thought, he still wasn't well enough to travel too far on his own.

Frank tried his best to reassure me. 'Maybe he's just nipped to the shops or something? I'm sure he won't be far.'

But I still felt uneasy.

'Look,' he said, taking my coat from the peg. 'I'm sure Peter's absolutely fine, but if you're this worried, then you should just nip home and check.'

I looked at my coat in his hands and back at his face.

'But what about work?'

'Oh, don't worry about that,' Frank replied. 'I'll man the phones and hold the fort. You get yourself off because you won't rest until you know he's okay.'

I jumped to my feet. Frank was right; there was only one way to know for sure. I pulled on my coat, collected my bicycle from outside and rode home as fast as I could, taking side roads and snickets to make the journey a little quicker. It only took me 15 minutes to get there, and by the time I arrived I was sweating and exhausted. I propped my bike up against the wall and wandered around the back of the bungalow. As soon as I turned the corner I spotted the bedroom curtains. They were still drawn – exactly as they'd been when I'd left for work earlier that morning.

Peter would never leave the curtains drawn, I thought randomly. I glanced at my watch. It was 3 in the afternoon! My stomach flipped with fear. *Something was wrong.*

The palms of my hands began to sweat as I walked to the front. I didn't know what to do. I had to check on him but I was too frightened to go inside – I didn't want to find him on the bedroom floor. My mind raced as I looked around, and that's when I spotted it – Ernie's house.

Ernie, of course! He'll know what to do.

Ernie lived two doors away. He was a lovely bloke, in his mid-30s, almost 10 years younger than us, and he wasn't just a neighbour but a good friend too. Taking a deep breath, I knocked at his door.

'Hello, Joan,' Ernie said, smiling down at me on his doorstep. But his smile disappeared when he noticed how worried I looked. 'Is everything all right?'

'Oh, Ernie, it's Peter. I've been calling him all day but there's been no answer. I've just cycled back from work, but the bedroom curtains are still drawn, and Peter would never leave them closed, not in the middle of the day.'

'I see. Do you want me to go in and check on him for you?'

'Would you? It's just … I don't think I can. What if Peter's collapsed? What if …?' I said, my voice trailing off to a whisper as I imagined the worst-case scenario. I took a deep breath for courage. 'I can't, Ernie. I can't bear to go inside because I'm frightened.'

'Come on,' he said, closing the door behind him. 'Let's go.'

My heart was in my mouth as we headed back to the bungalow. Ernie stood on the step and tried the door handle. 'It's locked.'

A feeling of dread shot through me.

'I locked it when I left for work this morning,' I recalled.

'Have you got any keys?'

'Yes, I have. They're in my handbag somewhere.' I scoured the contents with trembling hands. 'Here,' I said, holding them aloft. The keys dangled and jangled between my fingers, but I remained rooted to the spot.

Ernie took them from me. 'You stay here while I go in and check on Pete.'

I watched as Ernie turned the key in the lock and let himself in. My ears strained as I listened for voices, for a clue as to what had happened to Peter. I heard Ernie's footsteps and the sound of doors opening and closing as he made his way around the property from room to room. I heard him call out Peter's name, but there was no reply. I steeled myself for the worst. Moments later, Ernie reappeared in the doorway.

'There's no one here,' he said.

Relief flooded through me but at the same time I felt confused. I looked around but there was still no sign of him. The garage door was closed, so he hadn't gone out in the car.

Ernie and I had just started to speculate where he could have got to when the sound of a car engine growled as it approached. Peter drove in and parked on the driveway. As soon as he saw us, he gave us a big, cheery wave, but as he pulled on the handbrake he glanced down at his watch and wound down the window.

'You're home early,' he said as he turned off the ignition.

'Peter, where on earth have you been?' I cried.

The passenger door swung open, and from behind his head another figure appeared. It was Wilf, an elderly neighbour. I must have looked shocked because Peter suddenly sounded really concerned.

'Has something happened? Are you all right?' he said.

'I'm fine. It's you!' I snapped. 'I've been really worried about you. I've been calling for over two hours, and I thought … I thought …'

My voice trailed off as emotion choked in the back of my throat. Now I knew he was okay, I wanted to kill him!

Ernie looked down at his feet and so did Wilf. They both knew how ill Peter had been.

'Well,' Ernie smiled, his voice breaking the tension, 'I guess all's well that ends well.'

'Yes,' Wilf chipped in brightly. 'And thanks again, Peter. I really appreciate it.'

Once we were alone, I fixed Peter with a steely stare. I couldn't help it – I was still so angry with him.

'It was Wilf,' he said, gesturing towards our neighbour who was busy making a quick exit down the garden path, followed by Ernie. 'He was going to the cemetery, but he was running late and he was going to miss his bus. You know where it is,' he said, pointing off into the middle distance. 'It's miles away and he had to catch two buses, so I told him I'd give him a lift.'

But I was still standing there with both hands on my hips. 'You should have let me know. You know I always call at 12.'

All the time I'd been fretting that Peter had collapsed at home when, in fact, he'd been busy visiting the dead. The irony wasn't lost on me.

'Why, you didn't think … did you? Is that what you thought?' Peter began to laugh, although I still couldn't see the funny side.

'I've been ringing you for two hours. I've been worried sick!' I shouted as I marched over towards the car. 'Come on, hurry up! You'll have to give me a lift back to work.'

Ernie and Wilf waved goodbye from the garden gate as Peter climbed into the driver's seat. He was grinning away because he thought the whole thing was bloody hilarious, which only served to infuriate me more.

'Don't you ever, ever do that to me again!' I yelled at him.

Looking back, I suppose I should've known better. Peter was just like me – he was the first to help anyone in distress. Only, I was his wife and his nurse, and it was my job to look after and worry about him.

Work continued over the next few years in a blur of medicals for each new intake of cadets. They would take place at the main Doncaster office, where the Coal Board doctors and the Mines Rescue Service (MRS) were based. The MRS was a team made up from the *crème de la crème* of miners. Not only were they physically in tip-top condition, they had an encyclopaedic knowledge of each mine and were all excellent first aiders.

The rescue team lived with their families in individual apartments close to the headquarters. The building also housed an aviary of canaries, which were used to detect harmful gases underground, particularly carbon monoxide. If there was a fire or explosion underground, the team would carry one of the canaries down in a cage. If the bird became distressed, it was a sign that the pit was unsafe and the miners should be evacuated. The canaries were lovely little things, and these big, tough men were crackers on them. In many cases they loved and treasured their little feathered friends more than they did their wives!

"Ere, you seen this one, Sister? She's a beauty,' one of the rescue team said, beckoning me over. He smiled as he pushed a fat finger in between the wire mesh and pointed at the little yellow birds.

'Which one?' I asked as they fluttered and chirped around inside. They all looked exactly the same.

'That one, over there. Can't you hear her? She's got a better voice than Shirley Bassey!' he said, grinning.

I laughed as I watched him. He was completely besotted with the delicate little things, yet, despite their soft, kind natures, these men were as tough as it got. They were on call 24 hours a day, covering a dozen pits throughout the Doncaster area. Wherever there was an accident the men would go. They not only had nerves of steel, they also had stomachs of cast iron. As a rescue team, they faced horrors that would have haunted the next man.

A few months later, I was asleep in bed when the telephone rang in the early hours of the morning. Bleary eyed, I went to answer it. There'd been a fatality at Bentley pit. Although I was the one on call, Jenny, the pit nurse at Bentley, was also on her way, even though she lived over 7 miles away from the colliery. By the time I reached Bentley pit it was 4.30 a.m. and still dark in the colliery yard. Jenny had already arrived so I went to find her. I was dressed in some old jeans and a T-shirt, but Peter had thought ahead and packed my overalls and pit boots in the boot of the car. The MRS was there and already hard at work. As I walked across the yard, a man approached me in the darkness; it was the superintendent of the rescue service.

'Ay up, Sister,' he called.

'What's happened?' I asked.

'It's a contractor. He was working in t'pit shaft doing some repairs. Somehow he's slipped and fallen all the way down t'sump.'

My stomach turned. The sump was right at the very bottom of the pit – the man must have fallen hundreds of feet to his death.

'His colleagues tried to pull him out,' the superintendent continued, 'but they couldn't reach him. Its t'sump, you see, it's covered in about 20 feet of water. We're pumping it out right now, but there's a lot of water. We'll get out what we can and try to recover t'man's body.'

'Okay,' I replied. These men were the experts. I just needed to be on hand to help. I instinctively bundled my overalls up in my hand – I had to get changed. I walked over to the medical centre, where I found Jenny.

'That poor man,' she sighed as soon as I'd opened the door.

She explained how the contractor had hit the side of the pit shaft on the way down. The impact had disembowelled him, and it had been down to poor Jenny to gather his innards from the pit bottom and place them inside a clear plastic bag.

'I've put them in the fridge,' she shuddered, still clearly shaken.

The body parts needed to be retained so that the doctor could certify the man's death.

'What a horrible way to die,' she added sadly.

I nodded and shivered as I thought of the unfortunate miner. He must have known he'd die as he plummeted to his death like a stone.

Although the situation was desperately tragic, as nurses we had work to do, and the rescue service still had to recover his body. Jenny and I travelled to the pit bottom to see what we could do to help. When we arrived, they were trying to lower men down in a makeshift metal cage in order to reach the sump, which was situated directly under the pit cage. The actual cage couldn't be lowered because it would've blocked their access, so the men had to improvise. To make matters worse, the sump was not only full of water, but rubbish too, because it had been used as a dumping ground for old mine cars and other bits of unwanted metal. It was painstaking work, but a few hours later the team had managed to partially drain the sump of stagnant water – a mixture of rain and moisture emanating from the pit shaft. They lowered the makeshift cage once again, but this time, as the heads of the team emerged, we heard the sound of retching. It was a young lad, probably in his mid-20s. He was part of the team, yet, unbelievably, this was his first ever rescue. I felt for him, because it was one of the most gruesome ones I'd ever been called out to.

'Are you okay?' I asked gently as the team stepped out of the cage onto the pit bottom. The poor lad was crying but waved me away, pretending he was okay. I could tell that he was mortified because he'd not been able to handle the situation.

'Look,' I suggested, 'why don't you take a moment out?' I led him away from the cage.

'No, honestly, I'm fine,' he replied with false bravado. 'I'll be okay.'

Only he wasn't fine, and I soon found out why. As the other men climbed out of the cage, I realised why he'd been throwing up. The team had recovered the body, which they'd placed inside a black body-bag, but the bag was half empty because they'd only managed to reach his torso. The superintendent explained that the deceased man's legs were still mangled up in machinery at the bottom of the sump.

'But because the water level's high, we're going to have to drain t'sump again to try to recover his missing limbs,' he said.

I heard the lad sob, so I turned to comfort him.

'Come on, love,' I said, wrapping my arm around his shoulder. 'You're very brave.'

'No, I'm not,' he wept, cursing himself. 'I feel so bloody daft for crying.'

I felt my heart break. I wanted to sit down and cry along with him, the poor, poor boy. I knew he was sobbing because he felt embarrassed at not handling it as well as he'd hoped in the company of some of the toughest, bravest men I'd ever met in my life. The shock of the rescue had affected him deeply and he felt ashamed, even though he had no reason to be.

'Listen, that was your first rescue and it's probably one of the worst ones you'll ever be called to, but you've done it. Look at you, you're here and you've survived it. And now it's over,' I said.

The lad wiped tears from his eyes, stood up straight and nodded gratefully. He took a moment to compose himself and then wandered back over to join the rest of his team. I felt for him because the introduction to his new job had been a baptism of fire, but he'd done it. There seemed little shame in allowing his emotions to flood through; after all, tears are what make us human.

A few of the contractor's colleagues were also standing at the side, waiting for news, but as soon as they spotted the body-bag they broke down. It was our job to calm them, even though Jenny and I were shaken ourselves.

'You couldn't have done any more than you did; you know that, don't you?' I insisted to one man who had his head in his hands, sobbing his heart out.

Jenny tried to console another of the man's colleagues: 'He couldn't have survived a fall like that; you did everything you could to help.'

It was a surreal situation, with the two of us acting as nurses but dressed like miners, comforting a group of grown men hundreds of feet underground, but in this job I'd come to expect the unexpected. Stuck in the underbelly of a pit, it's easy to lose track of time. I thought we'd only been there for an hour or so, but the reality was that we'd actually been underground for hours. The sump had to be drained a third time, but by now the rescue team were both physically and emotionally exhausted.

'We'll have to come back tomorrow,' the superintendent decided, looking around his men.

The area was sealed off for the rescue work to recommence the following morning, although, to my knowledge, the pit remained open. We loaded the body-bag into the cage and escorted the deceased man up to the surface. Jenny and I walked over to the medical centre with his body on a stretcher between us. When we arrived, we found a police officer waiting.

'I'm afraid they've only managed to recover his torso,' I warned, pointing down towards the half-empty bag. The officer seemed to pale before my eyes.

'Do you need to see the body to confirm the death?' I asked.

'Is it in there?' he said, pointing towards the bag.

'It is.'

'Well, in that case, I think I'll take your word for it.'

I understood his reluctance. It was a pretty gruesome task and one he'd decided against. The police officer left the yard, and arrangements were made to transport the body in the pit ambulance to the mortuary at Doncaster Royal Infirmary. The mood was solemn as we sorted through the necessary paperwork at the medical centre. I was busy looking through some papers when Peter appeared. After dropping me off at Bentley pit in the early hours, he'd realised it would be a long night and so had returned home. I glanced up at the clock on the wall – it was almost midday. Because we'd been awake so long, it felt much later. Peter dipped his hand into a bag and pulled something out.

'Here,' he said, revealing a bottle of whisky. 'I thought you could do with a nip of this.'

We never usually drank on duty, but by now our work was done. Besides today was different – it was exceptional circumstances so I took a small nip of whisky, for shock, if nothing else.

'It was horrible,' I told Peter, reliving it frame by frame inside my head as we drove home. 'I can't tell you how horrible it was.'

The following day, I returned with Jenny as the rescue service attempted to recover the man's remains a second time. Thankfully, they'd managed to successfully drain away most of the stagnant water, but its disgusting smell lingered in the still air. After an hour or so, the team was able to recover the man's remaining limbs, which were transported to the hospital mortuary. With his body now complete, he could be formally certified for death by Dr Macdonald.

The whole incident had been a truly horrible experience from start to finish, but it had made me realise, aside from their obvious toughness, just how compassionate these men were, and I had nothing but the utmost respect for them all. The Mines Rescue Service truly was a unique set of men. They not only saved lives, putting their own on the line in the process, but their work allowed relatives a form of closure as bodies were pulled from difficult and extreme situations.

Although the MRS covered all the pits in the area, each colliery also had its own part-time rescue service. I had a team of 10 such men working at Hatfield. A team from each pit competed against each other in competitions, and our team was led by a wonderful man called Tommy Chappell. One year, the lads came in to see me for their annual medicals. Tommy opened up a cardboard box and pulled out a brand new set of overalls from the top of a pile to show me.

'What do you think to this, then, Sister?' he asked, holding it up to the light. 'We've just got 'em through. Brand new, they are.'

'Very smart,' I agreed, as he lay them out proudly across the desk.

'Only trouble is,' he said, standing back to consider it, 'when we wear 'em, no one knows it's us. I mean, no one knows which pit we belong to.' He rubbed his chin thoughtfully for a moment. 'Wouldn't it be lovely if they all had Hatfield on them, then they'd all know where we came from?'

A thought popped into my head.

'I'll tell you what,' I said, stuffing the overalls back into the box and pushing them to one side. 'Leave them with me and I'll see what I can do.'

'Really?' Tommy asked.

'Yes, just give me a few days.'

That evening I took them home and, with a needle and thread, I painstakingly embroidered the word 'Hatfield' onto the arm of each and every one. A few days later I returned them to Tommy.

'Ooh, Sister,' he gasped. 'They look smashing!'

In fact, Tommy was so excited that he called the whole team together to draft a letter of thanks to me, signed by each man. But even that wasn't enough. A day or so later Tommy knocked on the medical centre door.

'The lads wondered if you'd do us the honour of posing for a photo with 'em. They'll be wearing their brand new overalls.'

'I'd be delighted to,' I said, smiling warmly.

An hour later, I was seated at the front of the team, who had lined up behind me, crossing their arms and proudly displaying their arm flashes for everyone to see. When the camera shutter fell, the moment was captured for ever.

As well as the Hatfield rescue team, we also had a team of trained first aiders. My team was made up of both surface and underground workers. All were equally as proud when it came to their work. They also competed against first-aid teams in the area from large companies including the Pilkington and Rockware glass factories. The first-aid competitions were usually a mock-up of an aeroplane or train disaster to see how well the men worked under stress.

Unlike the men in the rescue service, who had their kit paid for by the National Coal Board, the first aiders' gear was paid for by the pit, or through fundraising. One day, the lads got together to practise, but as I watched them I realised just how tatty their overalls had become. I didn't want them turning up at competitions looking scruffy, so I decided to raise some money for new ones by completing a sponsored swim. I swam 40 lengths, raising £46 – a small fortune back then – to buy 10 spanking new overalls.

Needless to say, they were thrilled with their new gear and desperate to show it off in the upcoming competition. Unfortunately, they didn't bring home the silver that day; however, they did manage to get the Hatfield name on a shield one year. Not that it really mattered, because not only were they all competent and highly skilled men, but they always got the job done. They respected me, as I did them. This became evident when I was asked to help out with the many 'sports' competitions that they ran. The men, it seemed, had a team for everything, be it cricket, football, darts or snooker.

The pit would also organise an annual gala in the village. It was always a lovely summer affair that included a series of decorated floats, complete with a beautiful gala queen, who had been especially chosen from the local community. Of course, I remained on duty throughout the day in case of injury or if anyone fainted during the heat of one of the hottest summers on record – 1976 – which had been dubbed as the 'drought of the century'. Thankfully, the day passed without incident.

With the long, hot summer and hosepipe ban a distant memory, and autumn on its way, the men got back to organising the next sporting season. I was in the medical centre one day when I heard a light tap at the door. Trev, a miner and member of the pit football team, walked in. He wanted to have a word.

'What's tha doin' this weekend, Sister?'

I looked up from my desk. 'Not much, Trev. Why?'

'Good, 'cos I've put you down for football on Sunday.'

'Not playing, I hope?' I said, shaking my head.

'Not really, you're the linesman … or lineswoman. I suppose that's what I should call thee.' He grinned.

My mouth fell open. 'But I don't know a thing about football!'

'Dunt matter, Sister,' Trev said, shrugging. 'They'll soon shout at yer if tha does owt wrong.'

I studied him for a moment.

If the men needed me, then so be it.

'Okay,' I agreed, 'you've got me. Put me down for it.'

'Don't worry,' he replied. 'I already have. In fact, I'm relying on you.'

With that, he closed the door.

Sure enough, early the following Sunday morning I was there, running up and down the line like a lunatic, waving my arms and blowing a whistle someone had strung around my neck. Besides being the lineswoman, I was also entrusted with a bucket and sponge. Although there weren't many bad injuries, only a few scuffed knees, I took great pleasure in squeezing ice-cold water down the necks of men who'd given me a hard time over the years.

'It's good. You need it – for the shock,' I insisted, with my tongue planted firmly inside my cheek.

But if I thought it would be all glory then I was wrong, because a week later I was called up again.

'Am I a linesman?' I asked eagerly when I arrived. It was freezing, and frost glistened upon the hard ground. Although I'd wrapped up for the occasion, I still needed to stamp my feet against the cold earth to keep warm. The team looked sideways at one another before turning their attentions to me. A gruff-looking miner spoke up from the rest of the pack.

'Don't be daft, lass. You're in charge of t'ice packs, in case of injury or foul play.'

My face fell as the breath from my mouth rose up in the air, forming small clouds. I'd obviously had too much of a good time giving ice-cold baths and I'd been stripped of my bucket and sponge.

'Although we thought you might like to bring on t'slices of orange at half-time,' one said, trying to placate me.

'Done,' I agreed.

And I had been, although the following week I slipped a few slices of lemon in just to keep them on their toes.

'Euueewwwk!' one of the lads squawked, almost spitting his teeth out.

I laughed my socks off. Whereas once I'd been the 'outsider', now I was at the hub of it all, and I loved each and every single minute. Of course, it was ultra-competitive with the NUM (mineworkers) taking on BACM (management) in the football matches. Even Ken Deeming, the pit manager, tried to court favour with me before the game.

'Remember, Sister. If it's management that's injured, use the sponge. If it's one of t'miners, you can throw a bucket of cold water over 'em.'

I smirked and shook my head. 'No way. You're all getting the same treatment.'

And they did.

With the men taking constant showers after football and their shifts down the pit, we had an outbreak of athlete's foot. It was a particularly nasty strain, so I decided to carry out a survey. I pinned up a notice asking men with foot problems to call in to see me at the medical centre. In the end, I selected 30 miners to take part, including one called Kev. I asked Kev to remove his pit boots and socks so that I could inspect his feet. He had one of the worst cases of athlete's foot I'd ever seen. It wasn't just between all his toes – it had transferred to both feet.

I knew I had three courses of action available. The first 10 men received permanganate of potash (potassium permanganate). It came as crystals, which I dissolved in water and the men had to soak their feet in the liquid for 15 minutes every day. The solution was an antiseptic and was drying on the skin, but it was also very effective. The second group of men were treated using gentian violet, which was painted on after showering to form an extra barrier against the skin. But Kev fell into the third group – of those whose feet needed something a little stronger.

'Here,' I said, handing him a small white tube.

'What is it?' he asked, taking it from my hand.

'It's a tube of Canesten. You need to rub it sparingly onto the affected areas. Do that a couple of times a day and you should soon see an improvement.'

'I've never heard of it before,' Kev said, eyeing the packet warily.

'No, that's because it's expensive, so we don't usually give it out. But in your case,' I said, looking at his feet, 'I think you'll need it. Now, just use that tube and see how you get on. If it hasn't cleared up and you need some more, then come back and see me.'

'Okay, Sister. Right you are, and thanks for this,' he said, waving the packet between his fingers as he clambered to his feet.

A week or so later, I walked inside the medical centre to find Bill sitting at his desk, shaking his head in despair.

'What's up?' I asked.

Bill put his pen down and shot me a sideways glance. 'Sometimes I think the men think we're running a chemists or summat.'

'What? Why?' I asked, a little baffled.

'I've just had a lad in through them doors asking for something for his wife!' he said, looking towards the entrance as though the miner was still standing there.

'You're kidding me.'

'I'm not!' Bill tutted. 'Some people never cease to amaze me.'

He picked up his pen and went back to work. I could tell he was really annoyed, so I decided not to press him further. The medical centre was there for the men, and they knew I was on hand to help out with family matters wherever I could, but even I'd been baffled by the odd request. A fortnight had passed but Kev and his infected feet hadn't returned. I presumed his fungal infection must have cleared up and I'd almost forgotten about him, until early one morning when he knocked at my door.

'How are you feeling, Kev? And how are your feet?' I said, looking down at them.

'It's come back again, Sister. That's why I'm here,' he said, taking a seat in the treatment room. Kev peeled off both socks to show me as I inspected his feet thoroughly. While they certainly didn't look as angry as they had before, it was obvious that the infection was still present.

'But the cream … didn't it work?' I asked, a little surprised.

'Yeah, it worked brilliant, but then I ran out.'

I was puzzled. 'So why didn't you come back to see me, like I told you to?'

Kev planted both feet flat on the floor and sighed heavily. 'I did. That's the problem.'

'Eh?'

He shook his head as he began to explain. 'I read all the instructions like you told me to, but when I called here I couldn't for the life of me remember what the chuffing stuff was called. I stopped by to have a word but you weren't in. There was only Bill here.'

'And didn't he give you the cream?'

'Nah,' Kev replied, shifting in his seat. 'I couldn't remember the name, so I asked him if I could have some more of that "itchy fanny cream".'

There was a moment's silence as I tried my best not to snort with laughter.

'Itchy fanny cream?' I repeated, the words coming out in a high-pitched squeak.

'Well, that's what the instructions said it was for,' Kev continued.

'And … and what did Bill say?' I said, my eyes beginning to water with laughter.

'You see, that was it. I think he thought I were winding him up or summat because he looked at me a bit funny and told me to come and see you.'

The penny suddenly dropped. I remembered how annoyed Bill had been about the miner asking for medication for his wife. I managed to contain my laughter even though my hands were shaking as I pulled out another tube of Canesten for his flaky feet. When I later explained it to Bill, we both fell about laughing.

'Oh, don't,' Bill said, clutching his sides, when I told him later. 'I wondered what he was on about. At first I thought he was a cheeky sod for asking, and then I thought he'd gone completely mad!'

'I know. I thought I'd die laughing!' I agreed, wiping the tears from my eyes.

Thankfully, Kev's feet recovered and, thanks to a letter drafted to the NUM by the men, a new and better floor was laid in the showers. It was much easier to clean, which helped prevent the spread of infection. It was good news for Kev who, to my knowledge, never had use for a tube of 'itchy fanny cream' ever again.

16

Bentley Pit Disaster

I was in the middle of a dream when I heard the sound of a bell ringing in the distance. Bleary eyed, I pushed myself up onto my elbows and tried to focus. At first, I wasn't sure if I was still dreaming, but then I realised that it was the noise of the telephone ringing in the hallway. I checked the clock on the bedside cabinet. It was 4.50 a.m.

Who on earth would be calling at this time in the morning?

I heard Peter sigh. He pulled back the eiderdown, got to his feet, yawning and stretching, and padded out of the bedroom and into the hallway.

'Hello,' I heard his muffled reply. He must have been holding the receiver to his mouth in an attempt not to wake me. But it was too late; I was already wide awake, bolt upright in bed and listening to every word.

'Who is it? Why, what's happened? What? Right, I see. We're on our way.'

It was an emergency at the pit – it had to be.

There was a slight clatter as Peter replaced the telephone and came back into the bedroom.

'Joan, there's been a paddy accident over at Bentley,' he said. 'You're needed now.'

'I thought so,' I said, climbing out of bed. I wandered over to my chest of drawers and searched for clothes. Although I wondered what would face me at the pit, I wasn't unduly worried because I'd been called to deal with paddy incidents before. Other than a few crushed limbs or missing fingers, they'd never really been all that serious, and they certainly weren't anything I couldn't handle. I pulled out some comfy underwear, a pair of jeans and a knitted jumper.

'Ready?' Peter asked a few moments later, the car keys already in his hand.

'As ready as I'll ever be.' I yawned, wiping the sleep from my eyes.

It was the end of November, so it was freezing cold. Peter went out to the driveway to scrape ice from the car windscreen and warm up the engine. I pulled my winter coat from the peg, grabbed my house keys and locked the bungalow door, before dashing over to join Peter in the car.

'Oh, it's freezing,' I complained, rubbing my ungloved hands together.

It was so cold that I could see my breath, even inside the confines of the car. I put a hand out and turned the heater to full blast. Our car was a cherry-red saloon we'd only had a few months – it was very reliable and the apple of Peter's eye. As warm air began to flow inside, making it a little more bearable, he paused for a second and stared hard at the steering wheel.

'What?' I asked.

'Nothing,' he said, a bemused look on his face. 'I was just thinking. This old girl,' he said, tapping the dashboard with his fingers, 'she must know her way to Bentley. I reckon if we jumped in and said "Bentley pit", she'd be able to drive herself there because we've been there so much recently.'

I threw my head back and laughed.

'You are daft,' I said, nudging his elbow. 'Come on, they'll be waiting for us.'

Peter took the back roads over to Bentley. The tarmac glistened in the moonlight as we sped along. The black road sparkled with its covering of ice, as though it had been sprinkled with glitter. I glanced out at the empty farmers' fields around us. The trees were silhouetted as strange, tall, dark shapes in the distance. Everything was still and cold. Unlike us, other folk were still tucked up in their warm beds.

The journey only took 15 minutes, and as we pulled into Bentley village we made our way over to the colliery. I immediately spotted the medical centre because its windows were lit up against the inky blue sky. The rest of the pit was momentarily illuminated in the beam of headlights as we turned into the colliery yard. I'd expected to see men wandering around, but the place seemed eerily quiet. Peter and I climbed out of the car and wandered over towards the medical centre, where Ken, one of the senior MRAs, was waiting. Ken was a lovely man, a paternal type in his mid-fifties, who wore glasses and was tall and stocky. I'd met Ken many times before with Jenny, the sister at Bentley, and had always found him easy-going and pretty unflappable. But as soon as we entered the room, he stood up. Ken was normally a cheery fellow, but his face looked so solemn that I sensed it was no ordinary call-out.

'Hello, Ken,' I began, waiting for his face to soften – only it didn't.

'Oh, am I glad you're here, Sister Hart. I've rung Jenny, and Dr Macdonald's on his way. The switchboard has rung the other sisters, who are all on their way over too,' he said, without pausing for breath.

'For a paddy incident?' I gasped.

Maybe I'd misunderstood?

'Yes, but it's way more serious than we first thought.'

'Why? What do you mean?' I said, trying to untangle my arms from the sleeves of my coat.

Ken gulped. 'Because there are seven men dead.'

The words hung in the air as I stopped what I was doing and looked up at him in disbelief. 'Dead?'

He nodded grimly.

I continued to stare, with my mouth slightly open, the shock registering on my face. We'd never had a disaster on this scale in the Doncaster area in the whole time I'd lived and worked here. I knew seven casualties in a pit village as small as Bentley would mean that each and every resident would know one of the deceased. This was unprecedented, but Ken hadn't finished.

'There are 19 serious casualties too,' he added grimly.

Although my stomach had sunk to my knees, I knew there was no time to waste – there was work to be done.

'Right,' I said, rolling up the sleeves of my jumper. I headed over to the sink to wash my hands. 'Let's see what needs to be done.'

It's hard to explain, but in situations like these the nursing instinct takes over and carries you through. With 19 serious casualties, and heaven knows how many walking wounded, I knew I had to get organised and quick. I went through all the drawers and cupboards, grabbing everything we'd need: bandages, dressings, slings and Entonox. I realised that the most serious cases would be treated using morphine from one of the locked boxes underground.

'Labels,' I suddenly remembered, turning to face Peter. 'We need to make labels, so we can identify each patient and what injuries he's sustained.'

'Right, I can do that,' he said, pulling up a chair.

Moments later, the phone rang; it was one of the underground first aiders. Normally, these men had nerves of steel and always kept their feelings in check, but this poor man sounded completely panic-stricken.

'It's really bad, Sister,' he began, his voice quavering with emotion at the sheer scale of it. 'How long is t'doctor gonna be? Is there anyone else coming down to help me?'

I desperately wanted to throw on my overalls and get down there, but I knew Dr Mac and Jenny were just minutes away. This was Jenny's pit and she would want to take charge underground.

No, I reasoned. *I'd be more use manning the medical centre with Ken, treating the wounded as they're brought up to the pit top.*

Sure enough, as soon as I put down the telephone I spotted car headlights and two vehicles swerved quickly into the yard outside. I heard the sound of car doors banging and saw Dr Mac and Jenny running over towards the pit shaft. The sun had yet to rise, and as I looked out of the window I realised just how unnaturally still the whole place seemed. Although the Mines Rescue Service had been alerted, most of the other men were either on their way or already underground trying to help out as best they could.

I looked over at Peter, who was busy cutting up labels out of cardboard.

'It's a bad one, Peter,' I said, voicing my concerns aloud.

Ken looked up as Peter nodded. No matter how hard I swallowed, I couldn't stop the wave of nausea from rising up in the back of my throat.

Would we cope?

I felt rigid with fear, although I couldn't let anyone see how scared I was. A few more minutes passed before other nurses started to arrive, including Sister Sarkar, the chief nursing officer. She took charge above ground and dispatched two nurses over to the medical centre to assist me. Three others remained with her at the shaft side, where she operated a triage system. She quickly assessed each miner as he was lifted to the pit top. Shocked and wounded men were sent over to me, while the more seriously injured were dispatched by ambulance to Doncaster Royal Infirmary.

The pit switchboard had already notified the police, who sent officers to man the pit gates and set up roadblocks so the injured could be transported as quickly as possible. But there were so many seriously wounded miners that each ambulance was forced to carry two men and a qualified sister on board to monitor them so that they didn't die during the journey. It was a conveyor system, but it worked. Meanwhile, news filtered through that a temporary morgue had been set up in the pit's garage. As soon as I heard, I felt physically sick.

Those poor, poor men.

Soon, a steady stream of wounded men had started to come through the doors of the medical centre, and, slowly, as each man recounted his story, we began to piece the whole picture together.

At approximately 4.45 a.m., just 5 minutes before I'd received the telephone call at home, a group of miners – around 65 in total – had finished their shift and climbed on board a paddy train. The men were taking a ride back to the pit bottom when the train suddenly veered out of control and crashed against the wall. The accident had killed seven miners. One lad – a coalface trainee – had only been 18 years old, while another had been three years older, aged just 21. The injured men had been travelling in the last two coaches of the train and were thrown out, hitting the rock side. Many had serious head injuries, while others had suffered deep lacerations to their torsos, arms and legs.

Jenny travelled underground with Dr Mac to deal with the most serious cases and identify the dead. It's an unwritten rule that whoever arrives on the scene first takes charge of whatever needs to be done, and that person happened to be me. The men's injuries were horrific. The run area for the paddy train is only very small, so when it had derailed the men had banged their heads against both walls and the ceiling. Thankfully, they'd all been wearing their helmets, so some had been protected from more severe injuries. However, others had ricocheted violently from one wall, losing their hard hats, to another, sustaining fatal injuries.

The timing had been terrible because, just as the train derailed at the pit bottom, the next shift of miners had arrived to start work. Miners had seen their colleagues fatally or seriously injured and had run over to help, so we not only had injured men to deal with, we also had to treat others for shock. With hordes of miners still waiting to be seen, Doncaster Royal Infirmary was put on red alert. I focused on what needed to be done and went into autopilot, treating the men in order of the severity of their injuries.

'Here,' I said, passing Peter a clipboard, paper and pen. 'Keep a log of who has been brought up from underground. List their name, check number and whether or not they've been given morphine. That way, if anyone asks, we'll know who's gone where.'

'Okay,' Peter agreed, taking it from me.

I knew we needed to remain organised and keep a central log. Peter wrote the men's details down onto individual labels, which he tied to their wrists using strips of bandage. Some of the miners were concussed, while others had drifted in and out of consciousness, so we needed to know who they were. The hospital also had to be clear about who had been given what medication. Besides head injuries and lacerations, some had sustained suspected fractures and required X-rays, while others had cuts that ran so deep they required sutures. Both groups had to be assessed and ferried to hospital, but only after the more serious cases, because those took absolute priority.

As the morning wore on, the pit became busier and busier as extra men were drafted in to help. While we worked away, tending to the injured, the police were frantically trying to keep the crowds under control outside. Worried families and friends vied for position at the pit gates, waiting for news of their loved ones. As the ambulances sped along neighbouring streets, news spread that there'd been a major incident at the pit, so more and more relatives turned up anxious for news of husbands, sons, fathers and brothers. Reporters also arrived, but the police kept them at arm's length too.

With Peter's help, logging each and every patient, we were able to concentrate on the job in hand – treating the injured. I felt for poor Jenny, because she had the worst job of all. She'd gone underground not only to assist with the rescue, but also to recover body parts so that the deceased could be fully identified. I thought of all those poor families standing outside in the freezing cold November morning, crying and waiting for news. We treated the men for hours at a time, but the queue seemed neverending. It felt like being in the middle of a battlefield. Just when we thought we'd got through the worst of it, more miners arrived.

Finally, the queue filtered away to nothing. It was only then that I allowed myself a moment out. I drifted over into a quiet corner of the room to try to compose myself. Whatever I'd learned throughout my years as a nurse, nothing could have prepared me for something like this. Tears brimmed in my eyes but I willed them to go away. Peter noticed and stepped forward to hold me in his arms.

'Peter, there are seven men dead, and God only knows how many injured,' I mumbled. My hands were sore, my legs and back were aching, and my head was pounding with stress and exhaustion. By now, tears were threatening to tumble out and I didn't know if I could stop them. Even though I'd managed to keep it together, now that it was finally over I felt overwhelmed with emotion.

'Don't cry or throw a wobbly, just keep calm and be there for them all – it's all you can do. Okay?' Peter said, squeezing me tighter.

'Okay,' I said.

'That's my girl!' He kissed the top of my head.

I smiled and went back to my duties, tidying up the medical centre. Somehow, my team and I had managed to treat around 50 men over the space of nine hours. No other nurse had her husband with her because the rest of them could drive, but I felt blessed to have had Peter by my side. Just by being there, he'd given me the strength to carry on and do my job. Peter was and always would be my rock.

With the Mines Rescue Service now in full attendance, the dead were recovered from underground and their bodies transported to the makeshift mortuary. A first aider was given the unenviable task of making each man look presentable for their relatives. The managers allowed one relative from each deceased man's family into the pit to formally identify them. Peter's list of injured men became invaluable – we were able to direct worried relatives to the right place because we knew where every man had been sent. Once all the men had been treated and duly identified, Sister Sarkar came over to thank us for our hard work. By now it was 2 p.m., and Peter had been due his heart medication hours before. With very little left to do, I asked Sister Sarkar for permission to leave.

'You get yourself home, Sister Hart,' she agreed. 'You look exhausted.'

She was right; I was both physically and mentally spent. It had been one of the most gruelling days of my life, and one that would remain with me in the years to come. Exhausted, we climbed into the car and Peter started up the engine. As we pulled out through the colliery gates, the police had to help direct us because there were still so many relatives crying for loved ones at the pit gates.

As we wound down the narrow streets of Bentley village I noticed hordes of neighbours gathered, hunched over garden fences and outside doorways, comforting one another. The whole village was grieving. It broke my heart to see them. Their faces continued to haunt me as we headed away from Bentley and back towards home, but still I refused to cry, even though I'd witnessed one of the most distressing things I'd ever had to deal with. I didn't cry despite being on site when men had passed away. I didn't even cry when I realised it had been almost 47 years to the day that Bentley had experienced a disaster on the same scale. But once the bungalow door had closed behind me, I broke down. I sobbed my heart out until I had nothing left to give. I wept for the brave and proud miners who'd been cut down in their prime, and for those who had died in the middle and at the end of their working lives. I sobbed for their wives, mothers, daughters and sisters. But most of all I grieved. Losing those men had felt like losing a member of my own family, because the mining community *was* a big family. The disaster had changed everything in an instant. It had wounded an entire community and, while it would eventually heal, the scar would remain in our hearts. Nothing would or could ever be the same again.

Time passed and, months later, like other families that day, I suffered my own personal loss. I was at work one day when a call came through to the medical centre. It was Bill, Mum's partner.

'It's your mum. She's really ill, Joan,' he explained.

Mum had been having the treatment for bone cancer, but because I was back living up north I didn't see her as often as I would have liked. Still, I telephoned her every week and tried to visit at least once every three months. Even though she had the willpower of 10 men, her frail body had begun to fail.

'They say it's gone into her brain.' Bill sobbed as the words caught at the back of his throat.

I didn't know what to do because Mum was hundreds of miles away, in London. After I put down the phone, it rang again. It was a staff nurse from the hospital, and it was obvious she didn't have a clue which part of the country I lived in.

'Can you get here in the next half an hour? It's your mother – she's very poorly.'

'But I live in South Yorkshire. I'll never get there in time,' I gasped.

I felt sick because I knew that, whatever I did, I'd never be able to reach her and say goodbye. Instead, I sat at my desk in a daze, numb and unsure about what to do. Within the hour, Bill had called back to say that my mother had passed away. I wandered from the treatment room back into my office and closed the door. Frank heard what had happened and went to see Ken Deeming. Moments later, Mr Deeming knocked at my door.

'Are you okay?' he asked, wrapping a comforting arm around my shoulder. His kindness made me break down even more because I'd felt so utterly helpless. I hadn't been there when she'd needed me most.

'You stop here while I go and ring Peter,' Ken suggested.

A short while later, Peter arrived to drive me back home.

'Our Ann, and Tony – someone will have to tell them,' I panicked.

'It's all right,' Peter said. 'I've already made the call.'

Mum's death hit us all. We'd not always seen eye to eye, but she was my mum and I loved her. I was glad I'd made contact all those years before. Despite the numerous rows and her obvious disapproval of my marriage to Peter, I knew deep down that she'd always loved me. I'd also like to think that I'd made her proud.

17

Rubber Gloves

Despite the pit disaster, life carried on, although the mood at Bentley and the surrounding pits remained sombre and never seemed to recover. The men realised that the job they did day in, day out was both gruelling and dangerous, and the derailment of the paddy train reminded them just how much it was.

The years passed by, and with them came more rules and regulations than you could shake a stick at, and soon the 1980s were upon us. A new decade had begun, and with it, supposedly, new opportunities. Margaret Thatcher and the Conservative Party were voted into power in 1979, and the country had its first-ever female Prime Minister. Where once there had been talk of trade unions and strikes, now there was talk of entrepreneurial spirit, opportunities and greed. To be honest, I tried not to get involved with politics because I was far too busy concentrating on my job and caring for my men. I'd often hear grumbles from the miners about the way the country was being run.

Despite the change in the political landscape, something else was soon on everyone's minds. There was a new disease and threat to public health called HIV – human immunodeficiency virus – that we medical professionals were being educated on. We were told it could lead to something called acquired immune deficiency syndrome, or AIDS.

The disease brought with it a kind of mass hysteria in the media and new medical safety practices, namely the introduction of rubber gloves. Soon, they became the norm, but every time I was called to examine a miner I wouldn't use rubber gloves because I knew just how sensitive they were about them. It'd taken me years to gain their trust and I didn't want to offend them. It was a strange situation because I'd insist that all the first aiders wore them when working underground.

It's hard to explain, but back then there was still a lot of ignorance, and people didn't understand or want to know anything about AIDS, especially not in a pit environment. The miners were very traditional and old-fashioned, and they couldn't fathom what on earth this 'strange new disease' had to do with them. I knew that if I'd worn rubber gloves, they'd each have taken it as a slight on both their character and their sexuality.

However uncomfortable they felt speaking about it, I knew I'd have to tackle it in the end, because rumours had started flying around that someone at the pit had been diagnosed with HIV. I had a word with the NCB's education and health department, which said it'd make the necessary arrangements, and days later we set up a video camera in the middle of the medical centre. It was a big, black, cumbersome thing, which took up an awful lot of room, but I knew a safety film was needed not only to quash rumours, but also to educate the men that the gloves were there for their own protection.

'What's all this, then? Have we got ITV in?' one of the lads chirped as soon as he saw the camera in the middle of the room.

'No, we're making a safety film, so don't be so cheeky. Now, clear off!' I scolded, shooing him out of the door.

I wasn't usually one for make-up, but that day I decided to make a little bit of an effort for my film début. In fact, I'd dolled myself up to the nines. Wearing my trademark navy-blue nurses' uniform, I sat down behind my desk and cleared my throat as the video recorder whirred.

'You may have noticed that we have introduced vinyl gloves in all of the underground first-aid boxes. New legislation has been brought in, whereby everyone in the medical profession now has to wear rubber gloves to stop cross-contamination of blood or other bodily fluids ...' I spoke in my poshest voice. With my eyes still on the camera, I walked over to a cabinet and pulled out a file with *Prevention of cross-infection* marked in big letters across the front to hammer the message home. Then I pulled out a pair of vinyl gloves and dangled them in front of the camera.

'So, you see, we need to wear them, not only to protect ourselves, but also to protect you because your health and safety in the workplace is paramount,' I finished.

The health-and-safety official waved his hand and called 'cut'. It was, as they say in showbiz, a 'wrap'. It was hardly Hollywood standards, but the 15-minute film said everything it needed to say without being patronising, and with the emphasis on safety. I knew that if the men understood the reasons behind it, then they'd accept it. We screened it on the two televisions, one in the checks room and one in the canteen, so I knew all the men had seen it.

Over the next few months, Peter's health continued to go downhill. It had been 10 years since his heart operation and I worried what the future held. In particular, I fretted about how I'd get him to hospital in an emergency.

'I've been thinking,' I announced one morning as we sat at the breakfast table.

Peter was busy smearing margarine onto a piece of toast.

'Oh, what's that?' he asked, without looking up.

'I was thinking it's about time I took my driving test.'

Peter stopped what he was doing and dropped the knife down on his plate, which clattered against the porcelain.

'But you're 51!' he cried.

'It doesn't matter. Besides, I think it'd be handy if I could drive. It'd take some of the pressure off you.'

Peter thought for a moment and nodded his head. 'Suppose so. When do you think you'll start?'

'No time like the present,' I said, putting my dirty plate in a bowl in the sink.

I didn't want to tell Peter the real reason, that one day I feared I'd have to get him to hospital quickly in the middle of the night. If I couldn't drive then we'd be stranded, waiting for an ambulance.

I asked around, and through the miners I heard that a former deputy from Hatfield pit called Barry had set himself up as a driving instructor. I rang Barry and arranged my first lesson.

'If you can teach me to drive, then you deserve a medal!' I laughed.

Barry was patient but determined, and, after months of driving around the streets of Doncaster, I finally put in for my test. He kept his fingers crossed that I didn't get a particular examiner, who, Barry reckoned, had it in for all the students he'd taught.

'He's a right so and so,' Barry grumbled.

I thought he'd been exaggerating, until the day arrived and I did indeed get Mr So and So. Barry grimaced, his eyes rolling back in his head when the man approached the car. As I prepared to set off, I decided to try to charm my way into the examiner's affections.

'Would you like a Polo mint?' I asked. 'It's just that I suck them all the time – it helps with my concentration.'

The examiner turned sharply towards me in his seat with an appalled look on his face.

'That's bribery!' he said.

I knew then that I was doomed.

I began my test along Doncaster High Street, but as I approached a pedestrian crossing, a man, who I'm sure must have been a plant, kept stepping on, off and back on it again.

'I wish he'd make his bloody mind up!' I huffed, not knowing whether to stop or start.

But the examiner didn't possess a sense of humour.

'That's harassing the public!' he sniffed as he made a note against the piece of paper on his clipboard.

We carried on further up the road, where I started to slow down. The examiner turned to me. 'Mrs Hart, the lights are on green.'

'Yes,' I agreed, pulling the car to a halt, 'but they're going to change any minute, and I don't want to be caught in the middle of the road.'

Unsurprisingly, I failed, so Barry put me forward for another test six weeks later, this time in Gainsborough.

'Just drive as though you're on your test with Barry,' the second examiner advised. Unlike the first, he was a kind and patient man. He gave me enough confidence to pass.

Of course, the miners had thought it was hilarious that I was taking my test at such a late age.

'Clear the roads, lads! Sister Hart's taking her test again this afternoon!' one had teased.

'Good luck, Sister. And don't forget yer Highway Code!' another had added.

'Listen,' I'd told them. 'If you see me coming down that lane later on my bike, then don't say a word because I will have failed.

But if you see me driving down the pit lane in my car then you can all bow!'

With my driving test passed, I drove my bright red Ford Fiesta into work later that morning. So, you can imagine my delight when I turned the corner to find a group of miners all lined up, clapping, cheering and bowing towards me.

'I did it, lads!' I said, waving at them through the open window. 'I only went and passed.'

'Flaming hell, Sister Hart's behind the wheel!' they shouted as laughter rang out in the air.

After that, I began to drive myself into work, which took some of the pressure off Peter.

Not long afterwards, I was sitting in the medical centre when the phone rang. It was one of the deputies calling – from underground.

'Is that Sister?' he asked. 'I've got a man down here who's got his finger trapped in some machinery. It looks right nasty.'

'Are the first-aid men there?'

'Yes, but its t'miner, you see. He dunt want anyone else treating him. That's why I'm calling – he only wants you.'

In other circumstances I would have felt flattered, but it actually made me feel more nervous. I'd had the same situation before. I'd travelled underground to treat a man, only for all the big, burly miners to stand back and wait to see what I'd do. It made me anxious because I was only human and sometimes they expected me to perform miracles. In reality, all I could do was put my nursing training into practice. I donned my overalls, pit boots and hard hat, and ran to collect my metal checks, lamp, battery pack and self-rescuer. All kitted up, I hopped inside the empty cage as the banksman pulled down the chain-mail shutter, sealing me in.

'Ay up, Sister. You got another one?' he asked as he slammed closed the outer metal door.

''Fraid so,' I cried as the cage lowered and I descended into the darkened pit shaft.

As soon as I reached the pit bottom, I was greeted by one of the workmen, who took me to the miner, a lad called Simon. By the time I arrived, one of the first aiders had already managed to free him from the chock. Somehow, he'd sliced the top of his finger off, right down to the first knuckle on his index finger.

'It's all right, everybody. Sister's here,' a man called out in the darkness.

I felt the responsibility weigh heavily on my shoulders.

'Now then, love. What have you done?' I asked as I kneeled down next to Simon. I began to examine the stump of his finger.

'I'm not sure, Sister. I got it caught, up there,' he said, gesturing with his other hand. 'It all happened so fast … it's bloody killing me. Why, is it bad?'

Although he was a big, tough miner, I realised that Simon was in a lot of pain.

'Listen, love. I'm going to put this mask on your face. It'll release something called Entonox, which will help with the pain.'

He nodded gratefully as I unpacked the equipment and placed it by the side of him.

'Has your wife had any children?' I asked, trying to take Simon's mind off his nasty injury.

He seemed a little baffled but nodded. I stretched a piece of elastic around the back of his head and anchored the mask over both his nose and mouth.

'Well, she's probably had something like this because it's also called gas and air,' I said.

Simon tried to smile but I knew I'd have to act fast. I grabbed a clean dressing, wrapped it around the stump and held it tight inside my hand, applying pressure to the wound. When someone suffers a traumatic amputation the capillaries tend to shut down, so, although you get some blood and fluid loss, it's not as much as you'd expect. However, I knew the real risk was that the patient could go into shock, so I watched Simon like a hawk, checking all his vital signs. As the Entonox took hold and relieved his pain, I examined his half finger. Some blood had oozed through the dressing and there was a bit on my overalls, but it wasn't anything I couldn't handle. His finger had been found and loaded into a tub of ice, but it had macerated and so was useless to him. Of course, I'd completely forgotten my safety talk about vinyl gloves throughout all of this. The first aiders loaded him onto a stretcher, and I walked alongside, clutching his hand, as we brought Simon back up to the pit top.

'I'll be all right from here,' he insisted, climbing off the stretcher onto his feet. 'I'll walk t'rest of way to t'ambulance.'

The pit ambulance was waiting, so Simon and I climbed in and we made our way to hospital. By the time we arrived I was soaked in his blood because it had seeped out through my ungloved fingers and dripped down into my lap. But the staff in A&E knew me well, so we were attended to almost immediately by a staff nurse.

'Could you both take a seat there,' she said, directing us over towards a bed. She pulled the drapes around us for privacy, and knelt down to take a better look at the wound. I was still clutching Simon's hand because I was frightened to let go until she'd brought a clean dressing to put over it.

'Can I have a look?' she asked.

I uncurled my fingers just enough to let her see what he'd done. She peered at the open wound before straightening up again.

'Have you got the other bit?' she asked, pointing to the tip of her own finger.

Unlike the other sister, who I'd once had words with, this nurse was both polite and extremely efficient.

'No, because by the time I reached him it was all mangled up. They'd placed it in ice but it'd macerated. He'd managed to free himself from the machine, so I gave him some Entonox.'

'I see,' she said, nodding her head. 'Right, I'll just be a minute. I'll just nip and get some gloves and a clean dressing for you.' With that, she disappeared off behind the curtains.

Simon turned towards me with a puzzled look on his face.

'What does she want gloves for?' he asked, a hint of offence apparent in his voice.

'Well, because that's what they do now – they all wear gloves.'

But the longer we sat there, the more I realised just how much the nurse had offended him.

'Look,' I said, trying to explain. 'You know that film we did about cross-infection with blood and other bodily fluids?'

Simon nodded.

'Well, this is to do with AIDS, and other things such as hepatitis.'

Simon listened and glanced down at my hand wrapped around his – the blood had covered us both.

'But you haven't got gloves on, Sister.'

I'd been caught bang to rights.

'Well, no, that's true, Simon,' I said, trying to search for the right words. 'That's because I know you. But they see hundreds of patients here, so they don't know you or your background like I do.'

He peered up at the cubicle curtain still drawn around the hospital bed.

'Well, can't you tell her that then, Sister? The bloody funny bugger!'

I tried not to laugh.

'Of course I will, but she has to wear them, Simon. It's her job; otherwise she'd get into trouble.'

He sighed and looked down at his hand where the missing digit had been. 'Okay. It's all right, I suppose, if you say so, Sister.'

Simon shrugged his shoulders as though he didn't care, but I could tell that he did. Although he wasn't entirely happy, he allowed the gloved-up nurse to treat him. He understood that she had a job to do. She expertly dressed and wrapped a bandage around his wound, and he was given an appointment to return to have a skin graft. Other than that, there was very little else anyone could do.

On my way back, I called in at the garage where Simon's wife worked to tell her what had happened.

'Oh,' she replied.

'He asked if you'd fetch him some fags in later,' I told her, relaying his message. But she seemed less than impressed by her husband's request.

'I will, but he'll have to wait until the end of my shift.'

I tried not to laugh. Simon might have lost a finger, but his wife had been furious that he'd bothered her at work to ask for a smoke!

The whole incident reminded me just how complex these men could be. They were tough on the outside, but scratch just below the surface and they were deeply sensitive souls. I'd seen it when their colleagues had been injured. The miners would try their best to disguise their fear, but it was always there. Some of the men treated me like God and thought I could perform miracles. Sadly, I couldn't.

This hit home a few months later, when my father was ill. I visited Dad every weekend, but his health had begun to deteriorate. He had started with a nasty cough that refused to go away. His GP insisted that it was nothing to worry about, but I suspected otherwise. Dad visited the doctor time and time again, but he refused to do tests. Frustrated at the lack of answers, I called a family meeting and suggested we all donate money to pay for him to see a specialist. Dad's cough had worsened, and he was struggling to swallow. The specialist carried out a bronchoscopy, using a device that looked inside his oesophagus and lungs. A subsequent biopsy indicated our worst fear – it was lung cancer. He was referred for radiotherapy treatment at Sheffield's Weston Park Hospital but, tragically, the cancer was already advanced. He was admitted to hospital as his condition worsened, but he hated anyone fussing over him. The day before he died, I realised the end was near, but, Dad being Dad, he was more concerned about me than himself.

'There's no need for you to hang around here, love. Get yourself off home,' he said.

I left, but as soon as I stepped out of his room I fell to pieces in the hospital corridor. A male staff nurse saw me and came running over. He guided me into a nearby office and told me to take a seat.

'You do realise the situation, don't you?' he asked gently.

I loved my work as a nurse, but in some situations it carried mixed blessings because I understood when the situation was desperate.

'Yes,' I told him. But then I broke down, until soon I was unable to speak.

The nurse looked at me. He turned and walked over to a cupboard, where he pulled out a bottle of whisky. He put a small tumbler on the table in front of me and poured out a measure.

'Here,' he said, pressing the glass in my hands. 'Have this. It'll help you.'

I was in such a state that I did as he said and knocked it back in one. It numbed both my throat and my mind, which was probably just what I'd needed. The nurse explained that there was very little else I could do other than go home and rest. The staff at Weston Park Hospital were absolutely wonderful and did everything they could to make my father as comfortable as possible. Sadly, a few hours later he slipped into a coma and never regained consciousness. At 6 o'clock the following morning the nurse telephoned to say he had died.

Peter phoned Ann and Tony, and broke the awful news. From that moment on, Peter took charge and organised the funeral. I felt grateful because I'd been left devastated by my father's death. He'd not only been a fantastic dad, he'd also been my role model and work colleague, who'd helped guide me through life and my career as a pit nurse. He'd been my world, and his death left a gaping hole in my life. Now I'd lost both my mum and dad, and I didn't know how much more I could take.

In his typically unselfish fashion, my father had been more concerned with the care of his wife Polly. Tragically, Polly had developed Alzheimer's disease and, up until his illness, Dad had been her main carer. When his health had started to fail he'd asked us to sort something out so that he could die in the knowledge that Polly would be well cared for.

After my father passed away, a family meeting was called. Only Tony didn't attend. Of course, the family looked to me to provide care. I think it was because I had a spare bedroom and no children living at home, but I also had a full-time job and a sick husband to look after. I knew that Polly would require round-the-clock nursing, so I told them she needed to be in a specialist care home. Tony backed me but, although I was speaking from years of nursing experience, Ann fell out with me. It was a thoroughly horrible situation because I'd lost Mum, then Dad, and now my sister. But I was also very stubborn and I refused to back down, so I battled on. Ten years later, on New

Year's Eve, the telephone rang at home. I picked it up to hear Ann's voice on the other end of the line.

'Whatever's happened, we're still sisters,' she began. A lump formed at the back of my throat and threatened to choke me because I realised in that moment just how much I loved and had missed her.

Ann and I arranged to meet in a café in the centre of Doncaster. We ordered two pots of tea and talked long into the afternoon. We decided that, although we'd lost our parents, we didn't want to lose each other, so, after a 10-year silence the rift had finally healed.

Only two years after Dad died, something else happened that I could neither help nor control. It was early 1984, and there'd been a general sense of discord among the men for a long time. Rumours had been circulating about wages, pit closures and possible strikes. The usual upbeat mood in the pit yard had changed. Men spoke in hushed voices about changes afoot, which was very unsettling. I'd always refused to get involved in union matters. If there was an argument or incident, I'd ask the union representative to step outside so that he could discuss it with the men, because my medical centre wasn't a place for politics. I refused to side with either management or miners, because in my mind I was there to help them all, but soon something would happen to turn all our worlds upside down.

18

The Miners' Strike

Although I refused to get involved, I would have had to walk around with my eyes and ears closed not to pick up on the whispers of strike action at Hatfield. Despite a new government, two million manufacturing jobs had been lost over three years. Many blamed Margaret Thatcher. There'd almost been a pit strike in 1981, but it had been narrowly avoided. However, on 5 March 1984, following a government announcement that it intended to shut 20 coal mines, with the loss of 20,000 jobs, local strikes began at Cortonwood Colliery and other Yorkshire pits. Arthur Scargill, President of the National Union of Mineworkers (NUM), told the men that the government's long-term plan was actually to close 70 pits, and he called a national strike on 12 March 1984. The miners, fearing their livelihood was about to be pulled from under their feet, staged a mass walkout across the country, including all the pits in South Yorkshire.

Early one morning, Eddie, a COSA member (Colliery Officials and Staff Association), was waiting to see me.

'Hullo, Sister,' Eddie said as soon as I stepped inside the door.

'Hi,' I replied, a little startled. It was early and I wasn't expecting anyone to be there. 'Is everything okay?' I asked, looking at him. 'Are you well?'

Eddie smiled and nodded. 'Yeah, I'm quite okay, thanks, Sister. It's not that. I'm here because I wondered how you were going to get into work tomorrow.'

I looked at him, a little bemused. No one had thought to ask me that question in years, not since my early days at Hatfield when the van would come to collect me.

'Oh, I'll probably cycle in,' I said, pointing towards my bike, which was chained to the barrier outside.

'Er, I don't think that's wise.'

'Why ever not?'

'Because tomorrow everyone's going to be out – they won't be in work.'

'What do you mean?' I said, turning back to face him as I undid the buttons of my overcoat.

'It's t'men, you see. They're going on strike.'

'Strike?'

'Yes, so that's why I was wondering how you're gonna get in.'

I pushed a hand through my hair and tried to think. There'd been talk of it for ages – threats of a walk-out – but I'd dismissed it. Now it seemed I'd been wrong to.

'All of them?' I asked.

Eddie nodded. 'So, how are you going to get in, then? Tomorrow, I mean?'

I thought of my options. I could drive but my car had been on the blink. Peter could run me in but I didn't want to drag him out of bed early. If a bike was out of the question then I only had one other choice.

'The bus,' I replied. 'I'll catch the bus.'

Eddie shook his head.

'Nah, I don't think that'd be a good idea either,' he said. 'Things could get a bit … difficult, tomorrow. Listen, why don't I bring you in? I'll pick you up about 6 a.m.?'

'Okay,' I agreed, although little did I know what would happen.

The following morning, Eddie pulled up in his car outside my bungalow, as he'd promised. I ran out and climbed inside the passenger seat. I had butterflies in my stomach. As the car neared the top of the pit lane, I gasped. There were what seemed to be a hundred or so men waiting, and they appeared to be stopping vehicles from going in to the pit.

'Blimey, you weren't joking, were you?' I said, turning to face Eddie before looking back at the hordes of men.

I recognised most of the faces because, over the years, I'd spoken to or treated each and every one of them. As we drew closer, a group of miners formed a semi-circle around us. Eddie wound down his window and the elder of the group stepped forward to greet him.

'Nah then, where tha think tha's going, Eddie?'

I'd never felt intimidated before, but for the first time in my life, sitting in that little car, I felt extremely vulnerable. Not that I thought any of the men would harm me. It was the sheer number that unnerved me.

'We're going in to work,' he told the miner. 'Me and t'sister,' he said, pointing at me.

A dozen pairs of eyes swivelled to look in my general direction through the car windscreen. As they did, I slid down in the passenger seat, held up a hand and waved weakly back at them. The miner in charge considered me before turning his attentions back to Eddie.

'Nah, you're not, because COSA are on strike too.'

'Since when?' Eddie asked.

'Since this morning – didn't yer know?'

Eddie shook his head.

'Ah well, that changes things then,' Eddie said to the men. He shifted uneasily in his seat and turned towards me.

'You'll have to get out here, then, Sister,' he said, 'because I can't cross t'picket line.'

'You're joking me!' I shrieked.

I glanced out of the car window. There was a huge group of men crowded along the top of the pit lane. I knew I'd not only have to walk through them, but at least another hundred yards to reach the colliery yard. It was a dark and bitterly cold morning. Although the group had congregated at the top of the lane in a human bottleneck, there were others milling around in the shadows.

But Eddie had stopped listening.

'Right, I'll back up and park over there,' he said, putting the gear stick into reverse.

'But what about me?' I asked.

'Sorry, Sister, but if we're out, we're out. If you want to go in, then go,' he said.

I sighed as I reluctantly climbed out of Eddie's car and slammed the door. While I never allowed myself to get caught up with politics, a huge part of me agreed with their reasons for the strike. The miners deserved better. They worked long hours, often in dangerous conditions, so they deserved better wages, not pit closures. However, although I didn't really understand all the reasons behind it, I thought the timing was a little odd. With spring just around the corner and summer fast approaching, people were already stacked up with coal, so there wouldn't be as much demand. When it came to it, it didn't matter what I thought because I was employed by the management and therefore forbidden to go on strike. If I had stood alongside my men, I would have lost my job – it was as pure and simple as that. Despite my reluctance on the other side of the fence, I reasoned that as long as I was on site, if anyone was injured either inside or outside the gates, then I'd be on hand to treat them.

'Right, it looks as though I'm walking the rest of the way then,' I huffed as I watched Eddie reverse his car out of the lane.

I smoothed down the hem of my coat, held my head high and began to walk down the darkened path towards the pit gates. Although I didn't show it, inside I was scared stiff. Despite my position and the fact that I was heading into work, the miners at the top of the lane were courteous and let me pass without comment. I'd just reached halfway down when I heard voices – the sound of miners walking towards me in the darkness. Fear rose in the back of my throat. At first I wondered what they were doing coming out of the pit instead of standing at the top of the lane, and then it dawned on me: these were men who'd gone in for the early shift. But now they'd marched out, so that they could join the rest of their colleagues. It didn't matter what the circumstances were, the miners were a united family and their loyalty knew no bounds.

'Ay up, who's this, then?' a voice whispered in the darkness. 'Someone's walking in t'wrong direction.'

I gulped again. Deep down I was frightened because I didn't know how the men would react to the fact that I'd crossed the picket line. Although they knew I'd had very little choice, some felt so passionate and angry about the strike that I was worried I'd set myself up as a target. Holding my head high, I focused on the pit as I tried to walk through the group of men.

'Well, what have we got here, then?' a miner said. He stood in front of me as the others crowded behind him.

My heart plummeted like a stone.

Was I in danger?

But I should have known – these were my men, men whose wounds I had tended, men whose marital problems I'd helped fix, men who had nothing but the utmost respect for me. Men who were also complete and utter wind-up merchants.

'Shut your cakehole, John,' another voice called out. 'It's Sister Hart.'

'Yeah, you're all right,' another man said, laughing and jostling John out of the way. 'It's only Sister. I don't reckon she'll give us much trouble, eh, lads?'

The men began to laugh and parted in the middle to let me through.

'You daft 'aperth,' I smirked, pushing John out of the way.

In many ways the first day of the strike felt the worst. Normally, the colliery yard would be a bustling hive of activity, alive with laughter, jokes and friendly banter. The miners had been the beating heart of it all, but now they'd gone, and it all felt as broken and empty as a ghost town. I didn't realise it then, but that moment, standing alone in the empty yard, was a premonition of what was to come. Unsure what to do, I wandered over towards the control room. Inside, it was packed with men who were all members of the British Association of Colliery Management (BACM). There'd always been a few other women on site, namely the secretary and canteen ladies, but most were members of COSA, and so they were on strike. For the first time, I was the only woman, and I'd never felt so alone.

Ken Deeming was seated, but when I entered the room he stood up to address us all.

'Right, I want everyone to stay in here because we're expecting trouble,' he said. Eyes widened as we absorbed the news that we were under threat of an attack.

'Is it safe? I mean, are we going to be okay?' someone asked from the back of the room.

Mr Deeming looked over at him. 'Yes, but I've taken the precaution of calling the police. They're on their way.'

For the next hour or so, we sat there, feeling anxious, waiting for trouble. When it didn't happen, I wondered if Mr Deeming's information had been wrong. But at around 12.30 p.m. someone was looking through the window of the control room when they spotted something.

'Hold on to your horses, everyone. Here they come!' he cried.

I stood up and craned my neck. I saw what looked like a hundred men coming over the pit top, heading straight towards us. They were angry, their voices loud, shouting and chanting abuse at the managers inside the control room. A few rocks and bricks were thrown, and I automatically flinched and ducked down to protect myself. I heard the missiles thud as they smashed loudly against the outside wall. A few hit the windowpanes, showering the floor with glass, but thankfully they had metal bars against them, so no one was injured. Moments later, the local police arrived. They managed to control the crowd, and within half an hour the men had backed off. The anger simmered down and peace was restored outside, but fear remained inside the room. We stayed that way for the rest of the day.

Finally, Mr Deeming stood up to speak.

'Nobody is allowed to leave the pit buildings,' he said. 'No one must walk about on the pit top. It's for your own safety. We will all stay in the control room. We must stay together.'

His words would have sounded a little melodramatic before the stone-throwing incident, but now they rang true. Suddenly, it wasn't safe, not any more. By mid-afternoon, trapped and unable to leave the colliery, we were absolutely starving. A call was made, and an hour or so later an NCB van arrived from Doncaster with a few plates of cheese sandwiches. The sandwiches had certainly seen better days.

'Is this all they've got?' I asked, picking up a slice of stale white bread between my fingers.

The van driver shrugged as though we were lucky to get them. But the sandwiches were so bad that everyone had lost their appetite. Then I remembered something – a small Breville toaster I had stashed away in a cupboard in the medical centre. One of the undermanagers escorted me as we ran the gauntlet to go and look for it. Luckily, we weren't targeted. With a bit of heat, the curled-up sandwiches were soon transformed into heavenly cheese toasties – it'd been simple but effective, making the unpalatable palatable.

'Hmmm, these are gorgeous,' one of the men murmured, licking his lips and the tips of his fingers.

'Hmmm, lovely,' another agreed.

It was hardly cordon bleu, but it filled a hole in our stomachs.

The rest of the day passed without further incident, but the afternoon dragged by. I'd been due to leave the pit early, around 4 p.m., but the police advised us to stay a little longer, so I picked up the phone and called Peter at home.

'I don't know what time I'm going to get home because we're trapped at the pit,' I said.

'Do you want me to come down and pick you up?' he offered.

'No, that's the last thing I want. You should see it here. The top of the pit lane is like a madhouse – it's bedlam. You keep away. Promise me that you won't come down.'

'Okay, I promise. And Joan …'

'Yes.'

'Promise me you'll not do anything daft.'

'I won't.'

'Okay, good. But how will you get home?'

'Don't you worry about me. I'll sort something.'

And I did. In the end, one of the managers gave me a lift home at around 6 p.m. As we drove out I glanced back at the top of the pit lane as it disappeared off into the distance. The men were still at least a hundred strong, and for the first time in my life I'd felt intimidated by their presence. We'd already discussed how we'd get into work the following day, and a plan had been formed. Although it all seemed very cloak and dagger, I knew it was necessary because now everything had changed. Things would never be the same again.

19

Bird Woman

It was early, around 4.15 a.m., and I was waiting at the agreed meeting point, a supermarket car park. I saw someone approach in the dark, and I squinted my eyes to see – it was Ken Deeming.

'Morning, Sister Hart. You'll be travelling with me this morning,' he said, opening up the passenger door of his car. Mr Deeming already had two undermanagers in the back seat, so I slid into the passenger seat beside him. If truth be told, I was a little startled by the stealthy nature of our travel arrangements, but soon there were around 20 people crammed into six cars, with Mr Deeming's car leading the convoy, and we left the remaining vehicles in the car park.

Without warning, Mr Deeming pulled out of the supermarket car park and turned right, away from the pit.

'Er, where are we going?' I asked.

'The public telephone box. It's just up here,' he said, pointing ahead towards a small parade of shops on the left-hand side. 'I have to telephone the police stationed at the pit to ask which route we need to take this morning.'

Half a mile down the road, he parked the car.

'Is all this really necessary?' I asked as he undid his seat-belt and climbed out.

'Absolutely!' he replied. 'Tomorrow we'll take a different route, and the day after that, because you can't be too careful!'

Although it all seemed a little dramatic, Mr Deeming was right. Afterwards, the route was changed every single day to ensure that we wouldn't be ambushed on our way into work. I'd hoped there would be safety in numbers, and at first there was, as we were led in by police escort, which would meet us on the way. But after a few days, things began to change and the striking miners became more hostile towards us. I wondered why the pit manager always asked me to travel with him in the first car, up front, until Peter pointed out something obvious.

'As long as you're sitting next to him, he knows the men won't stone his car. The miners would never hurt you, Joan.'

Peter was right, although the amnesty only lasted for so long. At first, the miners would dip down to see who was inside the car. Upon spying me, they'd stand back and leave us alone. I knew they respected me, but the pit manager was a different matter. A few days later, the miners still didn't touch the car, but they started to spit at it. It was upsetting to be on the receiving end of their anger, even though I knew it wasn't directed at me.

On the second day of the strike a picket line had formed. A hut had been erected and a fire lit, and suddenly it seemed as though this wasn't something that would go away overnight. The damage had already been done. The miners knew that coal had been stockpiled in the yard long before the strike, almost as though management had pre-empted the whole situation. The miners despised them for it and for forcing their hand. Shortly afterwards, the cars following behind us were pelted with stones. A few vehicles had their windscreens smashed as we made our way down from the top of the pit lane into the colliery yard, but Mr Deeming's car had only been spat at. The damage hadn't been carried out by our men, or anyone I recognised; I suspected that it was carried out by organised pickets who had come to Hatfield to try to stoke up trouble. Once we reached the yard, we were given designated jobs. It was only 4.45 a.m., but I was told to cook bacon and eggs for all the managers on site.

'It's a bit early,' I commented.

'Doesn't matter. The men have had a tough time just getting here, and they can't work on empty stomachs.'

I shook my head.

What about those poor souls freezing to death on the picket line, fighting for their livelihoods? I wondered, although I never said it out loud.

A few times, when we were short staffed, I was told to watch the dials in the control room, which measured levels of gas and air pressure in the pit below. To be honest, I didn't understand what half of them did because it was a highly specialised job and one I shouldn't even have been doing. If any of the needles went into the red, I had to call one of the surveyors as soon as possible. Half the time, I didn't know what I was supposed to be looking for, but I watched those dials as though my life depended upon it. One day, one of the needles blinked over into the red. In a panic and fearing a nuclear-type explosion, I grabbed the phone and dialled the number I'd been given.

'It's the dials,' I gasped. 'One's flickering over into the red.'

'Okay, I'll be right over,' the voice on the other end of the line replied.

Minutes later, one of the lads from the Safety Department wandered over. He tinkered with something until the needle shot back over into the green.

'You shouldn't have any more problems from now on, but if yer do, then just gie us a call,' he said.

It was hardly the reassurance I'd been hoping for, but at least I knew help was on hand should I need it.

My other duties included keeping the place clean and tidy, and the unenviable task of shovelling coal from the compound into a wheelbarrow so it could be tipped and stored closer to the offices. This was so management could keep a watchful eye on it and prevent it from being stolen. I also mopped out the men's showers, even though they'd hardly been used since the beginning of the strike, and I tended to the garden.

One day, I was in the medical office when I spotted a police car park up outside the window. The back door of the car opened and I watched as two officers dragged out an 18-year-old miner who had been at the pit since he was a cadet. His name was Nigel.

At the start of the strike, the relationship between the miners and local bobbies had been cordial. Some had shared sandwiches and cigarettes, baked potatoes over the barrel fire and even played football together. But after a few days, the powers that be realised this and took the local police off. I think they knew it wouldn't be good in the long term to have men policing miners who lived in the same community. Instead, other officers were drafted in from further afield, namely Metropolitan Police officers.

Stories had been rife along picket lines of Met police waving £10 notes in front of striking miners, goading them about how much overtime money they were earning. I'd heard tales of Met officers being actively aggressive and argumentative in a bid to stoke up trouble, confident that they had the manpower, equipment and the full backing of the courts behind them.

Up until now there had been minor scuffles and skirmishes, but nothing serious, until the Met police arrived. In June, at a place called Orgreave in Sheffield, striking miners were beaten down by batons as they tried to escape police on horseback. It was a battlefield. Hundreds were arrested and thrown in cells, with many facing the prospect of trials based on trumped-up evidence. As a result, the striking miners neither liked nor trusted Met police officers. So, when I spotted Nigel being dragged from a police car, my senses were on full alert.

'Are you the sister here?' the first officer asked, pulling Nigel roughly behind him.

'I am,' I replied.

'Right, well, I need you to look at this man for us before we take him in. He's sustained a cut to the back of his head.'

I looked at Nigel. His head was dripping profusely with blood and he looked terrified.

'Whatever's happened, love?' I asked, walking over towards him. I knew Nigel well. He'd worked at the pit for the past two years, and I knew he was a good lad and not the sort who'd get into trouble.

'He needs attending to,' the second officer barked, breaking my thoughts.

I led the three of them into the adjoining treatment room; as I did, I realised that Nigel had been handcuffed.

'Well, you can take them off for a start!' I said, pointing at the handcuffs.

'No chance. He's a prisoner.'

I rolled my eyes as though I had neither the time nor the patience for either of them.

'Yes, he's a prisoner outside,' I said, 'but this is a medical centre, so you will take those handcuffs off now.'

'But he's under arrest,' the second officer protested. 'You don't understand – he's our prisoner.'

'Well, right now, in here,' I said, pointing at the floor, 'he is my patient. And if you want me to treat him then I'll need those handcuffs off.'

We stood there for a moment, caught in a stalemate. I knew that they needed me to treat him before they could proceed, so I had the upper hand. More than that, I didn't agree with the way they were treating the poor lad, as though he was an animal.

'Listen, you can say what you like,' I said, standing my ground, 'but when you're in my medical centre you abide by my rules. I don't care who you are or where you've come from. That lad needs treatment, but I'll not treat him trussed up like that.'

Realising they'd met their match, the officers' resolve softened. Reluctantly, the first officer stepped forward and unfastened the metal cuffs on Nigel's wrists.

'Thank you,' I sighed as he stepped back to let me take a proper look. I half expected them to leave, but they remained standing there in the doorway.

I felt a little on edge. I wanted them out of the treatment room so I could speak to Nigel in private and ask him what had happened. But I knew better than to push my luck, because these were Met police officers. I knew Nigel was a good lad from a nice family, so I was baffled as to what he'd done to warrant a baton to the back of his head.

'Whatever's happened?' I whispered, pulling open a drawer to look for saline solution to clean his wound with.

The gash to the back of his head was nasty. It was deep and approximately 2 inches long, so I knew it was no ordinary injury. Head injuries bleed excessively, and Nigel had been hit so hard that his scalp was oozing blood like a tap. Some had dried and matted into a mass in his thick brown hair, and the rest was dripping, soaking his neck and shoulders. I took out some gauze, wet it with saline solution and tried to clean it up. Nigel flinched and winced beneath my touch as he began to explain what had happened.

'I was just nipping t'shops for a paper when I saw all these people running past me,' he said, his voice a little shaken. 'Next thing I knew, I felt a sharp crack to back of me head and I went down like a sack of spuds. That's when I saw 'em, police standing over me. I wasn't anywhere near t'pit but they brought me 'ere to see you. They've told me I'm under arrest, although I haven't done owt wrong. I was bloody scared stiff, Sister,' he admitted as his hands trembled against his lap.

I felt a fury boil up inside me. Nigel's dad worked at the pit and I wondered if he knew what had happened to his son. I stopped what I was doing and held the wad of gauze aloft in my hand. I looked at Nigel and ignored the officers standing directly behind me.

'Have you been in touch with your dad?' I asked loudly.

Nigel shook his head.

'No, I've not had time,' he replied, his voice cracking with nerves. It was clear that the poor lad was completely traumatised.

'Right, you phone your dad now,' I said, handing him the telephone receiver.

'No, he can't do that,' the first officer said. Nigel glanced over at him warily, but I was adamant and refused to be intimidated by the two bully boys.

'Look,' I said, turning to the policeman. 'It's my medical centre and he'll do what I say.'

But they refused point blank, so I made the call myself.

'It's Sister Hart,' I said as their eyes bored into me. 'I've got your Nigel here. He's been arrested. He has a nasty cut to the back of his head, so I'm going to tell the officers to take him straight to the hospital. Could you meet him there and make sure he's seen instead of being taken straight to the police station?'

You could've heard a pin drop as I put down the phone. I disposed of the gauze and packed away the saline solution. I had decided Nigel's head wound – which had quite clearly been caused by the blow of a police truncheon – was far too deep for me to treat.

'There's nothing I can do with this other than dress it,' I informed them. 'It's a deep cut so it'll need several stitches. He'll have to go to Doncaster Royal Infirmary because he needs immediate medical treatment.'

I could see the police officers were furious as they snapped the cuffs back on, but now they had no other choice than to take poor Nigel straight to hospital.

At the beginning of the strike the miners had been united, but as the months passed a few returned to work. I had no choice, but it didn't stop me empathising with the miners or indeed my own MRAs, Frank, Bill and Andy, who were on the picket line.

Although I'd asked him not to get involved, Peter would sit at the top of the pit lane along with the striking miners. He'd bring cigarettes and chat with them long into the afternoon. In many ways, I was caught up in a surreal situation because I could see the strike from both sides. However, no one blamed me – not like they did the management. It was as though, through my job as a nurse, the men understood that I had no choice but I would always be there for them.

One of my other jobs during the strike was to look after the pit canaries. We only had a handful at Hatfield, four in total, but each of them had its own cage. I knew the birds ate chickweed, but supplies had started to run low, so, one day, with very little else to do, I decided to take some bags and go out to collect some. With the sacks in my hands, I strolled past two policemen, who enquired where I was going.

'I'm going to pick chickweed for the canaries,' I explained. 'I thought I'd get a few sackfuls while it's quiet.'

'Where do you get it from?' one asked.

'Around the back, by the coal tips,' I said, pointing towards the rear of the building.

'Oh no, we can't let you go around there,' the officer insisted, rolling backwards and forwards on the balls of his feet, with his hands clasped behind his back.

'Why ever not?'

'Because there's no CCTV around there – it's out of range.'

'But I'm only going to get a bit of bird food; otherwise the poor things will starve to death.'

'Well, you can go,' he said, shaking his head to make it clear he didn't approve. 'But you'll have no protection.'

'Protection? Against what?'

'The striking miners.'

'Don't be daft! I'll be fine. They wouldn't hurt me; besides, I doubt I'll bump into any around there.'

'Well, you never know.'

'Oh, flaming heck,' I said, exasperated at how ridiculous the conversation had become. 'I'll only be a minute and then I'll be back. It won't take me long – we've only got four birds!'

The officers looked at one another and then at me. The first one, having considered my request, made a suggestion.

'Okay,' he said, looking at his wristwatch. 'You've got 30 minutes, but if you're not back within that time then we'll come looking for you.'

Realising it was the only way they were going to let me go, I agreed to their terms.

'I'll be back in half an hour, I promise.'

With that, I disappeared off towards the back of the coal tips. It was cold but I was dressed in my overalls, pit boots and an old donkey jacket, which I'd acquired *en route*. I wandered around the back of the outbuildings, trying to remember where the men usually picked the chickweed. I was lost in my thoughts when I turned a corner to be greeted by six men collecting waste coal from a heap. I recognised each and every one of them. I knew what they were doing was technically classed as theft, but with the cold winter months approaching they had little option if they wanted to keep their families warm.

'Ay up, look who we've got here, then,' one of the lads called as the others stopped what they were doing and looked up.

'Hello, lads,' I smiled. I knew I wasn't in any danger, but I was technically at work so I was uncertain what their reaction towards me would be.

'Bloody 'ell,' said the elder of the men, straightening up. 'It's Sister Hart. What are you doing here?'

'Never mind that,' another called. 'Look at them boots, and that jacket. I'll tell yer what, lads – you have t'boots, while I grab t'coat, eh?'

I looked over at the men. Their hands had been blackened from digging deeper for better coal at the bottom of the heap. They'd been desperate to steal it, but I also knew by the tone of their voices that they were also winding me up.

'Aww, shut up, you daft 'aperth,' I said, grinning.

We all laughed in the midst of this most unexpected situation.

'So, whatcha doing 'ere, then, Sister?' one asked.

'I'm looking for chickweed.'

The men looked baffled.

'For the canaries,' I offered.

'Oh, right you are. And 'ave you found any?' the older man asked.

'No, not yet. But I've only got half an hour before the police come looking for me, so you'd better watch yourselves out here, just in case.'

The men seemed worried. They glanced above and beyond me into the distance, but the coast was still clear.

'Don't worry, I've only just started looking,' I said, glancing down at my watch, 'but I'd better get a move on.'

'Is it for t'pit canaries? Our canaries?' one of the lads asked.

I nodded.

'Well, in that case, why didn't you say so? Come on, I know a good spot over here for chickweed.'

I followed him with the sacks in my hands, and then something remarkable happened. All the men began to follow us. Together, we picked enough chickweed to fill all four sacks and feed the canaries not only through the winter, but well beyond.

'Thanks, lads,' I said, stuffing the last bit in. 'You've been a great help.'

'You will look after 'em, the canaries, won't you, Sister?'

'Of course I will. Don't worry,' I insisted, 'they're in safe hands.'

I turned to leave, but one of the men put his hand on my shoulder to stop me.

'And what about us – I mean, us picking coal … will tha tell?'

'Me?' I replied, shaking my head. 'I didn't see a thing.'

I never said a word about the men or the missing coal. As far as I was concerned, it was none of my business. I wasn't there to judge or hand out punishment, I was there to look after and protect. I also kept a close eye on our feathered friends. With winter approaching, I insisted that their cages be moved from the cold garage into the heated control room. I continued to feed them and clean their cages out, until early one morning I noticed that one of the birds appeared to be lame. It was standing awkwardly, trying to grip its perch, but I could see that its right claw looked both sore and swollen. I knocked on the pit manager's door.

'I need to take one of the canaries to the vet because it's lame,' I said.

'Canary?' Mr Deeming replied, putting down his pen.

'Yes, I think it's infected and, if I don't do something about it, it'll die, and we'll be accused of murder or something!' I said, recalling my promise to the miners.

It all sounded a bit melodramatic, but I knew just how much the men loved those little birds, and if I were to let one get sick and die on my watch then they wouldn't be happy.

'Okay,' he said, rising to his feet. 'I'll come and have a look.'

Together, we watched as the tiny bird struggled to stay on two feet. Mr Deeming shook his head and said, 'Take him to the vet, Sister Hart.'

The striking miners knew our regular comings and goings in and out of the pit, but if a vehicle left at a different time it immediately raised suspicion. With this in mind, I popped in to see the police chief, who ran the control office in a boardroom situated next door to Mr Deeming.

'Can I have a word?' I asked, tapping lightly on the half-opened door.

The officer called me in.

'I need to take the canary to the vet but I'm not sure what to do,' I began to explain.

'If you drive a vehicle out of the yard then you'll need a police escort,' he decided.

I thought as much, although I didn't like to think badly of the men. I knew the picket line was being manned by strangers and other miners from outside the area. I wasn't sure how they'd react to me leaving the pit in the middle of the day. It was eventually decided that I'd carry the sick canary in its cage on my lap, in the passenger seat of the pit ambulance with a police escort.

An undermanager stepped forward, offering to drive the ambulance.

We made our way up the pit lane slowly towards the picket line, where I spotted the men in the distance, half-way down the lane. Half a dozen clambered to their feet and strained their necks to see what was happening. As soon as they spotted me, the canary and the police escort, they fell about laughing. Their laughter followed us all the way up the lane and along the main road as we headed towards the vet in the centre of Doncaster. The police escort peeled away once we reached the outskirts of the village. After a brief examination, the vet concluded that the canary did indeed have a foot infection and duly prescribed some antibiotics tablets, which I was told to dissolve in the bird's water at regular intervals. After reuniting him with his mates back in the control room, those four little birds made enough racket to wake the living dead. It wasn't long before the managers tired of their constant chirping and song.

'Can't you shut them bloody birds up, Sister? They're doing my head in!'

I refused because I knew that, as long as they were singing, they were happy. Whenever I nipped out, the men would sneakily cover them up with a bit of cloth, but I'd remove it as soon as I returned.

As for the lame canary, he made a remarkable recovery. He decided that he didn't care much for the odd-tasting water, but he must have had some understanding of his situation because he decided to stick his gammy leg in it. Remarkably, it worked. Within weeks his foot hadn't just healed, but he was back standing on his perch, chirping louder than ever, driving the management insane.

20

Noel

The strike dragged on. Most of the men had thought it'd be sorted within a fortnight, only it wasn't. Instead, the weather had turned bitterly cold as the men struggled not only to feed their families – many relying on soup kitchens set up specially by the miners' wives – but also faced the prospect of freezing to death in their own homes. I hated to think of the hardship they faced, but there were just so many that it was difficult to know what I could do to help them all. I was thinking about it one day when Peter came rushing through to the kitchen.

'Quick, Joan,' he gasped. 'Someone's just tried to blow up Margaret Thatcher!'

I ran through to the front room to watch the news on TV. A bomb had been detonated at the Grand Hotel in Brighton, narrowly missing the Prime Minister. Her cabinet had been staying with her in the hotel for the Conservative Party conference. Many had been seriously injured, including Norman Tebbit, who suffered multiple injuries. But his wife, Margaret, had been paralysed after being trapped by falling masonry. The IRA later claimed responsibility, saying Thatcher had been the target, and although she escaped injury five others were killed and a further 31 injured. The news shocked the nation, and for a moment the media spotlight was taken away from the striking miners. I was shocked that someone could do that to another human being, although, predictably, many of the miners weren't quite so empathetic.

'Pity she didn't go with the bomb when it exploded,' one remarked.

'Yeah, it's a shame they missed,' said another.

While I understood the men's frustration, I was shocked at just how deeply their hatred of her ran. Even though there had been IRA bomb attacks during the 1970s, I never expected something like this. The Brighton bombing happened on 12 October, seven months to the day since the miners had first gone out on national strike. However, a month later, in November 1984, a taxi driver called David Wilkie was driving a strike-breaking miner to work in Merthyr Vale, accompanied by two police cars and a motorcycle outrider, when two striking miners dropped a concrete block from a footbridge, killing the taxi driver instantly. The two miners were eventually convicted of murder, but the charge was reduced to manslaughter on appeal.

The attack caused widespread outrage. Even though it was condemned by politicians and miners alike, public sympathy towards the men began to wane. I remember feeling horrified when I'd read about it in the paper. I deplored violence and, except for newspaper reports and a bit of stone-throwing, I saw very little of it at Hatfield.

When the bus transported working miners to the pit down the lane there'd be some bad language, name-calling and a few stones being thrown, but that was it. The workers were shouted at by the striking miners' wives, rather than the men themselves. They labelled them 'scabs', and the name stuck, even long after the strike ended. The workers would be transported in a single-decker bus, with the windows covered with metal cages for protection.

At the beginning of the strike, there were only two men who broke the picket line. They were rebels who saw it as a way of sticking two fingers up at those on strike. But by Christmas that number had increased to eight. The bus would park up outside the medical centre because the management wanted them all in one place. They'd then be deployed to various jobs around the pit top. There were a few cocky men, but the majority of them had returned to feed their families. One day, I noticed that one man seemed particularly upset after he'd been dropped off for his shift. I watched until he separated from the rest of the group and wandered over to have a word. This particular worker had travelled in from Moorends, a small village outside Thorne some 8 miles from Hatfield pit.

'It's like this, Sister,' he said after I asked him what was wrong. 'I can stand most things, but when people spit on my kids in the street, well,' he said, pausing for breath to try to keep his emotions in check, 'it just breaks me heart.'

I felt for him and his family but I could feel the desperation from both sides. It was difficult for them all. The striking miners argued that, by standing together, they were protecting every man's job and the future of the pit, so the men who broke the strike were ostracised. Some even had 'scab' spray painted in red across the front of their homes so everyone would know who and what they were. The striking men despised the working ones because they believed they were playing straight into the hands of the NCB and the government, and weakening their strike action.

Slowly but surely, family, friends and communities were torn apart by what was considered a 'betrayal'. The working miners had taken an almighty gamble in coming back to work. Once a man had made the decision, there was no going back because he and his family would be cast out. Those who'd chosen to cross the picket line worked in the lamp cabin, charging lamps, or did odd jobs on the pit top. Despite popular belief, working miners never went underground at Hatfield pit. Instead, management would go down to maintain the pit, otherwise it would have flooded. It remained open for when the striking miners returned to work – whenever that would be.

I felt as though we were living in dangerous and unpredictable times, and it reached a point where I almost dreaded turning on the TV because the news had become so bleak. The world changed again when the BBC's Michael Buerk reported from Ethiopia of famine on a biblical scale. The images of starving babies and children were beamed halfway across the world into our living rooms. It was both shocking and heartbreaking to think that people were still starving to death in the modern world. In Ethiopia families were starving because of politics and an acute lack of food supplies. Back in England, where food was plentiful, the families of miners were also going hungry because of a political decision. Of course, the two weren't comparable, but I found it ironic that, while our hearts went out to families thousands of miles from our shores, we couldn't even look after our own. It was 1984, yet people were suffering unnecessarily.

One day, we received the dreadful news that two brothers, Paul and Darren Holmes, aged 15 and 14 years old respectively, had died collecting coal in South Yorkshire. They'd been trying to pick coal in Goldthorpe, near Barnsley, when the embankment had collapsed on them, burying them alive. Striking miners had tried to dig them out, along with the emergency services. Their father had dashed to the scene and, using his bare hands, had desperately tried to save his sons. Tragically, Darren died at the scene while his brother died on the way to hospital. When the funeral was held, a week later, the whole community lined the streets to pay their respects. I shuddered as I remembered the men I'd found digging through the coal tips at Hatfield. They weren't thieves; they were decent blokes trying to keep their families warm.

Soon, the weather worsened and the redundant Yorkshire pits were covered in a white blanket of snow. With Christmas fast approaching, and with the country turning its attentions away from the miners and towards the famine in Ethiopia, I decided to do something positive. I wanted to help the families, especially the children, so I made an announcement at work.

'I'm organising a collection for the children of the striking miners,' I told management. 'But it's got to be good stuff – we don't want to look as though we're giving them rubbish.'

I was a little unsure of the response I'd get, but, to my delight, just days later I was handed carrier bags full of board games, dolls, teddies, footballs and new clothes. Word had spread and local shops had got involved. Many wanted to donate food too, but I directed them to Stainforth Miners Welfare Club, where it could be distributed fairly by the NUM.

The donated goods were all good quality and, if it wasn't new or nearly new, then it didn't go in. The appeal took on a life of its own, until soon I'd managed to fill half-a-dozen bin liners. With the Christmas presents in place, I wrote to the NUM secretary to ask if I could donate it to the miners' families. The NUM agreed and dispatched someone from the welfare club in a van to collect it all. I explained that, while some of it had been donated by management, most of it had come from the wives. They were mothers and hated the thought of children going without. I wasn't sure how it would be received, but a week or so later I received a letter thanking us for the donation. I didn't care about thanks or recognition, though – I just wanted to know that those children would have something nice to open on Christmas Day.

The plight in Ethiopia continued to dominate the news, wiping the miners' strike from the top of radio and TV news bulletins. A bunch of singers formed a supergroup called Band Aid, and they released a special charity song called 'Do They Know It's Christmas?', which rang out from the radio as Christmas neared. I felt far from festive because each day I'd battle my way into work, passing my friends on the picket line. It was an extremely difficult and tense time.

One bitterly cold December morning, I was walking across the pit yard towards the medical centre when I spotted a mound of snow outside the door by the step. I brushed it aside with my foot, but it moved. I noticed a pair of brown eyes looking up at me – it was a little dog. The stray Border Terrier looked half frozen to death as I scooped him up in my arms. He was as light as a feather and covered in snow, although underneath it he was absolutely filthy.

'Hello, there,' I whispered as he shivered in my arms.

I unbuttoned my coat and wrapped him underneath as I unlocked the medical-centre door. I wrapped him in a towel, filled a bowl with some warm milk and gave him some biscuits. Sitting beside the stove, I rubbed his fur with the towel until it was dry and warm. He was so exhausted that he curled up and fell straight to sleep once I was finished. I asked around the management in case he belonged to someone, even though it was obvious he didn't. Then I called the police station to ask if anyone had reported a missing dog, but no one had.

'Well, if they do, he's here with me,' I informed them. I put down the phone and stared at my new four-legged friend. 'What on earth am I going to do with you?' I asked as he nuzzled affectionately against the palm of my hand.

I found no collar or identification on him, so I decided that he needed a name.

'I think I'll call you Noel because I found you at Christmas,' I told him. Noel seemed to like his new name because his little black nose bobbed up as he licked me.

I went into the control room to ask if anyone had any spare sandwiches.

'It's for a little dog I found starving on the doorstep,' I explained.

Within minutes, everyone had crowded into the medical centre to look at my very own Christmas miracle. We all became so smitten that Noel was constantly fed everything from spare bits of chicken to pieces of meat pie! Noel and I became inseparable, but I knew he couldn't sleep inside the medical centre, so I set him up with a little bed inside the control room, next to the canaries.

'Bloody 'ell, Sister. It's like a zoo in here!' one of the managers moaned.

'I know,' I smirked. 'Just call me Doctor Dolittle.'

The following morning, I went in to check on Noel.

'I'm off outside – want to come for a walk?' I asked as he bounced straight out of bed with his tail wagging. He'd made a miraculous recovery.

'Who's your friend, Sister?' someone asked as Noel padded close behind me in the yard.

'He's a stray. I found him on the doorstep, and now he lives here,' I said.

'He's like your shadow,' the man said, grinning. He stooped down to stroke Noel behind the back of his ear.

I looked down at him. It was true; Noel refused to leave my side. I wanted to take him home but Peter and I owned two cats, which had once been strays, so I knew he wouldn't stand a chance. Instead, he remained at the pit like a little mascot, cared for by everyone.

'Can I give him a biscuit?' a police officer asked one day.

'Go ahead.'

He knelt down as Noel gently took the biscuit from his finger-tips. But, instead of eating it, he ran off to bury it deep in the snow.

'I think he's keeping that for later,' the bobby grinned.

But it happened again and again. Every time someone gave Noel a treat, he'd take it and stash it away. It was as though he'd decided he never wanted to go hungry again.

Instead of a ball, I took a rubber nursing glove and puffed into it until it was fully inflated. I threw it around for him along the pit top. Noel loved chasing it as it bounced along the yard but, unlike his food, he always brought it back. He was a lovely little thing but no one ever claimed him. Soon, he was adored by the working miners, police and management alike. His presence helped lighten the mood as the strike wore on. Animals have a unique way of uniting people, even in the most desperate situa-tions, so in many ways it felt as though Noel had been sent to us for that purpose.

When Christmas week arrived, the management informed us that the pit would be protected by a security firm over the holi-day period. The only problem was that they'd be bringing Alsatian dogs with them to patrol the yard. I knew the dogs would kill little Noel, so the time had come for him to move on.

'I think I need to find you a new home,' I whispered as he nuzzled against the side of my neck.

I asked the men if anyone could offer him a permanent home.

'I'll have him,' one of the surveyors offered. 'We've already got a few dogs at home but I reckon the wife would love him.'

That evening, as we prepared for shutdown, Noel licked the back of my hand as I bid him farewell. I felt choked up watching him leave, but I knew he'd be fine – and he was. I'm glad to report that Noel not only settled down well into his new home, but he also went on to live a long and happy life. However, there was a twist in the tail. Noel wasn't the little man we'd all thought he was, because a few months later 'he' gave birth to a litter of two pups. It certainly explained her need to hide the food supplies in the snow. When I returned to work in the New Year, the snow had started to melt away and I could see just how much the little dog had left her mark. Various dog biscuits, rolls and pieces of meat pies that she'd buried only a month or so before were still there, dotted in the most peculiar places across the pit yard.

21

Target

Even though the men were on strike, the colliery nurses took it in turns to cover the night shifts so that there was always someone on site. One week, I was called to Rossington pit, to cover three nights. Rossington was still in the Doncaster area but it was on the other side of town, so Peter offered to drive me over. By this time, he'd swapped our old cherry-red saloon car for a white Vauxhall Astra, which, from a distance, looked a little like a police car. It was the end of winter and it was dark as we approached the main pit gates just before 8 p.m. In the dim light the striking miners sitting quietly on the picket line around an open fire must have thought we were in a police car, because, without warning, they suddenly jumped to their feet and started throwing glass bottles.

'What the …?' Peter shouted as the glass smashed against the road. He turned to me in a panic. 'I can't go down there, Joan. I'm not risking losing the car,' he gasped, pushing the gear stick into reverse.

The miners were still coming towards us, but instead of reversing down the lane, Peter pulled up and wound down the window. One of the men approached the driver's side.

'Who have you got in there?' he asked, dipping his head to get a better look.

'It's Arthur Scargill,' Peter snapped, looking at me. 'Who does it look like?'

The miner grimaced and straightened up. It was obvious that he wasn't amused. I piped up from the passenger seat to try to break the tension.

'It's Sister Hart. I'm doing a night shift here.'

'Okay,' the miner grumbled, nodding towards the others. 'You can go down, but the car stays 'ere,' he grunted, eyeballing Peter defiantly.

But Peter wouldn't give up.

'I don't like the idea of her walking down there,' he said, gesturing towards the pit lane.

'No one will hurt her,' the man interrupted. 'She'll be safe with us, won't she, lads?'

The group nodded, so I opened the door and climbed out. Peter still wasn't happy but I didn't want any trouble, so I told him to go back home.

'I'll be fine,' I insisted.

He didn't look convinced.

'As long as you're sure,' he said.

'I am. Now take the car and go home.'

Peter didn't move. Instead, he remained and watched until I'd reached the safety of the pit gates. I turned and waved him good-bye. I knew the men wouldn't hurt me because I wasn't a threat; however, unlike the men at Hatfield, they didn't know me, either, so I understood why they'd been suspicious. The pit was empty, apart from managers, and there was very little to do other than check that the medical centre was fully stocked. I spent the rest of my shift inside the warm control room, doing odd jobs and helping to keep things ticking over. The following morning, when I'd finished my shift, one of the managers offered to drive me back home.

'Are you sure you don't mind?' I said.

'No, not at all. I'd rather know you got home okay.'

I was grateful because I knew there'd be a new set of men on the picket line and I didn't want to risk Peter's white car again. Thankfully, the following nights passed without further incident.

A few weeks later, I was back at Hatfield when I received a call to say that one of the undermanagers, who'd gone to carry out general maintenance duties, had collapsed underground. Unfortunately, he was miles out because he'd travelled inbye to one of the districts to pump out water. There were three others with him but we'd lost contact with them. Shortly afterwards, the deputy manager received a vague telephone call from one of the team. The undermanager was okay, but he was suffering from chest pains. The deputy manager turned to me because he was unsure what to do.

'What do you think, Sister?'

There wasn't time to think.

'Well, I'll have to go down there,' I insisted, grabbing my pit boots and overalls. I got changed and pulled out a portable tank of oxygen and some Entonox to take with me.

'Right, I'm coming with you,' the deputy manager agreed.

We looked like Little and Large striding across the yard – the deputy manager standing well over 6 feet to my diminutive 5. However, he was about as much use as a chocolate teapot. He was tall but not very thoughtful. Not only was I having trouble keeping up with his giant steps, but he'd also left me to carry all the equipment.

'Look,' I gasped, coming to a sudden halt as I tried to catch my breath. 'I'm not carrying all this gear on my own!'

The deputy manager huffed, turned back and picked up half of the stuff and set off again, this time at double the speed. In the end, I had to run just to keep up. The cage was waiting to take us underground. For me, it would be the first time I'd been down the pit since the strike had started. But without the men and general hustle and bustle of a working pit, it felt unnervingly quiet. Usually, the air would be filled with sound – laughter and sometimes a bit of colourful language – but now there was nothing, only a stillness weighing heavily in the air.

'This feels so weird. It's so quiet,' I commented. But the deputy manager wasn't listening because he'd already set off.

It seemed strange, almost alien, as though it was my first-ever time underground. The silence was deafening because there was only him and me, and the four missing men.

'This equipment's heavy, isn't it?' he complained out in front.

'You're telling me,' I replied.

He stopped and glanced back. That's when he realised I was still struggling.

'Here, let me take the rest of that,' he said as he unburdened me of my load. I'd never felt as grateful to anyone in my life. 'Yeah, I'd better take it 'cos it's still a good few miles yet.'

'Wait, there's still a few more miles to go?'

'Aye.'

My heart plunged to my already aching knees as he set off once more. But now I'd been relieved of the oxygen tank, I found it much easier to keep up with the giant deputy manager.

'Not far now,' he called as I squinted in the dim light coming from my headlamp.

Where on earth were they?

With no qualified men to operate the underground paddy train, we walked for another 20 minutes without stopping.

If that man dies down here, miles from the pit bottom, I'll bloody kill him, ill or not! I cursed silently to myself.

Then I began to fret.

How on earth will we manage to lift him out between us?

I was just starting to lose the will to live when I spotted the dots of headlights and the outlines of shadowy figures in the distance.

'There they are!' the deputy manager called as he quickened his pace.

I ran after him, but he turned around sharply, bringing me to a sudden halt.

'No, Sister. You stop here for a minute because there's gonna be some foul language,' he warned, holding the palm of his hand up to stop me.

I shook my head.

'I'm sure I've heard it all before,' I argued, but the deputy manager was adamant.

I did as I was told, but it defeated the object because I could still hear the men effing and blinding from where I was standing. The deputy manager eventually came to fetch me.

'He's okay,' he said. 'He's still got chest pains, but he's not too bad.'

I attended to the man and administered oxygen, which seemed to bring him back around. We'd planned to stretcher him out, but one of his colleagues was a trained paddy driver so, while I administered first aid, he returned in a diesel train. We climbed on board and travelled back to the pit bottom. I was just grateful that I didn't have to do any more walking.

The ambulance was waiting at the pit top. It transported the undermanager to hospital, where he was diagnosed with unexplained chest pains. It hadn't been a heart attack, after all. Relief flooded me because goodness only knows how he would have survived if it had been.

22

End of the Strike

I was told that the men would be returning to work the following morning. It was 3 March 1985, and they'd been on strike for almost a year. Dr Macdonald told all the nurses that he wanted us to go to the area office in Doncaster to discuss the return to work. To this day, I still don't know why he didn't want us to remain at our own pits.

Maybe he expected trouble?

As soon as I told Ken Deeming, he forbade me to leave the pit. Instead, he picked up the telephone, called Dr Mac and told him in no uncertain terms that I wouldn't be coming.

'I need her here. The men are back today and she's been here all the time they've been off, so she will be here when they come back,' he insisted.

I'd never known Mr Deeming to refuse Dr Mac before, but I was glad he had because I desperately wanted to be there to see the men. For the first time since the strike began, management had decided that there was no longer the need to meet in supermarket car parks to be ferried in.

'You can all make your own way in tomorrow,' Mr Deeming announced.

That night, I found it difficult to relax because I was worried there would be trouble or bad feeling. Exhausted and anxious, I eventually fell into a fitful night's sleep, until the alarm clock woke me sharply the following morning. I got up and dressed, and pulled my bicycle out of the garage. I'd decided that the fresh air would do me good, and that the journey would give me time and space to think.

'Are you sure you'll be okay?' Peter asked as he watched me wheel my bike down the drive and prop it up against the side of the house.

'Yes, I'll be fine. We're not expecting trouble, although I'm not quite sure what the general mood will be like when I get there.'

It felt strange. After a year of being ferried in under police escort, we were suddenly back to normal, although, deep down, I knew it wouldn't be like it was before. The first thing I noticed as I cycled in that morning was that the picket line had gone. It had become such a familiar sight over the past year that it felt strange to see the top of the pit lane deserted. I cycled into the yard, pulled up in front of the medical centre and chained my bike up. The place was still quiet, with no sign of the men.

A few hours later, at around 10 a.m., I was in my office when I looked out of the window. There were hundreds of men walking united down the pit lane towards the colliery yard. The entire workforce had decided to walk back to work together in a dignified silence. I felt choked up as I watched them approach. Despite the bitter strike and eventual defeat, I realised that these men weren't out, not by a long chalk. Instead, they'd marched back as a family, something they'd always been. The sight of them left me humbled because the men had been to hell and back. They'd been starved and almost frozen to death, but they'd survived it all. Although some felt humiliated by the defeat, they'd come back with their heads held high. I choked back tears of emotion as they passed by my window.

I was pleased to see them back, but I was aware that, for many, life would never be the same again. The strike had not only divided friends and families, but it had also managed to destroy marriages along the way too. Some wives had left, while others, who up until that point had been full-time housewives, had suddenly found themselves the main breadwinners. This had empowered many women, giving a few of them a newfound resolve to leave for good too.

However, the majority of wives were proud of their men and supported them, both financially and emotionally. The miners' wives had managed as most women do in a crisis – they'd become the backbone of the strike. Without them, and their food and money collections, many families would've starved to death. There'd been no real financial help, other than minimal payments from the NUM, because families had been unable to claim benefits.

Of course, the bad feeling between the miners who had worked and those who had not remained. The end of the strike had been a terrible blow to the many who had lasted a full year without wages and had suffered extreme poverty. But a distinction was made between those men who had broken the strike early on, and others who'd felt forced to return. At other pits, carnations had even been strewn at the gates – the flower being symbolic of a hero.

As the crowd passed by, the door of the medical centre opened and in walked Bill, Frank and Andy. I'd kept in touch with them throughout the strike. We'd often stop for a chat in the village, and Peter and I had paid Andy to do the odd gardening jobs for us. I'd like to think the money had helped keep him afloat when times were tough.

'Right, we need to sort out who's working when,' Bill said, getting straight down to business.

We didn't talk about the strike or what had been, because it didn't feel appropriate. I was in a difficult position as I'd worked throughout, even though my heart had always been with the miners. Now they were back, all that mattered was that they remained safe and well under my watch. However, not all of them felt the same, and there were one or two who refused to let me treat them.

'No,' one grunted, to stop me from approaching. He'd caught his hand in some machinery, but he made it clear he didn't want me to examine him. 'I'd rather have Bill.'

'Oh,' I replied.

His rejection was like a knife in my side. I glanced over at Bill, who stepped forward. It felt horrible but I tried not to take it too personally, because I knew he blamed me and lumped me alongside management. For a long time, some of the men presumed I'd belonged to the NUM and had crossed the picket line. In truth, I was employed by management, under the BACM (British Association of Colliery Management) union. I'd decided not to elaborate because I didn't feel the need to explain myself to them or anyone else. After all, it hadn't been my battle. I was there in a medical capacity to ensure everyone's safety.

Apart from that particular miner and another stalwart union man, the majority of men were as courteous and respectful towards me as they'd been before the strike. To be honest, nobody wanted to discuss it, even though it was always there, like the elephant in the room. Surprisingly, we had quite a few men pass through the centre during those first few weeks. Apart from the usual trapped fingers and blackened nails, many suffered headaches, as their eyes strained to get used to working underground again. Others complained of backache because the work was tough and many hadn't done anything as physically strenuous for a year.

While I was able to ease aching muscles with my miracle heat lamp and rubs, I was unable to erase the awful atmosphere that hung over the colliery like a permanent black cloud. It took a month or so, but slowly things began to settle down, although they never returned to normal. During this time, I helped many men who were suffering from depression. It had been as an obvious result of the strike, although they didn't recognise it at the time. I began to notice that quite a few were calling in at the centre more than usual, with unexplained headaches, so I began to ask questions.

'Is there anything else? Are you sleeping okay?' I questioned one miner.

'It's just I keep getting these terrible headaches, Sister.'

'And when did they begin?'

'Months ago. I can't shift 'em. I've taken painkillers but nowt seems to work.'

'And what about sleep? Are you sleeping okay?'

The miner shook his head.

'Not for ages,' he said. 'I wake up all times of night, and then I can't get back off again.'

'Would you like to see the pit doctor, or your own GP?'

'Why, Sister? What do you reckon it is?'

'I think you may have depression, but you need to speak to a doctor about it.'

The man looked at me glumly and cast his eyes to the floor. It was obvious he'd been under a lot of pressure, but he didn't know how or even where to start.

'Yeah, I think you're right,' he said. 'I think I'll see t'pit doctor.'

A gentle line of questioning was usually all it took to open the floodgates. Lots of the men had split up with wives and partners, so some of their problems were emotional, but in many cases their depression was related to the financial burden they'd found themselves in. They'd lost a year's wages, and in some cases their cars and homes had been repossessed. Although it had been a long slog for many, once the financial pressure had lifted, the depression eventually followed. Soon, the pit was functioning once more, but while the men were back at work their hearts remained on the picket line.

I often thought about my father and what he would have made of it all. He'd died two years before the start of the strike, but I knew his sympathy would've been with the miners. He'd gone out on strike himself as a lad, during the general strike of 1926. The strike, called by the general council of the Trades Union Congress, lasted for 10 days, and was an attempt to try to improve wages and working conditions for 800,000 coal miners. During this time, and for a long time afterwards, my dad sang in nightclubs to earn a wage. He'd be accompanied by his sister Ann on the piano, and he'd sing old baritone favourites such as 'Bells of the Sea'. Dad survived the strike, and he supported the Jarrow March 10 years later, in 1936. He'd strongly believed that you should always fight for what was right, just as the miners did during 1984–85. Unfortunately, for both them and me, the writing was already on the wall.

23

Loss

Peter had undergone his first heart bypass in 1974, but his health had continued to deteriorate. It reached the point where I worried about him constantly; I knew that, in time, he'd need another operation to prolong his life. In many ways, it felt as though we were living on borrowed time, but I also knew that, with his advancing years – he'd just celebrated his sixtieth birthday – a second operation could kill him.

Things had changed at work too. Michael Heseltine had announced that many pits would shut. Some of the older miners took voluntary redundancy to try to preserve the jobs of their sons and grandsons. Divisive character though he was, Arthur Scargill had been right about the sweeping pit closures all along.

With Peter's health worsening, I knew I needed to be at home more. Peter insisted that I'd be bored stiff, but when I was offered voluntary redundancy from the pit I decided to take it. It was 1988 and I was 56 years old. I'd worked at Hatfield for 14 years. I loved my job, so I felt saddened to be leaving. But the strike had changed everything, and the bitterness from it had had a lasting effect on Hatfield. The trust between the men and management had been broken and nothing could fix it – not even time. Things were different, and somehow I could no longer find my place, so I left the job that I'd loved and cherished. Of course, once the men heard, they all made a tremendous fuss of me. They clubbed together and bought me a padded, flowery sunlounger so that I could relax, although I had no plans to sit still. On my last day, dozens of men called in at the medical centre to say goodbye.

'We're gonna miss yer, Sister,' one said, gripping me in a big bear hug.

'Yer right there, she's a grand lass,' another piped up from the back of the room.

It meant the world to me.

Sadly, Ken Deeming had transferred to another pit, so the new pit manager called me into his office to present me with a bouquet of flowers. I struggled to compose myself as I glanced down at the beautiful flowers in my hands, but before I could speak there was a knock at the door – it was the deputy.

'Can you come downstairs for a moment, Sister Hart?' he asked.

I was a little bemused as I followed him downstairs into one of the boardrooms. As he opened the door, a huge cheer erupted from inside.

'Surprise!'

'Well, you didn't think we'd let you leave without a party, did you?' the deputy grinned, giving me a wink.

The room was packed with people wanting to give me a good send-off, and they'd even laid on a small buffet. It was a kind gesture and it touched me greatly. It also seemed a fitting end to my working life at Hatfield. Even though I was sad to leave, I'd not been the first, which had convinced me that I was doing the right thing – it was time to go.

However, I underestimated the impact both the loss of my job and old way of life would have on me, because, initially, I found it hard to adjust to my new position as a practice nurse at a doctors' surgery. Moving from an all-male working environment to a quaint public-service position was a huge shock to the system. My role had reversed overnight – instead of advising men, I now offered advice on smear tests and hysterectomies. I'd worked at the surgery for a few years when the doctor called me into her room for a chat.

'I'd like you to read this smear test and let me know what you think,' she said, handing me a piece of paper.

I studied it thoroughly before making my diagnosis.

'Well, she'll obviously need a hysterectomy because these results are bordering on first-stage cancer,' I concluded. 'I can have a chat with her, if you like?'

'Joan,' the GP said, gesturing for me to sit down. 'Read the name at the top of it. It's you, Joan. These are your test results.'

'Oh,' I gasped.

I'd previously had a couple of suspect smears but, other than a cone biopsy, I'd not needed any further treatment. However, now my results told an entirely different story – I needed a full hysterectomy.

'You need to look after yourself,' the GP insisted.

I tried not to worry. Even though it was in the early stages, it was still a shock. For the first time in my life, I was the one who needed looking after. I underwent a full hysterectomy at the start of 1990. Everyone had warned Peter that I'd be depressed after surgery, so he secretly booked a coach tour of America and Canada to cheer me up. A few months later, we flew into New York City, where we boarded a bus and began our tour. It was an action-packed trip and we didn't stay more than two nights in one place.

I noticed how exhausted and out of breath Peter had become, so, on our return three weeks later, I booked him in to see the heart specialist. He'd become so breathless that the doctor ordered various scans and tests at the Northern General Hospital in Sheffield, where he'd had the original surgery. The tests concluded that the original bypass grafts in Peter's heart had broken down. Unfortunately, the consultant's list was full and we weren't sure how long Peter could wait, so, rather than risk his life, we decided to have the operation done privately. The bypass cost us thousands of pounds, but I knew I couldn't put a price on Peter's life.

He underwent heart surgery at the Thornbury Hospital in Sheffield, which undoubtedly saved his life. But this time, although the techniques used had been more refined, Peter was older so it took him longer to recover. After the operation, he developed a large hernia in his chest cavity because he'd been cut open so many times. Even though the doctors repaired it, Peter's health continued to worsen. Despite my round-the-clock care, he suffered permanent chest infections. Then he began to have trouble with the circulation in his legs, where the veins had been removed and attached to his mammary artery to keep his heart pumping. Despite everything, Peter rallied on. We rented a flat in Bridlington, which we used for our summer holidays because he wasn't well enough to travel abroad.

I continued to work at the doctors' practice in Stainforth. It was only a few miles from home, so I was able to nip back at a moment's notice. I'd often pop home to check that Peter had everything he needed. In many ways it felt like I was holding down two jobs. In spite of the pressure at home I grew to love my role as a practice nurse.

The surgery set up a new clinic, visiting and caring for the over-75s in their own homes. The irony wasn't lost on me because by now I was 60 years old, and my patients called me the 'wrinkly nurse'. I had 600 patients on my books and I'd visit them all at home once a year to check on their needs. This ranged from chiropody or a new walking stick, to a home help or a wet room. I'd also keep a regular check on their blood pressure because most of them had problems but didn't like to bother the doctor. I carried out memory tests for Alzheimer's disease, and even helped a few fill in attendance-allowance benefit forms to ensure that they received everything they were entitled to.

I loved my job and my patients, so I was upset one day when I encountered a problem. I'd been visiting a family, but every time I arrived their son would refuse to leave his parents alone with me. He was rude and became verbally aggressive, so I left the house to report him to the doctor. I was just heading to the front gate when his elderly mother caught up behind me.

'Nurse Joan, please don't go,' she begged.

'I'm sorry, but I won't tolerate being spoken to like that.' I glanced back at the house and her son, who was scowling from the doorway.

I was just about to leave when the lady explained that the reason her son had been so abusive was because he was convinced I wanted to take his parents away and put them in a care home. I couldn't believe it. I'd spent my whole life trying to help, not hinder family life. But the son, it seemed, had an attitude problem and was well known for it in the village. Everyone, even his parents, lived in his shadow.

A few weeks later I visited an elderly man in a remote farmhouse. His son greeted me outside as I pulled up in my car.

'Ay up, Nurse,' he called, lifting his flat cap in greeting. 'He's waiting inside for yer.'

'Rightio,' I replied.

I grabbed my bag, knocked on the door, and entered to find the pensioner sat in a threadbare old armchair. He was wearing a flat cap and had his trusty walking stick propped up at his side. As soon as I walked in, the old farmer looked up momentarily, before turning away.

'What does tha want?' he asked suspiciously.

'Well,' I said, putting my bag on the floor. 'It's not what I want – it's what you want and need.'

But the man seemed wary.

'Like what?' he said.

'Like, who cuts your toenails, for starters?' I said, pointing at his feet.

'Son. He does 'em, every now and again.'

'Okay,' I nodded. 'But would you like a chiropodist to come and do them properly for you?'

The old man sniffed, clearly unmoved by my offer of help.

'How much?' he grunted.

'Nothing. It's free.'

He looked up at me, making eye contact for the first time.

'Right, I'll have him.'

As we chatted, he explained that his hearing aid had also broken.

'No problem. I'll arrange for someone to come out from Doncaster to fix or replace it.'

'How much?'

'Nothing.'

'Oh, right. I'll have that too.'

By the end of the day I'd organised a chiropodist, a new walking stick, a new hearing aid and I'd even got him pushed up to the top of the cataract operation list.

The following year, I returned once more to find him sitting in the same chair, wearing his flat cap, only this time with a new walking stick at his side.

'What does tha want now?' he grumbled.

'Nothing, I just wanted to see that you're okay.'

The old man looked up.

'But what does tha want?' he asked.

'Nothing. I've come to see what you want or need.'

The old farmer took off his flat cap and scratched his bald head with the tips of his fingers. 'Well, tha can go then. I dunt need owt 'cos I've had it all, so tha needn't come and bother me any more.'

I didn't take any offence. Yorkshire men are blunt by nature, so I was used to it. I'd also been toughened up by my days working at the pit. As soon as I climbed inside my car, I started to laugh, and I didn't stop until I'd reached my next patient.

Another man was similar. He too lived in a remote house in the middle of nowhere, but, unlike the other chap's, his house was filthy. After much discussion, his daughter moved him into a spotless granny flat. She even allowed him to bring some of his old furniture with him. When I arrived, the flat was clean but his hands and feet were filthy. As soon as I nipped into the bathroom I realised why – the whole bathtub was full to the brim with coal.

'Why on earth is your bath full of coal?' I asked.

The man shrugged his shoulders as though it should be obvious.

'So I don't run out, of course,' he said.

He would've had a point, if it wasn't for the fact that he had a gas fire.

Inside the front room, dozens of seed boxes had been scattered on the carpet, tables and every available surface. He'd water the plants religiously, not caring if he soaked the carpet through. In truth, the flat was absolutely stunning, but he treated it like a garden.

'It's too posh,' he grumbled. 'I preferred it back home.'

I didn't know what to say or where to start. The place would've been stunning if not for him and his plants. I could only imagine his daughter's frustration, but there was little I could do other than offer advice. I told him it'd be far better to store his coal outside.

'No, it's all right where it is.'

He was a stubborn old goat, so I knew I was fighting a losing battle. I got up to leave.

''Ere,' he said, suddenly getting to his feet as he rooted about in the front room. 'I've got something for yer.'

'Oh,' I said, turning back, 'that's kind. What is it?'

With that, he turned and handed me two enormous cauliflowers. We later ate one for our tea – it was absolutely delicious.

With Peter's health worsening, I retired from the doctors' practice at the age of 62. It was finally time for the 'wrinkly nurse' to call it a day.

Four years later, during Christmas 1998, Peter, who was now 70, caught the flu. When he failed to recover in the New Year, I insisted that something was wrong, but the GP wouldn't listen. I demanded that Peter be referred to the cardiologist at Doncaster Royal Infirmary who had treated him as a private patient.

'Well,' the doctor replied, 'if that's what you want, then I suggest you ask him yourself.'

So I did. I picked up the phone and rang his wife, who told me her husband would call at our house on his way to the hospital. He took one look at Peter, and within the hour he had my husband admitted to the coronary care unit because his heart wasn't beating properly.

Sadly, Peter never came home. I sat with him every single day for three weeks as his life ebbed away. I'd arrive at 12.30 p.m. and not leave until 8 p.m., during which time I'd wash and change him. I didn't want the other nurses to do it because he was my husband and I'd always been his nurse. One day, I received a call from the hospital, asking me to come quickly because Peter was gravely ill. I ran to Ernie's house because I was in far too much of a state to drive myself there. Although we reached the hospital in double-quick time, Peter had already died. His body was placed in a quiet side ward, beside a little table with a candle and bible on it. Often, in moments like this – and I'd witnessed it many times over the years – the deceased loved ones are in shock. I certainly was.

'You'll have to give him some more pillows,' I said. 'He can't lie down flat, you know, because he won't be able to get his breath.'

Even though the nurse knew me well, she was gentle and professional.

'I don't think he needs pillows any more, Joan,' she said softly.

And that's when it hit me. Peter had gone. I was so crippled with grief that Ernie drove me home and telephoned Ann, who arrived shortly afterwards.

'What's that?' I asked, numb with grief. I pointed towards a carrier bag in her hand.

'It's a sleeping bag. I'm here for as long as you need me.'

It felt good to have my family around me, but after a few days I knew I needed to be on my own.

'I understand,' Ann said, giving me a hug. 'But you know where I am if you need me.'

I nodded gratefully, but I had to face it – life without Peter. I needed time and space to grieve alone. He was, without doubt, the love of my life, and I still miss him every single day. The bungalow we'd bought together suddenly seemed empty without him. Before he was admitted to hospital, Peter hadn't been able to get to the supermarket, so I'd fetch the shopping and he'd put it away. It was his job and he loved it because it'd made him feel useful. After he was gone, I'd go through the motions of buying and bringing the shopping home. I'd place the bags on the side, but I couldn't even empty them; instead, I'd leave the house

– my loss so acute in that one small task. The shopping would remain until I'd mustered up enough courage to unpack it.

I even stopped walking through the village. Everyone knew Peter and word had spread about his death. I simply couldn't face people. Instead, I'd drive to the supermarket, so that no one could stop and offer their condolences. It was a particularly horrible and lonely time. Only after his funeral was I slowly able to accept the fact that Peter had gone.

A few months later, I was sorting through a box full of old papers when I stumbled upon an envelope containing two small pieces of Barnsley Bright coal. It's the finest coal you can buy and is used by the Royal household. Peter brought it out of Brodsworth Colliery on an underground visit there in 1956.

That afternoon, I cried, not only for my husband, but for my father too. I wept for all the boys I'd known at school, the generations who'd devoted their lives to working down the pit. I sobbed for the communities and their residents whose lives had been ripped apart by the bitter year-long strike. But most of all, I wept for the lives that had been divided by that same bitterness. Villages had been decimated when the pits had shut – the hearts ripped out of both the community and those living within them. There had once been camaraderie, and the village working men's clubs had been the central hub of it all. They had teams for everything, be it darts, snooker, football or even cards – there was always something for everyone. But all that slowly disappeared. Afterwards, those same villages fell to pieces. The whole sense of community vanished and there was nothing to replace it. Life would never be the same again because the coal mines had gone for ever.

Many years later, I joined a writers' group where I met a man called Brian Gray, and we became good friends. We had lots in common because Brian had once been a miner. One day, Brian handed me a poem he'd written after the pits had shut. When I read it, I almost cried because, to me, it summed up perfectly the hopelessness we'd felt when the pits had gone and were no more.

GONE
A Miner's Poem by Brian Gray

The darkness and the grime,
The heat and dirt, and the slime,
GONE.
The laughter, the mates, and the hot canteen,
The showers, the lockers, and the scrubbing clean,
GONE.
The dust, the bile, and the smell that makes you ill,
The face, the gate, and the roof that can kill,
GONE.
The union, the strikes, and the rage,
The defeat, the humiliation, the wage,
GONE.
The deputy, the overman, and the boss,
The union man who was always at a loss,
GONE.
The certainty, the dignity, and the grit,
The friendship, the community, the pit,
GONE.

24

Eternal Nurse

Even though I was now alone, the nurse within me remained. I felt it was my calling – I'd been born to look after others, and I still did so. At Christmas, I'd open my house up to my friends and neighbours, but during the remaining winter months I'd feel lonely. I'd spent my whole life being a nurse, and suddenly I found myself a retired widow with too much time on my hands. I still had my friends, and Ann and Tony, but I felt at a loss. So when I heard Doncaster Royal Infirmary was looking for volunteers, I stepped forward.

It was 2006, seven years after Peter's death, and despite being 74 years old I felt the need to return to work and make a difference. Even though I'd been a nurse for over 58 years, I was deemed far too old to do my job. Instead, I was given monotonous tasks such as filing, photocopying or, if I was really lucky, I was asked to run errands for the Occupational Health Department. I felt despondent and completely under-used. I considered leaving, but then I moved again, this time to day-care theatre admissions, where patients underwent cataract operations. I was given a little more responsibility, but I still wasn't allowed to administer eye drops or even take blood pressure. The hospital insurance wouldn't cover me because I was too old. Once more, I became a general dogsbody. I cleared away laundry, showed people to the wards and took bloods to the haematology department.

In a bid to get a bit of excitement back in my life, I decided to enter a competition run by Age Concern. I reasoned that, even with my advancing years, there was plenty of life still left inside me. The competition posed the question, *What have you always wanted to do?* So, as a bit of a joke, I wrote, *Wing walking and flying a glider.* I posted my entry and forgot all about it. So, you can imagine my surprise when I received a phone call a month later saying I'd won and I needed to travel to an airfield in Cirencester for the flight! I'd done a few terrifying things over the years, including riding on top of the cage during the pit-shaft inspection, but being strapped to the wing of an aircraft was a first, even for me.

'Smile!' the cameraman shouted from an adjacent plane as I flew alongside him, hundreds of feet up in the air, strapped to a glorified bicycle seat!

My neck craned as I glanced across and grimaced. I wondered what on earth had possessed me to do such a crazy thing as the wind blasted against me, stealing my breath. Once I had both feet back on the ground I began to shake, and I didn't stop until hours later.

It had been quite an adventure, and I'd been bitten by the bug. A year later, I travelled in a hot-air balloon and tried my hand at skydiving. Nothing, it seemed, could stop me. Maybe I'd been missing the adrenalin rush from my days at the pit and my airborne activities were a way of filling the void – I really can't say. All I did know was that I wasn't going to let a silly thing like age get in my way.

I'd always been useful as a nurse, but as a hospital volunteer I faded into the background and felt totally lost. I left Doncaster Royal Infirmary in 2011, aged 79 – the oldest nurse in town. Hospitals had never held the same kind of job satisfaction that I'd got from working down a pit. I still miss those days now.

Hatfield Colliery remains open, but only just. After I left in 1988, the pit passed through many different companies and was even featured in the 1996 film *Brassed Off*. It is the last viable deep pit in the country. Today, it's run by Hatfield Colliery Employee Benefit Partnership, but only last year (2014) the NUM had to step in to prevent the pit from closure with a £4 million loan. The union came forward after the colliery failed to secure cash from either the government or the banks, even though the pit stands on 50 million tonnes of coal reserves. At 1.2 million tonnes a year, it means there's still another 40–50 years' worth of coal mining left at Hatfield, but it is being threatened by cheap coal imports from as far afield as Russia and America. At its peak, Hatfield employed 2,000 men. That number has now dwindled to just 434 employees and 60 contractors. In early 2015 the government gave Hatfield Colliery a commercial loan of £8 million to help avoid immediate insolvency and support its managed closure by 2016. Two other deep coal mines, Kellingley in Yorkshire and Thoreseby in Nottinghamshire, are due to close in October 2015, leaving Hatfield Britain's last remaining underground coal mine. It is a very sad time for a once proud industry.

My old medical centre has been demolished and replaced with a new brick building, which houses a reception, offices and a couple of vending machines instead of a canteen. It also contains a much more compact medical centre. The nurse, who is also a redhead like me, is the lovely Sister May Justice. Sister Justice and I once worked together, albeit at different pits, during my last three years there. She is supported by one MRA, the very knowledgeable Gary Dexter. Together, May and Gary treat and tend to the entire workforce. As is the way with modern life, their jobs are now contracted out. There's no pit ambulance, either, and there hasn't been for years. If there's a serious medical emergency they have to call 999.

Although May and Gary both do fantastic jobs, the changes are sadly a sign of the times. I belonged to an era where a job was a job for life, and a time when village life and pride were paramount. The men are still proud of their pit, and they should be, but some of the miners are now employed from outside the surrounding villages. Both the old way of life and job security are being taken from them, piece by piece. I find it all terribly sad.

I belong to a different time, and I miss it greatly. I miss the banter of the men, the miners' jokes and their (often) filthy language. It's something I would never have experienced working inside a sterile hospital. The miners were and still are the bravest and most remarkable men I've ever had the privilege of working with. At times, caring for them was a hell of a responsibility, but it was a role I cherished and carried out with pride. My men knew that if they were ever trapped and injured down the pit, no matter how bad their injuries were, I would always go to them. Over the years, I became a mother, sister, confidante and friend to the 2,000 men in my care.

Today, I'm 83 years young, and although my legs aren't what they used to be, I have no plans to slow down. Sadly, many of the miners I worked with have since passed away. I miss them all. But, if anything, it spurs me on to seize the moment, because life is for living, and I plan to enjoy each and every moment of it.

Acknowledgements

This book has been a complete labour of love for me; I do hope you've enjoyed it. Please remember that it has not been written by a pit manager, surveyor or even a miner, but a female pit nurse, so if I have got some of the mining technology wrong, then please forgive me. Quite simply, it has been written through my eyes, as I witnessed and lived it. There are so many people who have helped me along the way that I don't really know where to begin, so I'll start with my husband, Peter – the most loving and patient man in the world. I miss him with every breath I take, but I'll never forget his love and support. Thank you, Peter – you were always my rock.

I'd also like to mention my family: my brother Tony, his wife Joyce, my sister Ann and her husband John. Thank you all for your continued help and encouragement.

I'd like to thank the miners and management of Hatfield Colliery, without whom there would be no book. My special gratitude goes to Tommy Chappell, who sadly passed away before the book was finished. When Tommy died, I not only lost a colleague but a great friend too, but I'd like to thank him for his support and advice over the years. Also to my nursing-sister colleagues, Dr Macdonald and the medical staff of the NCB in Doncaster – thank you all.

To Keith Argyle, from my first creative-writing group, who always had faith in my writing ability. Also, to all my friends and colleagues at the Bentley Writers' Group, especially Caren Fox, for their encouragement. Without them I would never have finished the book.

To my ghostwriter, Veronica Clark, who not only put the whole story together for me and suffered my emotions and memory losses, but also became a good friend.

To the rest of my friends and colleagues who have encouraged and pushed me to put my memories into words and write them down on paper before they are forgotten and lost for ever, I am eternally grateful.

Finally, thank you to my agent, Eve White, and Jack Ramm, and Vicky Eribo at HarperCollins for believing in my story and allowing me to share it with you.

Glossary of Mining Terms

BACM British Association of Colliery Management.

Banksman The person in charge of the surface/pit top and the cage.

Cage A compartment/lift, single-, double- or triple-decked, used to transport men or materials up and down a pit shaft.

Checks Brass discs with the miner's unique number on to identify when he's underground.

Chock A short prop or roof support made of timber or steel.

Coalface A solid area where coal is extracted.

Contractor A miner employed for a contracted period of time.

COSA Colliery Officials and Staff Association.

Deputy A qualified official in charge of a district.

District An underground area of the mine where coal is extracted, usually with a name and number.

Engineman A person employed to operate a winding engine at the surface or underground.

Gob A term used for waste or abandoned area.

Inbye A term to denote the position of someone in the mine towards the coalface.

Main A word used in Yorkshire colliery names where the principal seam was originally the Barnsley bed.

MRA Medical Room Attendant.

NCB National Coal Board.

NUM National Union of Mineworkers.

Onsetter The equivalent of the banksman, but at the pit bottom.

Overman A senior official of higher rank than a deputy.

Paddy An underground train used to transport miners.

Self-rescuer A small metal canister containing a portable short-term oxygen source.

Shot-firer A qualified person who fires shots of explosives.

Skip A large coal container, which is raised up the pit shaft.